WORLD ENOUGH & TIME

World Enough & Time

On Creativity and Slowing Down

CHRISTIAN MCEWEN

BAUHAN PUBLISHING
PETERBOROUGH, NEW HAMPSHIRE
2011

Library of Congress Cataloging-in-Publication Data

McEwen, Christian, 1956-
World enough & time : on creativity and slowing down / Christian McEwen.
   p. cm.
Includes bibliographical references and index.
ISBN 978-0-87233-146-4 (pbk. : alk. paper)
1. Creative writing. 2. Poetry--Authorship. 3. Self-actualization (Psychology) I. Title.
PN151.M37 2011
814'.6--dc22

2011014727

A note about the cover from the author: "The photograph on the front cover shows the desk I used my first time at Macdowell, taken by their in-house photographer, Jo Morrissey. Out of the window, you can see a Scottish landscape in south west Galloway, taken by publisher, Sarah Bauhan."

Photograph of desk at McDowell ©2011 by Joanna Eldredge Morrissey; inset photograph of Galloway in Scotland ©2007 by Sarah Bauhan.

To contact Christian, please visit her website: www.christianmcewen.com

*For the unabridged audiobook of this title, please go to our website
or download at www.audible.com*

BAUHAN
PUBLISHING LLC
PO BOX 117 PETERBOROUGH NEW HAMPSHIRE 03458
603-567-4430
WWW.BAUHANPUBLISHING.COM

Printed in the United Kingdom

For the Absent Ones

She was someone who could not be rushed. That seems like a small thing. But it is actually a very amazing quality, a very ancient one. . . . She went about her business as if she could live forever, and forever was very very long.

—ALICE WALKER

CONTENTS

Introduction

For fast-acting relief from stress, try slowing down.

LILY TOMLIN

GEORGE'S STORY

Twenty-five years ago, I was teaching a creative writing class in London. Some of my students were young mothers, relieved to find themselves in adult company again after the unremitting demands of their small children; some were middle-aged, with modest private incomes, and the rest were older people, recently retired.

There was a man in this last group whom I'll call George, a creaky, lanky, doubtful sort of fellow, perhaps in his mid-seventies. I don't remember his real name. But I do remember his response to one of my assignments. It was the sort of lesson, at least for me as teacher, that I hope I will never forget.

I had asked the class to take some ordinary task—washing the dishes, tidying up the children's toys—and to tackle it at less than half the usual speed. "Look at the bubbles on the knife-blade as you rinse it," I told them. "Feel the hot water on your hands. Enjoy that moment when the room is clean, and every single toy is put away."

The point behind all this, of course, was *slowing down*: slowing down enough to be there in the present moment, enough so they could notice and describe. I didn't know much about eastern religions in those days, but what I was proposing was in fact a very basic exercise in what Buddhists would call "mindfulness."

Several mornings later, everyone gathered around the long oval table to report back on what had happened. George was one of the first to speak. He had a part-time job, he told us, even though he was officially retired. It was a job he had been doing for a great many years. He always walked home along the same few streets, taking the shortest possible route. But the previous afternoon, fulfilling the assignment, he had walked home from work a different way. His face creased with pleasure as he described what he had seen: the pink geraniums in someone's window-box, the unfamiliar houses. It had taken him perhaps half an hour longer than usual. But he had enjoyed every minute. For the first time in thirty or forty years, his journey had seemed fresh to him, and new.

We live in a culture that is obsessed with speed, a culture wracked by strange illnesses and persistent low-level fatigue. "How are you?" one friend asks another, and the answer is the same, across almost all categories of age and race and class and gender. "I'm just *so busy*," people tell each other, half proud, half overwhelmed. "Really, I'm crazy-busy. How are you?"

That it might be possible to arrange one's life so as to be slightly less frantic has somehow become unimaginable. To claim, like my good friend Arthur, that "I *do* have time—to go to the gym, to have lunch with a friend," is looked at slightly askance. It is as if *busy* had come to equal "interesting" and "important," and being hard to get hold of translated, seamlessly, into "social cachet." This is a world where a reputable catalogue can advertise a program called "Meditation in a New York Minute," selling stress reduction, energy, and "intense mental clarity" all at the same time. "You can be super busy, super successful, and super calm," says executive coach Mike Thornton.

But what if you don't want to? What if you have come to believe, like the Trappist monk Thomas Merton, that "the frenzy of the activist neutralizes his work for peace," or that "the rush and pressure of modern life are a form, perhaps the most common form, of its innate violence"? What if you'd prefer, in Thoreau's terms, a "broad" (or at least broader) margin to your days? Then please keep reading. Like George, you may find yourself delighted to take the long way home.

A BIG HERE & A LONG NOW

When I began work on this book, back in 2004, friends would assume it was somehow connected to the Slow Food movement. This is the oldest and best known branch of what Europeans call Slow Living, and is centered on good local food, eaten at a comfortable pace and in sympathetic company: in conscious resistance to the solitary grab-and-go of so much American-style eating. In recent years, the Slow Movement has found its way into almost every corner of our culture, manifesting in numerous different ways, including Slow Cities, Slow Art and Slow Design, even, most recently, Slow Money.

My own interest in slowing down came from a very different place: less practical and product-oriented altogether. From the beginning, I was concerned with how slowness might intersect with happiness, and then again with creativity. I wanted to explore the space in which small, almost invisible habits might have the chance to flourish, seeing them as nourishment both in terms of "making," and as antidote to our usual frantic rush. Like the English composer Brian Eno, I wanted to find a way of living in a "Big Here and a Long Now." It was obvious from the start that this would not be easy.

The book you're holding in your hands came together over several years, as I wrestled with my own relationship to time, noticing what really gave me joy, and how that might act as springboard to creative work. In writing it, I drew on poetry and art and literary history, Buddhism and contemplative practice, along with a smattering of sociology and statistics. I also included interviews with a number of practicing artists: poets and writers, painters and calligraphers, dancers, musicians, folklorists and storytellers. Some of those I quote are famous and familiar: poets like Wordsworth and Coleridge, Walt Whitman, Emily Dickinson; writers like Emerson and Thoreau, John Ruskin, William James, Virginia Woolf. Some are our own elders and contemporaries: the poets William Stafford, Adrienne Rich, and Mary Oliver; the avant-garde singer Meredith Monk; the artist and dancer Paulus Berensohn. Others again are friends and colleagues of my own, little known outside their own immediate circles.

As we follow in these artists' footsteps, reading, writing, dreaming, telling stories, it should gradually become apparent that through the door of the ordinary, when treated with curiosity and respect, the extraordinary can appear: *a song, a tale, a painting, a new poem.* Each anecdote becomes its own little parable, modeling inspiration and advice. Because I myself think best in terms of story, these things have found their place inside a larger narrative of my own, organized in twelve lightly linked chapters, opening up like the petals of a daisy from a golden disk of slowness and creativity. You may read straight through, or dip and pick among the various chapters, focusing in turn on different themes. Each chapter is itself made up of eight to ten shorter sections, which means that the book can also be used as a source of daily reading, so-called *lectio divina* or divine reading, giving you the chance to muse and ruminate, and acting as encouragement for your own creative work.

Expert or apprentice, *maker* of whatever kind, writer or gardener, artist or teacher: my hope is that this is a book that will be of practical use to you, and to which you will return again and again. It was written for my friends and students, which is to say, for a wide-ranging general audience, most of whom remain chronically over-worked. But it was written with the fierce conviction that despite the daily onslaught of racket and distraction, it still remains possible, even now, to turn things around: to spin straw into gold, time into eternity, anxiety into ease and inspiration.

Tactics

↬ Choose any routine activity and allow it to become an end in it-self. Pay attention to how this feels.

↬ Finish the sentence, "If I had more time I would . . . " and then, at some point in the coming week, *find the time.*

↬ *Consider the following quotations:*
"It is in our idleness, in our dreams, that the submerged truth some-times comes to the top."

VIRGINIA WOOLF

"Art is the means we have of undoing the damage of haste. It's what everything else isn't."

THEODORE ROETHKE

CHAPTER ONE

Hurry Sickness

The minute rages in the clock.
THEODORE ROETHKE

Hurry Sickness

WHEN THE LILLIPUTIANS FIRST SAW Gulliver's watch, that "wonderful kind of engine . . . a globe, half silver and half of some transparent metal [glass!]," they told themselves it had to be his god. After all, "he very seldom did anything without consulting it: he called it his oracle, and said it pointed out the time for every action of his life."

Gulliver carried a single time piece with him, one small imperious deity, no doubt an old-fashioned turnip watch on a silver chain. Such watches could be slipped into one's fob or waistband pocket when they were not needed. Nowadays, time is not so easily disposed of. It eyes us from the edge of our computer screen, or the dashboard of our car; ticks away the minutes on the clock beside our bed. There are clocks set into our ovens, our smart phones, our ipods: a pantheon of tiny fretful gods, each one berating us under its breath for not meeting our commitments right this minute. *Tick. Tick-tock!* Or *click!* as the numbers shift against the grayed-out screen. *If you are lucky enough to survive the full stretch of your allotted span, you have approximately . . . thirteen million minutes left.* No wonder we feel overscheduled, overwhelmed.

Even vacation time can be eaten up by speed. My friend Joan lives in the country, far from family and friends. She and her sister had not seen each other since Christmas. But when Ellie came to visit, along with her two young daughters, "It was like a washing-machine experience—and then they were gone." They climbed a mountain, they shared a barbecue together, and everyone took lots of photographs. But Joan and Ellie "didn't have a single decent conversation," and there was no time to talk to her nieces either. When they left, she told me, she felt absolutely bereft. She thinks it's because they live in the middle of the city, and "they just don't know how to stop."

Joan lives on the west coast of Scotland, and her sister is based in Edinburgh. But their story is all too familiar, perhaps especially in the United States. As the sociologist Juliet Schor points out, we "work too much, eat too quickly, socialize too little, drive and sit in traffic for too many hours, don't get enough sleep, and feel harried too much of the time." Meanwhile the prices continue to rise: healthcare, childcare, education, gas. Despite the growing unemployment figures, the average U.S. citizen now works 270 more hours a year than his or her European counterpart, the equivalent of more than two whole months.

Not surprisingly Thoreau's "margins" (free time and leisure time, even tea and coffee-breaks) have continued to shrink—by as much as 37 percent since 1973. Vacations have diminished to two- and three-day mini excursions. The weekend is for crashing out, or catching up on household chores. The Sabbath is for shopping. For decades, "luxury time" has been at risk (the time to read or write a novel, to bake a birthday cake or tend a garden), but now essential human time is in jeopardy too. It doesn't help that most of us spend at least eight and a half hours a day bowed over some screen or another (TV, computer monitor, mobile phone), often simultaneously. In the States today, there is scarcely time to catch your breath and check your email, far less play with your children or talk in a leisurely fashion with your spouse. At least a third of us report that we have no time to reflect on what we're doing, that we almost always feel rushed.

Such "hurry sickness" (the phrase originates with Dr. Larry Dossey) speeds up our heart and breathing rates, leading to ulcers, hypertension and high blood pressure, along with a growing dependence on alcohol and cigarettes. The Chinese ideogram "busy" is made up of two characters, "heart" and "killing," and this is accurate: the new emphasis on speed and efficiency is, quite literally, damaging our hearts. Computers operate in nanoseconds, and we try, vainly, to keep up, like an old dog panting along behind his master's sports car. But a nanosecond is only *a billionth of a second*, and humanly cannot be experienced, so our effort to synchronize ourselves is doomed to failure. *Are we happy nonetheless? Are we enjoying ourselves?* We are moving too fast to come up with an answer.

Consider a world without sidewalks, a world where loitering is forbidden and musing is seen as a synonym for befuddlement or confusion. It's a world stuck in fifth gear, a world where there is no time to look forward or backwards, only the bleating nanosecond of the present. It is becoming, alas, the world in which we live.

THE BRIMMING CUP

There is a story about a western professor who comes to a Zen master in search of enlightenment. The monk offers his visitor some tea. But he fills the cup to the brim, and keeps on pouring, till the hot tea splashes out across the floor.

"What are you doing?" cries the professor.

"You look to me for wisdom," says the monk. "But you are already so chock-a-block with your own thoughts and opinions that there's no room in you for anything else."

And smiling, he pours more tea into the brimming cup.

More tea, and yet more tea. It's hot and sweet and comforting, but what's it worth, if most of it runs out across the floor?

OUTSIDE TIME

I grew up in Scotland, in the country, in a big old-fashioned house not far from Edinburgh. It was the sort of place Americans associate with *Brideshead Revisited,* or tired reruns of *Upstairs, Downstairs*; a place of beautiful shabby rooms and scented gardens, a perpetual drone of adult anxiety about school fees and taxes and the latest heating bill. But for the children who lived there—for myself and my brothers and sisters—Marchmont was a kind of paradise. We climbed to the top of the huge Victorian wardrobe, and leapt down, squealing, on the squashy beds. We seized the cushions from the sofa in the music room, and ran and skidded on the polished floor. We threw ourselves at the house with everything we had, meeting it, head-on, with our entire bodies.

Beyond the noise and laughter of each other's company, the house was cool and shadowy and empty. I spent immense amounts of time alone: hunched in the dark angle of the attic stairs, or mooching dreamily from room to room. There were days when it seemed like a palace in a fairy tale, each piece of furniture trembling with incipient life. I remember the gilded harp in the drawing room, with its strange lamenting face and broken strings, how from the mantelpiece a love-ly girl looked out, her long hair swirling into snaky rays. It used to seem only a matter of time before the dolls in the glass cabinet started to talk among themselves, or the dolphins leapt from the backs of the black and gold throne-chairs. Often I felt invisible, even to myself, as if I had drifted out of contemporary chronology altogether, and been reduced to some ethereal essence: a ghost child, some kind of passing spirit.

"Time had no home in me," wrote the poet Roethke in one of his notebooks. And though my parents had given me a watch for my seventh birthday (sturdy and serviceable, with a pale blue leather strap), time had no home in me either, at least during the holidays. There was breakfast and lunch and tea and supper, all at regular in-tervals. There was church and tidy clothes and remembering to do your homework. But there was silence too, and solitude, and calm, where clocks and watches mattered not at all: lying in the long grass behind the raspberry canes, listening to the roo-coo of the pigeons, self dissolved in wonder, lost in light.

FAST FOOD POETRY

I have been teaching now for almost thirty years, working with schoolchildren and college students, with teachers and with senior citizens. I have taught poetry and nature writing, biography and memoir, oral history. Most consistently, I have worked for a program based in Cambridge, Massachusetts, teaching teachers to use poetry in the classroom.

That work has taken me all over the United States. One month I find myself changing planes in Atlanta, Georgia, the next in Denver, Colorado. I've been to Boise, Idaho, to St. Cloud, Minnesota, to little windswept towns in northern New Mexico. Each time, I lead a pair of intensive weekend workshops, lasting a total of about forty hours. Such "fast food poetry" does not come easily to me. It is always a challenge to connect with a new group of students, themselves already well acquainted with each other. I try to get a grasp of their ideas and interests, their taste, their sense of humor, and then to pitch my teaching at that level. There are practical difficulties too: making my way from the airport to the hotel and from the hotel to the school, often in an unfamiliar car, along unfamiliar roads, hampered by jet-lag and exhaustion.

But my difficulties are nothing compared to what my students must endure. Most have families of their own, as well as a full-time teaching job. They get up early to grade papers and prepare classes; they stay on after school to finish crucial paperwork; they carve out time on weekends to complete their assignments. They are kind, warm-hearted, idealistic people, but they are also frantic and beleaguered. They must meet the requirements of "No Child Left Behind." They must deal with harassed supervisors, needy children, overcrowded classrooms, parents who themselves are often overtaxed and anxious.

When I was first sent to Las Vegas, about a dozen years ago, the city was expanding by some four to six thousand people every month. Ten new schools were being built each year: eight new primary schools and two new high schools. Wages were high, and eager young teachers were pouring in from all over the United States. On my most recent visit, in the spring of 2008, the population had reached a high of two million people, and houses were going into foreclosure left and right. Classes were being held in double shifts throughout the year, with special emphasis on Remedial English and English as a Second Language. One teacher told me that in her district, the children spoke 105 different languages. This was a culture of raging inequality: extravagance and affluence at one end of town, and screeching poverty at the other, with the teachers doing their best to walk between. It is not easy in such circumstances to preach the value of a liberal education, or the tender pleasures to be found in poetry. Children handed in poems whose lines were jammed with dollar signs, as if cash were the only alphabet that mattered.

"My son is working at one of those big casinos," one woman told me. "I've been teaching for twenty-three years now, and already he makes better money than I do."

Meanwhile the teachers themselves are often woefully under-educated, unable to spell reliably (to distinguish *there* and *their*, *its* and *it's*) or to write a simple book report. Many are afraid of poetry, which they know only at its most basic (Shel Silverstein, Jack Prelutsky), and which, apart from haiku and some saccharine inspirational verse, they feel certain "has to rhyme." I try to quiz them about their earlier experiences, and a name or two may emerge: Emily Dickinson, Robert Frost, Maya Angelou. Some have encountered couplets and acrostics, or the occasional Shakespeare sonnet. But that is rare.

Often several will admit, half bashful, half defiant, that they have always hated poetry, and done everything they could to avoid teaching it. Now that it is required they want foolproof recipes, lessons that will fulfill every possible criterion at one fell swoop: serving to test spelling and to teach alliteration, to cover rhyme and rhythm, and at the same time tip a hat to Black History Month and the jazz legacy of Langston Hughes. They want poetry with a vengeance, poetry as an all-purpose tool for use in any circumstances: a cell phone, a camera, a sewing kit and a Swiss army knife, its compass pointing north to that essential A.

I do my best to assuage these multiple anxieties, perhaps especially in places like Las Vegas. I lead the class through small, manageable, step-by-step assignments. I read them Sharon Olds and William Stafford, introduce them to Rumi in the Coleman Barks translation and to Neruda, translated by Alastair Reid. Over the course of our two weekends together, I try to shepherd them towards a more adult frame of reference, to show them books they might return to on their own.

But the teachers find it difficult to concentrate. After about twenty minutes, they begin to surf the web. They step out into the corridor to make a crucial phone call, rustle through their bag to find more pretzels. They want that A. But it is hard for them to read or write for any length of time. They are children of speed, of novelty, of distraction. It is a challenge for them even to sit still.

On one of my recent teaching stints, I went into a convenience store to buy something to eat. Behind the sliding glass doors were shelves of Coca-Cola and expensive bottled water, plump little flagons of pre-mixed cappuccino. There were mini-servings of cheese and crackers in a tidy plastic wrap. There were aisles of tuna fish and blotchy Spam, racks and racks of thousand-flavored chips. But with the exception of some nicely freckled bananas hanging up above the till, there was almost nothing "natural" in the store. This was convenience food carried to the point of nausea, food stale, freeze-dried, prefabricated, dead. It was "fuel" all right, but nothing more. All its savor, all its beauty, had been leached away.

That convenience store came back to haunt me as I thought about my teaching. *Convenience food, convenience poetry.* Surely there had to be a better way. It wasn't poetry *per se* I wanted to teach my students, so much as a life in which poetry might be possible, poetry in the form of slowing down. I had nothing to sell, no forty-dollar workbook, no esoteric rituals or complex promises. I just wanted my students to relax a little, to allow themselves to listen, to remember their own dreamy childhood selves. *Walking, talking, reading, drawing, praying, telling stories:* the nourishment is there, as close as our own breath. We only have to pause a moment, notice, and enjoy.

BUYING TIME

The Buddha predicted that a Dark Age would arise, when people's thoughts would move so tremulously fast there'd be almost no room left for inner stillness. That age is now upon us. The past snaps at our heels, the future drags us forward up a rocky road. Almost everyone I know, from five to ninety-five, is hungry for more easy, spacious time.

"What are you working on these days?" my good friends ask.

When I tell them I've been working on a book on slowness, they are hardly able to contain themselves.

"Oh, my husband (my wife, my cousin, my best friend) could make good use of *that*!" they all assure me. And, "Hurry up and finish that book on slowing down!"

It is as if there were some secret store piled high with longed-for time: the gold doubloons of pirate hours, a stash of silvery minutes, which could be ours if we only had the key. *Some people have the key*, of that we are convinced. The Carthusian monk tending the monastery garden. The child kneeling in the grass to watch a butterfly. We envy them their focus and serenity. We know so well the kind of help we need. We print it on our T-shirts or our greeting-cards, we read it on each other's bumper-stickers:

Work hard, be lazy —Nam June Paik
Beware the barrenness of a busy life —Socrates
There is more to life than merely increasing its speed —Gandhi

Meanwhile, we talk of saving/wasting/investing/buying time as if life itself were just another form of currency. We turn Carl Honoré's *In Praise of Slowness* into a surprise bestseller; we crowd into poetry readings by Mary Oliver and Naomi Shihab Nye. We play soothing ocean music before we go to sleep, and get up early to practice yoga and meditation. We turn our earnest purposeful consumer-oriented brains to slowness and creativity as if they too could be added to our current shopping list, and paid for with our gold American Express card.

All this is touching and humanly understandable. But the fact is that it is radically mistaken. We cannot buy what Nabokov called "unreal estate"—the treasury of invisible possessions, ranging from time to talent to contentment. Such luxuries are not for sale, which is not to say that they are unattainable. Slowness is an option for everyone on the planet, not just a privilege reserved for the very wise or very young or very rich. All of us can decide (and the phrase is a potent one) *to take our time.* But to do so, we have to set aside our busy competence and practicality, at least for a while, and adopt a gentler and more expansive way of being. For some of us here in the United States, the recession that began in 2007 has proved a surprisingly useful ally.

THE SILVER LINING

In the tumultuous years since the recession began, many workers have felt obliged to work harder than usual, and for longer hours, stringing together multiple low-paying jobs to make ends meet. Too often, their friends and colleagues have already been let go, and they're afraid their own positions are at risk. For these unfortunates, "hurry sickness" has actually been exacerbated. Others have come to realize, albeit with some discomfort, that for all its terrors and uncertainties, the silver lining to the recession may be the gift of time.

One of the curious facts about the Great Depression is that, despite the spate of suicides, most ordinary people were in fact healthier then than they had been in previous years. They also enjoyed longer lives. Quite simply, *they had more time at their disposal.* Such "time affluence," as the sociologists call it, is strongly correlated with human wellbeing (health, longevity, happiness, creativity) whatever the vagaries of one's private income.

It seems likely that our current recession may grant a similar boon.

As I write this in the early months of 2011, Americans are consistently buying less and spending more time with friends and family. We are starting to garden, to make meals from scratch, to read again, to visit museums, to take part in local community events. In a recent survey, more than a third of those questioned said that work just didn't seem as important to them as it once had. Our values are changing, and our priorities too. For many of us, the choices we're now making are the ones that we'll be living by for the remainder of our lives.

As we begin to clarify those values (and expand into a slower mode of being), we may find ourselves especially grateful to those elders and mentors who have gone before. The stark statistics of the sociologists are backed by centuries of anecdotal evidence, drawn from the letters, journals, memoirs, and biographies of creative people, for whom a rich sufficiency of time has always been essential. It would be foolish to pretend that there's some sort of all-purpose Artist/Bodhisattva/Scholar/Poet who can be used as model. Nonetheless, there is much to be learned, glancingly, obliquely, from such stories.

The practicing artist is, by definition, someone who is able to build a life around his or her own creative work. Inevitably, such a person will have considered his or her attitude to time. What matters is not how much they actually have, but how best to inhabit it and make it spacious: how to allow room in which attention can take root. Such choices are important for all of us, whatever we are trying to create. The philosopher Hannah Arendt wrote of a "timeless region . . . lying beyond human clocks and calendars altogether." It is a place that many of us have sought in vain, a place of patience and apprenticeship, and, finally, of creativity, a "small non-time space in the very heart of time."

TEMPO GIUSTO

For all our protestations about our crazy-busyness, most of us are not so comfortable with slowing down. The first boat built by Europeans on American soil was called *Onrust* or *Restless,* and that edgy restlessness is still a part of us, both a blessing and a curse. Even now, *slow* is often used as a synonym for "stupid" or "old-fashioned," "boring," "dumb," whereas *fast* is taken to mean "smarter," "sharper," "better on all counts." In recent years, that humblest of written links, the tiny hyphen, has vanished from some 16,000 words. "Fig-leaf" is now "figleaf," "pigeon-hole" is "pigeonhole," and "leap-frog" has catapulted into "leapfrog." The reason, says Angus Stevenson, who edited the *Shorter Oxford English Dictionary*, is that we *no longer have time to reach over to the hyphen key.*

It is as if any pause, however modest, had the power to trigger us, thrusting us forward into anger and impatience, the desk equivalent of road rage. But slowing down need not be so excruciating. Our sense of time is among the most malleable of all the functions of the brain. The "velocity" involved in paying the bills is very different from the "velocity" of love-making, as most of us understand extremely well. The things we value most, we almost always try to do with some nimbus of timelessness around them: the opportunity to get lost and found again, to dissolve into what can feel like eternity. Such timelessness can be profoundly inspiring, even on an ordinary weekend.

Some years ago, graduate student Katja Schindler was taking a class at Antioch University Seattle. Her professor asked her to come up with an assignment that would alter her perception in some way, and then to try to put it into practice. Schindler decided to devote her whole weekend to the experience of slowing down. She would do everything she always did, but with a difference: she would do it all v-e-r-y, v-e-r-y s-l-o-w-l-y.

"It was amazing," she told her friend Rowland later. "I felt so happy, so focused and alive. I thought I'd find it boring. Not at all. And you know what? I got so much done! Far more than in a normal speedy run-around weekend. Suddenly there just seemed to be so much time—"

Schindler's experiment allowed her to give each task its *tempo giusto*: its own right or appropriate amount of time. To her astonishment, she found both pleasure and efficiency in slowing down. Her experience has much to teach us in our own unfurling lives. Whether we simply clean our house and do our chores, or spend our precious weekends making art, finding our own *tempo giusto* will help us to enjoy ourselves, bring us back on track, and at the same time allow us to reclaim the modest satisfactions of our own body, our own inventive spirit. The choice is ours to make. As William Stafford wrote in one of his poems,

There is a thread you follow. It goes among
things that change. But it doesn't change.
People wonder about what you are pursuing.
You have to explain about the thread.

PARIS, 2006

On New Year's Eve, 2006, hundreds of demonstrators marched through the streets of Paris, protesting the arrival of the coming year. They brandished signs reading "Now is Better!" and "No to 2007!" and called on the United Nations and other international leaders to "stop the mad race of time." When the clocks chimed at midnight, proclaiming the arrival of 2007, the protestors were unfazed.

"Now is better!" they chanted. "No to 2008!"

It is hard to imagine such a demonstration being held in Washington, D.C. It is too zany and playful, too obviously impractical, altogether too *French*. And yet the truth is that we have a lot to learn from those Parisian crowds. In terms of taking back our time, the first essential tool is saying no. No to our own greed and self-importance. No to the extra work we carry home. No to hearing without listening, looking without seeing; no, above all, to the insistent voice of advertising, which thrives on our restlessness and dissatisfaction, and does everything it can to exacerbate them. A Brobdingnagian NO to all those things makes space for an even more gigantic YES.

My private code for this is *to refuse and choose.*

We may not want to join the crowds outside the Champs Elysées, but we too can refuse to participate in the "mad race of time." We can choose to talk face to face with our friends instead of via email or on the telephone; we can play with our children, now, this very afternoon; we can go off for long walks across the hills. We can turn off the television once and for all. In short, we can rejoice in being one of the elite who actually *does* have the privilege of choice instead of complaining endlessly about our lack of time.

Of course it can feel difficult to drop out of the rat race: to stand at the side of the road while our friends and colleagues race on across the horizon. But that doesn't mean that it's impossible. In Matisse's painting, "The Red Studio," the clock has no hands. We need to find a "red studio" of our own, the studio of our own insistent heart, perhaps, in which to set up an easel or a writing desk, or pull a dreaming daybed towards a broad, wide-open window. It sounds so simple—almost too simple to be worth saying—but slowing down can be a tremendous source of joy.

Tactics

↪ Be conscious of your pace as you go about your day. Experiment with functioning at different speeds.

↪ Make a list of slow activities: *a long train ride, a hand-written letter, gardening,* etc. If possible, do at least one such "slow thing" every week.

↪ *Consider the following quotations:*
"What was lost? Time varied, elastic and colored. Time local, mischievous and ribboned. Time seasonal, haphazard, red-lettered and unpredictable was gone. Time was . . . colonized. Mapped. Leveled. Privatized. Enclosed. Counted in and accounted out."

JAY GRIFFITHS

"Slow down, our sages advise, slow down all the way to the pace of stone and shadow."

DIANE ACKERMAN

CHAPTER TWO

The Infinitely Healing Conversation

The ear draws forth the story.
ITALO CALVINO

Time to Talk

A T SIXTEEN AND SEVENTEEN, AND ON into my early twenties, I had a friend called Kenneth Armitage. He was forty years older than me, a sculptor, a working artist, with a string of professional successes to his name. He had, for example, been asked to represent Britain at the 1958 Venice Biennale. Not that he talked much about such things. The work was what mattered to him, both the act of making it, and the world from which he drew his inspiration: the strange contorted trees in Richmond Park, or the creamy cobbled look of certain clouds.

We had met in Scotland, in the country, when he came north to visit my uncle Rory, himself a painter. Later, back in London, we met up for meals and talks and the occasional out-of-town excursion. I remember one trip to the South Downs, and another to Avebury, wandering round the ancient stones and talking, talking, all day long. He was amused by me, I think, by what people called my "intensity," and did what he could to encourage me, to help me find my way. And I, for my part, was filled with admiration for his vigor and originality, his immense gusto. I loved listening to him. I would come home from a day we'd spent together, and write down everything he'd said.

On one such visit, I found him in his studio, blue overalls and square lined face and iron gray hair, stocky and robust. "Well, I never see you for ages, and then you come in as cheerful as ever," he said, pouring out tea in the kitchen/sitting room upstairs. "That's right, that's *right*." I gazed around me, enjoying the books and photographs and battered chairs, the fieldstones and twists of dried wood, the

Wellington boots, the Indian masks. Two shiny painted arms (one of his sculptures) stuck out from above the mantlepiece, their splayed fingers greeting me or seeking help.

> Kenneth talked about the Burren (a rocky limestone area in the west of Ireland) and the other visitors there, mostly French. How when he's there, he forgets all about the art world, and once he's back in London, he can hardly draw. He talked too about Spain (the Prado) and about his work, and the difficulty of combining it with family life. *Intake*, for example: how much is enough? He talked about gods and goddesses, and why they are thought to exist. About women and men and how some trees (not all) are hermaphrodite. The elm tree stump he sits on while he works. About Richmond and the way trees "clot" in the autumn. He showed me the green industrial wax he uses to model them. Later they are cast in bronze.
>
> And he talked about fellow artists: he taught Howard Hodgkin, for example, and likes his work. About Arts Council grants. About a possible show in New York City. How nothing is better than the happiness that painting/writing can give you.

I was young and ardent and eager, and I drank in every word: *So this too was possible, this too.*

Years later, living in New York, I had another such friend. His name was Arthur Strimling. He was the director, I the writer, for an intergenerational theater group called Roots & Branches. Early each Thursday we would meet for breakfast: bagels and cream cheese, a tall cup of coffee. We would go over the script together, devising improvisations, laying out our plans. Our meetings were purposeful and highly focused. And yet somehow there was space in them as well: room to talk about books and movies or the latest dastardly politics, to share an anecdote or a couple of lines of poetry, to tease out a little more about each other's lives.

New York was the perfect place for such conversations, chock-a-block with lively projects, interesting people. But all too often, *there simply wasn't time.* One could spend three weeks trying to make a date with a friend, which would then be canceled at the last minute, or shrivel to a fifty-minute lunch, shadowed by exhaustion and neurosis. I used to long for a conversation that was *not* about work or shrinks or real estate or the rehashing of a bad, unhappy childhood. I thought of Kenneth's kitchen–sitting room on a Sunday afternoon: the smell of freshly ground coffee, his sturdy working hands. To give over an entire day to such lavish wide-ranging enthusiastic discourse had come to seem entirely unimaginable. It shone forth like a beacon from some other world.

Meanwhile, my friends and I spent hours on the phone. We all insisted we'd "no time" to get together, but we would sit at home for most of an evening, talking, talking, far into the night. This was pre-handset, pre–mobile phone, so one was, in effect, tethered to the desk for the duration of the call. One morning, I sprang awake in panic. I'd been dreaming that my phone was on fire. The flames leaping out from it were two feet high. It was as if all the desperate repetitive stressed-out news that sped along its wires had finally caused it to ignite. I was panicked, but I cannot say I was surprised. *Well, yes,* I thought. *Of course. That's really how things are.*

FASTFORWARD COMMERCIAL

In *The School Among the Ruins,* Adrienne Rich has a strange staccato prose poem called "USonian Journals 2000," in which she reports, ruefully, on recent changes in American culture:

> Could I just show what's happening. Not that shooting, civil disturbance, whatever it was. I'd like you to see how differently we're all moving, how the time allowed to let things become known grows shorter and shorter, how quickly things and people get replaced.

That speed, that almost instant obsolescence, has affected language too. Rich mourns the slower, more capacious ways of speaking, the "pause in conversation when time would stop, an idea hang suspended," or when talk would suddenly surge into its own crescendo, everyone talking at once.

The current mode of speaking is a fiercely different one. There is something relentless about it: *"I am here and talking, talking, here and talking."* [Rich's words and emphasis.] Its practitioners have grown up under the perpetual assault of the media, and they have developed a curious style of their own, breathless and urgent and self-absorbed, as if they saw themselves as characters in an ongoing comic strip or radio drama:

> "I thought she'd never call and I went aaah! to my friend and she went give it a week, she'll call you all right and you did"—"And you went waowh! and I went, right, I went O.K., it's only I was clueless? so now can we grab something nearby, cause I'm due on in forty-five?"

For Rich, with her trained poet's ear, such mangling of the language is intolerable. Even the pitch and timbre of the words has changed.

> Men of the upwardly mobilizing class needing to sound boyish . . . pirate lad's nasal bravado. . . . Voices of girls and women screeking to an excitable edge of brightness. . . . Male, female voices alike pitched fastforward commercial, one timbre, tempo, intonation.

One does not have to be a poet to recognize what Adrienne Rich is saying here. Court reporters document that we do indeed talk faster than we did in the 1960s, just as we write faster (and less legibly), work and eat faster, even make love more speedily. Meanwhile the ear is greedy for yet greater speed. The average fast talker speaks 150 words per minute, but listeners can comprehend up to 600 words a minute, as much as four times faster. Children find class boring because their teachers talk so slowly. Adults snap or cut each other off, because a colleague has taken so long to get to the point. Patience becomes a rare old-fashioned virtue. It is as if the cost of paying attention had become more than most of us can easily afford.

The Italian Futurist Filippo Marinetti foresaw this outcome back in 1913. Futurism, he wrote, was about "the acceleration of life to today's swift pace." The new man would communicate by "brutally destroying the syntax of his speech." He would "despise [the] subtleties and nuances of language." His thought would be marked by a "dread of slowness, pettiness, analysis and detailed explanations. 'Quick, give me the whole thing in two words!' "

The contemporary businessperson strives to do just that. In 1968, the average length of time a presidential candidate was able to speak uninterruptedly on television was 42.3 seconds. By 1988, it had shrunk to 9.8 seconds. Public speakers hire experts to help them trim their thoughts to the allotted sound bytes. Small margin is left for humor, irony, or playfulness, let alone genuine complexity. Efficiency is king, and in the process the glory that was English (or American) shrivels to the English of computer programs, *computinglish*, with its stringently simplified structures and commands. The writer Jay Griffiths describes this with scathing authority:

> Speed adversely affects language; as the ltle bk of txt abuse called "IH8U" shows all too well. "The pen is mightier than the sword—but the keypad is swifter," it advertises itself. The abbreviated words of text messages represent abbreviated emotions, vowel-less and thoughtless, the clichés of mindless juvenile communication, with its tawdry insults of ScmBg, SaDO and Nrd. The phenomenon is MnDNmn.

Meanwhile, many of the teachers I work with, and the students too, live their lives in thrall to just such speed. Asked to slow down enough to write a poem, or to draw a map of a favorite childhood place, their eyes fill up with tears. They haven't had time to muse, to remember, for they cannot say how long. They are proud of their cell phones, their new computers, but at the same time, they are dissatisfied. They have spent good money on the machinery of communication, but its pleasures continue to elude them.

One woman told me sadly about a friend with whom she used to sit and talk each Saturday morning, spaciously, companionably, over cakes and coffee. Now the friend calls her on her cell phone as she barrels down the freeway.

"She *thinks* she's keeping in touch," the woman said. "She *thinks* it's just the same. But not to me, it isn't."

It is easy to be seduced by the new media. They will answer any question you might ask; they provide a kind of ersatz companionship 24/7. With iPods and cell phones, computers and BlackBerries, Netflix and the Internet, let alone film and video, television and radio, no middle-class American need ever be at a loss for entertainment. Ten percent of those under fifty are so attached to the internet that, if it were possible, they'd be willing to have a connective device implanted in their own bodies. But when 43 percent of all free time "goes down the tube," part of ourselves goes with it. We lose the time we need to recover ourselves, to hear ourselves think, time to talk to each other and listen to each other's stories.

THE GREAT GOOD PLACE

Until recently, we in the United States were known for our gregariousness. "Americans of all ages, all stations in life, and all types of disposition are forever forming associations," wrote the French visitor Alexis de Tocqueville in the mid-nineteenth century. "Nothing, in my view, deserves more attention than the intellectual and moral associations in America."

When the spirit is there, such associations can find a way to flourish even in the most unlikely circumstances. The writer Howard Mansfield tells a lovely story about a group of southern gentlemen in the Smoky Mountains of North Carolina. He'd been doing some research in the area, and asked if he could meet with them. "Sure," they said, "We'll meet you at McDonalds." When he arrived the next morning the old men were out in force: all of them gathered around those small, awkwardly shaped plastic tables, each with a paper cup of coffee. They had taken over that fast food franchise, and totally transformed it, made it into their club, their private hangout, required it to move at their own slow-as-molasses pace. This was not something that had been consciously planned. As Mansfield explained, "It was just their habit of being."

But such stories have become increasingly rare. De Tocqueville's associations continued to flourish well into the twentieth century, but in the last thirty years, they have, in many cases, died away. People visit each other less often now; they are less willing to go out for drinks after work, or to organize a block barbecue on a hot summer evening. "We spend less time in conversation over meals," writes Harvard professor Robert Putnam. "[W]e engage less often in leisure activities . . . we spend more time watching . . . and less time doing."

Immigrants are frequently taken aback at the narrowness of our social world. Here, for example, is Arthur Gulkarov, a young dancer of Russian Jewish heritage, recently arrived from the Central Asian state of Tajikistan:

> Over there, childhood was really friendly. We play outside. We play inside. You know what we did in our building in Dushanbe? First floor, we did this big room for wintertime, all neighbors can go downstairs, drink tea, watch TV, and each neighbor cook something. Summertime, they did outside the same thing, make a special place.

In Astoria, Queens, things are very different:

> All neighbors friendly, but here is little bit boring and more alone. Now, I'm used to it. But before I was like, *My God, where is everybody? C'mon everybody, come down!*

That big room in Dushanbe was the kind of place Ray Oldenberg describes in his classic text, *The Great Good Place: Cafés, Coffee Shops, Bookstores, Bars, Hair Salons and Other Hangouts at the Heart of a Community*: the welcome "third place" after the inevitable home and work. The third place is where one goes to hang out, to shoot the breeze, to talk to friends and strangers in a relaxed and easy atmosphere. Because of the sheer diversity of its clientele, the conversation tends to be more lively and surprising than it is elsewhere. Like the old gentlemen in North Carolina, the regular visitor has the luxury of seeing friends by the set instead of singly, and often reaps the benefit of casual advice and practical help, even what Oldenberg calls "a spiritual tonic."

Unfortunately, many of us in the States (the middle class especially) do not recognize the value of the "great good place." We try to get by on what Oldenberg calls "a bipod" made up of home and work, behaving as if a beautiful house and a small group of like-minded friends could substitute for an entire community. Arthur's father, Ishak, an accomplished drummer, is especially contemptuous of this point of view. His English is broken, but the passion and emphasis are clear:

> America is free country, is working, working, working.
> Is money, money, money.
> After saving their money, money, money, they die.
> No good.
> Money is die.
> . . .
>
> After working should go to restaurant.
> Drink, I like you, you like me—enjoy!
> After working, working, working,
> you must kiss your husband, kiss your wife.
> Okay.
> Make music. Love family.
> Then can die.

Contemporary theorists concur. Social isolation is, quite simply, bad for one's health, undermining one's basic sense of equilibrium, and over time, one's happiness. Depression and anxiety, anger and violence have all been linked with loneliness, as have drug and alcohol abuse. Lack of friends reduces one's immune function, and lowers one's life expectancy. Joining a group—any group, from yoga to philately—gives an immediate boost to one's longevity. Luckily, some immigrants have made the effort to create just such opportunities for themselves. Ali El Sayed owns the Kabab Café on Steinway Street in Astoria, clearly a dazzling example of a Great Good Place:

> I was the first one to start a café on the block. Now they're calling the neighborhood Little Egypt. Other people I know, artists and musicians who come to my place, have been here for a while too. What we do, we make the area nice. We don't have much, so we create a state of mind to enjoy ourselves. . . . We get together and talk about literature and art.

> Every night I go home and I think about the conversations I had that night. It gives me hope that we might have a better universe. Like Picasso was Spanish and Braque was French and Gertrude Stein was American, but they met in the cafés in Paris. It was a place to exchange ideas. Astoria is becoming a place like that.

THE ART OF CONVERSATION

Literary historians like to claim that the "art of conversation" reached its peak in eighteenth-century France and England, with the opening of the first cafés and coffeehouses. Certainly an impressive roster of writers and talkers emerged on both sides of the Channel: what the philosopher David Hume once called "the conversible world." There were several thousand clubs and coffeehouses in London alone. Customers would gather together round the one long table, talking and smoking and reading the papers.

"What a lesson," remarked a visiting cleric, "to see a lord or two, a baronet, a shoemaker, a wine-merchant, and a few others of the same stamp poring over the same newspapers."

Literary men had their own special venues, like Will Unwin's on Russell Street, or Button's coffeehouse across the road. The poet John Dryden favored Will's, while Joseph Addison and Richard Steele, old friends from Oxford, helped to establish Daniel Button's. The work they did together, writing and publishing *The Spectator* and *The Tatler*, did much to establish a literate readership—what Coleridge would later call the "clerisy." Indeed, Addison claimed there were twenty readers for every copy of *The Spectator*. He himself could be seen at Button's every afternoon, talking and hobnobbing with his friends, and often stayed there deep into the night.

The flavor of the time is beautifully captured in Steele's short essay, "Twenty Four Hours in London." Steele gets up at four a.m., takes a boat upriver, and spends the rest of the day wandering about the city, quietly enchanted by the changing spectacle. Here, for instance, he is at Strand Bridge at six o'clock in the morning:

> Chimney-Sweepers passed by us as we made up to the Market, and some Raillery happened between one of the Fruit-Wenches and those black Men, about the Devil and *Eve*, with Allusion to their several Professions. I could not believe any Place more entertaining than *Covent-Garden;* where I strolled from one Fruit-Shop to another, with Crowds of agreeable young Women around me, who were purchasing Fruit for their respective Families.

Later, he takes a coach in pursuit of a young woman he describes as belonging to the family of "Vainloves," meaning she is something of a flirt. His driver has another name for her: in his terms, she's a "Silk-Worm." Steele is surprised at the phrase, but learns that it is slang among the drivers for their best customers: Women who ramble twice and thrice a Week from Shop to Shop, to turn over all the Goods in Town without buying anything.

The Silk-Worms are, it seems, indulged by the Tradesmen; for tho' they never buy, they are ever talking of new Silks, Laces and Ribbands, and serve the Owners in getting them Customers, as their common Dunners do in making them pay.

In other words, their conversation is itself respected as a driving force. By now it has reached two or three o'clock: high noon for the "People of Fashion." Steele's coach proceeds towards the business district, "and gay Signs, well disposed Streets, magnificent publick Structures, and wealthy Shops, adorned with contented Faces" fill him with delight as he is drawn into the center of the city, the "Centre of the World of Trade, the *Exchange* of *London*." He counts himself "the richest Man that walked the *Exchange* that Day," for he is brimful of impressions, and (feelingly, at least) shares in the profits of every bargain that is struck.

It seems only right that he should end the day at Will's, listening quietly to several simultaneous conversations having to do with "Cards, Dice, Love, Learning and Politicks." This last subject keeps him up till past two in the morning, before he finally retires to bed, ready to write the very essay we are reading. The conversible world indeed! What could be more affable and easygoing, more immediately productive and convivial?

The writer Jonathan Swift, one of Steele's great contemporaries, described conversation as "the greatest, the most lasting, and the most innocent, as well as useful Pleasure of Life." He had only one suggestion for improving it: *women should be admitted too.* He himself set great store by his learned "Stella" (Esther Johnson), though he belonged to a club from which women were excluded. This was not uncommon. Despite the galaxy of brilliant female conversationalists, among them the writers Fanny Burney, Hannah More and Lady Mary Wortley Montagu, the pleasures of the eighteenth-century coffeehouse were almost entirely restricted to "clubbable men."

On at least one occasion, Lady Mary Wortley Montagu asked her husband to leave a letter for her at a coffeehouse in Salisbury. But that did not mean that she could sit there at her ease as a man would have done. In Viennese coffeehouses, where women were made welcome, she enjoyed the kind of conversation she described as "the greatest happynesse of Life"—the "chosen conversation compos'd of a few that one esteems." In her late forties, she left the British Isles, along with an arid, unhappy marriage, and spent much of her remaining life abroad, in Venice, Avignon, and Rome, not returning till 1761, after her husband's death.

A PASSION FOR FRIENDSHIP

Emerson once said that he would walk a hundred miles through a snowstorm for one good conversation. In his lecture on "Table Talk," he advises his audience to "Seek society. Keep your friendships in repair. Answer your letters. Meet good-will half-way." There is much to be learned, he thinks, from casual conversation with close friends. More wit and insight is "dropped in talk and forgotten by the speaker" than gets into books. It behooves us therefore to pay attention, not just for courtesy's sake, but for our own.

> The wise man comes to this game to play upon others, and be played upon. He is as curious to know what can be drawn from him as what he can draw from them.

And again, "Sincere and happy conversation doubles our power. In the effort to unfold our thought to a friend we make it clearer to ourselves."

But not all friends, however admirable, are capable of the kind of fluid reciprocity that Emerson describes. It is entirely possible to be a brilliant writer and talker without also possessing what one might call "the art of listening." The poet Coleridge is a case in point. "My friend C," wrote Hazlitt, "could go on in the most delightful explanatory way over hill and dale a summer's day, and convert a landscape into a didactic poem or a Pindaric ode." In a letter to his brother and sister-in-law, Keats gives a hilarious account of one of these effusions. They had met in London, in the vicinity of Highgate, and Keats had walked with

Coleridge "at his alderman-after-dinner pace" for nearly two miles.

> In those two Miles he broached a thousand things—let me
> see if I can give you a list—Nightingales, Poetry—on Poeti-
> cal Sensation—Metaphysics—Different genera and species
> of Dreams—Nightmare—a dream accompanied with a sense
> of touch—single and double touch—a dream related—First
> and second consciousness—the difference explained be-
> tween will and Volition—so many metaphysicians from a
> want of smoking the second consciousness—Monsters—the
> Kraken—Mermaids—Southey believes in them—Southey's
> belief too much diluted—a Ghost story—

Clearly there was no end to this. "I heard his voice as he came
towards me" wrote Keats, "I heard it as he moved away—I had heard
it all the interval—if it may be called so."

There is something wonderfully invigorating in such a display.
When I think back to those long days with Kenneth Armitage, I realize that he too was not much of a listener. But to be with him was
sustaining, nourishing. There are talkers whose gift is to exhilarate
and inspire, and others, like Emerson himself, whose chief gift is one
of sympathetic understanding. For the apprentice artist (writer or
painter or poet) such encouragement is worth its weight in gold.
W. B. Yeats wrote in glowing terms of his friend Arthur Symons,
who was able to "slip as it were into the mind of another."

> [M]y thoughts gained in richness and in clearness from his
> sympathy, nor shall I ever know how much my practice and
> my theory owe to the passages that he read me from Catullus
> and from Verlaine and Mallarmé.

The Beat poet Allen Ginsberg spoke in similar terms of his friendships with Burroughs and Kerouac and Corso. Because these were
men he knew well, "whose souls [he] respected," he was able to speak
to them very openly, and that openness inspired him when he came

to write. He realized that all he had to do was to transfer to paper (tell the Muse) what he was already telling to his friends. The key was "to commit to writing—to *write*, the same way that you . . . are!"

In terms of their literary endeavors, and indeed, their public status, the philosopher Bertrand Russell and the writer Joseph Conrad could hardly have been more different. But their friendship blazed into tremendous intimacy from the very first. "We seemed to sink through layer after layer of what was superficial," Russell wrote, "till gradually both reached the central fire. It was an experience unlike any other I have known. We looked into each other's eyes half appalled and half intoxicated to find ourselves together in such a region."

Cicero would have understood what Russell was describing, as would Montaigne and St. Augustine. From their point of view, such friendships were among the great joys of human life, at least for the educated adult male. One wrote, one studied, one honed one's spirit, in the hopes of being worthy of just such a passionate connection. Marriage, with however bright and amiable a woman, was contaminated by its own utility, and could never match such heady, all-male glories.

A 2008 survey in the *Journal of Socio-Economics* claimed that the psychological benefits of friendship were equivalent to a pay-rise of eighty-five thousand pounds (some $127,000 in today's dollars). But modern writers tend to disparage such alliances, or to judge them all, mistakenly, as homoerotic. It is as if the traditional romantic relationship has become the only one that really matters. Man and wife rise up like two colossi in a trampled landscape, in which friendship (shrunk to pygmy size) seems scarcely to intrude. Many couples (preoccupied with work and children, pressed for time) do in fact operate along just these lines. They may chat on occasion with a colleague from work, meet casually with an acquaintance from the gym. But that is all. Such "differentiated friendships" (the phrase originates with the sociologist Georg Simmell) are specialized, fragmented— and inevitably shallow.

Simmell believes that most of us no longer have time for deep, wide-ranging, loyal, old-fashioned friendships, far less for the astonishing, almost violating intimacy Russell describes. Other experts concur. In the United States at least, the number of close friendships has declined since 1985, from an average of three to an average of only two. A quarter of the population claims to have no close confidant at all. All too often we blunder forward on our own, lacking those whose casual sustenance would have steadied and enriched us, "double[d] our power," and drawn us back into alignment with our own best selves.

WOMAN TALK

Classical accounts of friendship, like those of Cicero and St. Augustine, take small account of women. Cross-gender friendships were for many years extremely rare, owing to the pressures of romance, as well as the imbalance in training and education, and women's own alliances were just not taken seriously. Nor, as we have seen, did the "conversible world" offer much of a welcome. Words like "gossip" and "babble" and "tattle" were being used in 1674, and are still being used today, along with such variants as "blether" and "blather," "natter" and "tittle-tattle," many of them derived from the same (contemptuous) root. "Blather," for example, derives from the Old Norse *blathr*, meaning "nonsense," and "tattle" from the Middle Dutch, *tatelen*, "to babble" or "stammer." In comparison to the sturdy, logical, clear-headed talk of men, the implication is that the "second sex" just isn't worth listening to. The Scottish poet Liz Lochhead makes the point all too well in her poem, "Men Talk":

> *Women*
> *Rabbit rabbit rabbit women*
> *Tattle and titter*
> *Women prattle*
> *Women waffle and witter*
>
> *Men Talk. Men Talk . . .*
> *Women gossip Women giggle*
> *Women niggle-niggle-niggle*
> *Men Talk.*

Even now, men interrupt women far more frequently than men (or women) interrupt each other, and parents (alas) are far more likely to interrupt their daughters than their sons. Research shows that when women speak in class precisely 50 percent of the time, both sexes feel that they speak more. From a woman's point of view, one of the true advantages of cyberspace is that there, at least, we are finally permitted to have our full, unhurried say. But the snap-exchange of text-messaging, email's tireless reciprocity, even the domesticated narcissism of Facebook or Twitter, offer few of the satisfactions the best talk provides.

For years I have been haunted by a line from Adrienne Rich in which she describes the human longing for the "infinitely healing conversation," the joyful and restorative exchange in which both parties feel truly heard and understood. The point of this, she explains, is not just to say what one has determined on ahead of time, but rather, to "hear each other into speech;" in other words, to draw forth from one another what we scarcely knew we thought or had to say. This is, perhaps, the most delicious and surprising thing about a thoroughly good talk: that we depart from it filled with affection not only for our interlocutor, but also for ourselves. The sense of gratitude, of homecoming, can be very strong.

One thinks of such exhilarating talk as shared mainly between lovers and close friends, and (ideally) family members. But professional colleagues can provide this boon as well. Rich first met Audre Lorde, fellow poet and lesbian-feminist, at a time when such identities were rarer and more precious (and considerably more beleaguered) than they are today, and knew at once that she had found "a remarkable new poet and . . . also a colleague," someone she might actually be able to talk with. Meeting by chance at the City College of New York, they "began a conversation that was to go on for twenty years, a conversation between two people of vastly different temperaments and cultural premises, a conversation often balked and jolted by those differences, yet sustained by [their] common love for poetry and respect for each others' work."

Ann Patchett writes in similar terms about her friendship with the writer Lucy Greeley. Both, in this case, were straight women, but,

> We shared our ideas like sweaters, with easy exchange and lack of ownership. We gave over excess words, a single beautiful sentence that had to be cut but perhaps the other would like to have. . . . We didn't so much discuss our work as volley ideas back and forth until neither of us was sure who belonged to what.

And again:

> I loved to listen to her talk. I was never happier than on the nights we stayed home, lying on the living room rug. We talked about classes and poetry and politics and sex. . . . Iowa City in the eighties was never going to be Paris in the twenties, but we gave it our best shot.

For twenty years, I had the pleasure of such a friendship with a woman I'll call Rosie. We talked back and forth on the telephone. We wrote letters to each other, often. We visited each other in Massachusetts and New York City, took long weekend jaunts together. Our friendship enlarged and clarified my daily life, gave me steady purpose and direction, as well as a reliable source of oblique, ironic humor. The dead phrases of the psychoanalysts, which praise friendship as giving rise to "greater self-awareness," and an "enhanced capacity for agency and moral action," suddenly felt alive to me, and true.

The disembodied friendships that we now endure, in which a long unwinding chat over an endless pot of tea is replaced by a hasty five-minute email, the tactile pleasure of an actual birthday card by a virtual one which must be painstakingly downloaded, are, by contrast, pitifully insufficient.

SOUND AND SILENCE

In *The Spell of the Sensuous,* the writer David Abram describes two friends meeting again after a long time. If we should chance to overhear them, he says, we might well notice "a tonal, melodic layer of communication" beneath the explicit meaning of the words, "a rippling rise and fall of the voices in a sort of musical duet, rather like two birds singing to each other."

Each voice mimics a portion of the other's melody, at the same time adding its own inflection, which is then echoed by the original speaker, "the two singing bodies tuning and attuning to one another, rediscovering a common register, *remembering* each other." This tuning and retuning, this remembering, is what is called "entrainment."

It is hardly surprising that human beings should attune to one another in this way. After all, we live in a rhythmic universe, in which the earth revolves around the sun and the moon around the earth. Our bodies are rhythmic organisms, containing breath and pulse and heart beat. If you put two grandfather clocks in the same room, their pendulums will fall into unison within a couple of days. In the same way, when people talk or sing or move together, we tend to "entrain," or synchronize our pace with one another. This is one of the delights of good conversation: not just the stated theme, the surface content, but the underlying pleasure of entrainment, the half-conscious *pas de deux* with someone else's mind.

Every piece of music is made up of sound and pause, sound and pause, which is to say that *it also includes silence*. The trumpeter Miles Davis was praised for creating good music because he "opened up the space between the notes and stepped inside." Martin Buber, philosopher and mystic, accomplished something similar in his speech, as a member of his audience reports:

> I was fascinated by the *way* Buber spoke. Too mannered, perhaps, but entrancing—the way he lowered his head into his arms after saying something, waiting for the next revelation. He took time between utterances, time to pause, to listen. For Buber, speaking was a way of listening. *Shema Yisrael.* "Hear, Israel." Buber heard, and when he heard, we heard. By speaking, Buber was teaching listening.

In a predominantly visual and verbal culture, there is both relief and opportunity in such an opening to silence. (It seems magically apposite that the word "listen" is an anagram of "silent," and of course vice versa.) Buber's slow attentive self is little honored in our present world. But for those who are capable of such serenity, the rewards are vast. It can build a bridge not only to our living friends and to the writers we admire, but to the dead also, including our own ancestors. T.S. Eliot said it well in "Little Gidding":

> *And what the dead had no speech for, when living,*
> *They can tell you, being dead: the communication*
> *Of the dead is tongued with fire beyond the*
> > *language of the living.*

Here too, is the Scottish poet, W. S. Graham, in "A Note to the Difficult One," written to a friend who had recently died:

> *This morning I am ready if you are,*
> *To hear you speaking in your new language.*
> *I think I am beginning to have nearly*
> *A way of writing down what it is I think*
> *You say. You enunciate very clearly*
> *Terrible words always just beyond me.*
>
> *I stand in my vocabulary looking out*
> *Through my window of fine water . . .*
>
> > . . .
>
> *I see your face speaking flying*
> *In a cloud wanting to say something.*

"I stand in my vocabulary looking out / Through my window of fine water"—the welcome here, the patient readiness, is all. We are used, perhaps, to opening to our friends in this way, even to our beloved dead. But what of the non-human world? Can we listen to that too?

THE LANGUAGE OF THE WILD

For eons, human speech has been enriched, inhabited, by the language of the wild: the seethe and gush of rainwater, the tinkle of icicles, the song of the birds. But as the outside world has been blasted and subdued, as the songbirds are silenced, and the streams diverted into culverts, that aspect of our language is being wrenched away. As David Abram has said, "[W]hen we no longer hear the warbler and the wren, our own speaking can no longer be nourished by their cadences."

A friend who lives in the hills of western Massachusetts, close by a tumultuous little brook, told me of the visitor who arrived on her threshold eager to identify that "curious sound." She literally *did not recognize* the music of the stream. But that music is still there, for those who listen. Thomas Merton, for one, was not afraid to find words for what he heard:

> The rain surrounded the cabin . . . with a whole world of meaning, of secrecy, of rumor. Think of it: all that speech pouring down, selling nothing, judging nobody, drenching the thick mulch of dead leaves, soaking the trees, filling the gullies and crannies of the wood with water, washing out the places where men have stripped the hillside. . . . Nobody started it, nobody is going to stop it. It will talk as long as it wants, the rain. As long as it talks, I am going to listen.

And the English poet, Alice Oswald, who makes her living as a gardener, says that listening is what she enjoys most about her work, and what actually leads her into poems:

> I try to keep listening, letting each line grow slowly out of the landscape. I have my left hand cupped like an ear, and it feels as if I'm holding my mind in my right hand and a garden in my left.

For the Inuit people, as for many others, there was a time when human beings and animals were understood to speak the same language. In those days, "words were like magic," as a woman called Nalungiaq explained:

> *A word spoken by chance*
> *might have strange consequences.*
> *It would suddenly come alive*
> *and what people wanted to happen could happen—*
> *all you had to do was say it.*
> *Nobody could explain this:*
> *That's the way it was.*

"A word spoken by chance / might have strange consequences. / It would suddenly come alive." This is the "life" we seek in our tireless effort to communicate: the miracle of that infinitely healing conversation. But as so often it depends on listening. Can we listen to each other, can we listen to the dead? Can we listen to the birds in the rain-drenched garden? Can we allow some time to pause, some time for silence?

Tactics

↬ Make at least one personal call a day, and if possible, actually see (and walk with) friends and family.

↬ Allow time for a lengthy conversation with someone you care about. Make an agreement that you will allow each other "enough time" to follow the talk wherever it wants to go.

↬ *Consider the following quotations:*
"And this is what we mean by friends. Even when they are absent, they are with us . . . even when they are weak, they are strong; and . . . even when they are dead, they are alive."

CICERO

"He had a genius for intimacy, a genius for making one feel singular and worthy and interesting."

PAULA FOX of her friend WILLIAM MAXWELL

CHAPTER THREE

Child Time

Tomorrow, will we have hundreds of times to play?

GEORGIA McEWEN, AGED 4

Doing Nothing

I REMEMBER LYING IN THE GRASS, LOOKING UP into the flaming autumn glory of the spindle tree. The berries were a fiery orange-scarlet, each one shaped like a tiny four-cornered hat. I was six or seven then, the oldest child, with two younger sisters and a younger brother. Nursery life was noisy and demanding. But I felt happy there, under the spindle tree, watching the old horse, Snowball, ambling about, or listening to the wind in the thin straps of the leaves. I went back over and over again.

In the same way, I returned to the barn, pushing past the dock-leaves and the stinging nettles to the damp space underneath where the forget-me-nots grew. I used to sit there for what seemed hours, while the chickens scratched and scrabbled from the chicken coop, and the forget-me-nots gazed back at me with all their thousand bright blue eyes. I dug in like a little animal, full of the clenched pleasure of being alone. "*I am myself*," I thought, "*myself*," free of the grownups, of all inside obligations, and at the same time (perhaps contradictorily) at one with the soft waving of the grasses, the looming presence of the trees.

"All children want to crouch in their secret nests," writes the Irish poet Seamus Heaney, remembering his boyhood in County Derry in the early 1940s. He himself had a special affection for the boxwood hedge in front of his house, the fork of a certain beech tree, and "the soft collapsing pile of hay" at the back of the byre. But most of all he loved the throat of an old willow tree at the far end of the farmyard.

It was a hollow tree, with gnarled, spreading roots, a soft perishing bark and a pithy inside. Its mouth was like the fat and solid opening in a horse's collar, and once you squeezed in through it, you were at the heart of a different life, looking out on the familiar yard as if it were suddenly behind a pane of strangeness. Above your head, the living tree flourished and breathed, you shouldered the slightly vibrant bole, and if you put your forehead to the rough pith you felt the whole lithe and whispering crown of willow moving in the sky above you.

From an adult point of view, such experiences can look almost negligible. There's a book on the subject by Robert Paul Smith. Its title is *"Where did you go?" "Out." "What did you do?" "Nothing."* But for years now, artists and writers have praised this "nothing," recognizing it as a source of inspiration and delight.

> *There are in our existence spots of time*
> *That with distinct pre-eminence retain*
> *A renovating virtue . . .*

wrote Wordsworth, in his long autobiographical poem, "The Prelude." John Muir, too, wrote winningly of nature's "wonderful glowing lessons," and remembered his childhood on the raw edge of the North Sea. "Here, without knowing it, we were still at school; every wild lesson a love lesson, not whipped, but charmed into us."

In his mid-seventies, the art historian Bernard Berenson looked back over his life, remembering the times of greatest joy. One moment in particular stood out:

> Was I five or six? Certainly not seven. It was a morning in early summer. A silver haze shimmered and trembled over the lime trees. The air was laden with their fragrance. The temperature was like a caress. I remember—I need not recall—that I climbed up a tree stump and felt suddenly immersed in Itness. I did not call it by that name. I had no need for words. It and I were one.

EARTH CHILD

Time to muse and dream and do a blissful kind of nothing must always have been something of a privilege, a sleight of hand and heart, abstracted from work or daily chores. Depending on their age and class and race and family background, most children have been required to work; some 246 million work full time even now, the bulk of them in agriculture. But even without formal paid employment, child and adult time are set at odds. The child is curious and alert and interested, eager and impulsive; the adult, for the most part, "wants to get things done." One of the first hard lessons most of us learn is how the bitter grid of scheduling bites down across our own joyful, unselfconscious ease of being.

This is especially obvious in the case of school.

"My life changed abruptly when I started school," wrote the Italian novelist Natalia Ginzburg. Until then she had never needed to know what time was. "Now, when I woke up I checked the clock a million times, both the alarm clock on the night table and the huge clock on the street corner just opposite my window. I hated those two clocks. My life was gradually being taken over by things I hated." By the time a student graduates from high school, he or she will have spent some twelve thousand hours in school: close to five hundred weeks of childhood. Along with math and history and social studies come the more subtle lessons in hierarchy and compliance, in delayed gratification, in the honoring of rewards and competition. But first and last and always is the impress of the timetable. It is a lesson that can take a lifetime to unlearn.

But until very recently (some would say as recently as the 1970s), there has almost always been a happy margin at the edges of the day: a time of independence and adventure, in which it was possible to take off and explore. "Go on outside," thirty million American parents told their children every weekend morning. "Go on out and play." And play they did, on the stoops and sidewalks of New York City, in the grassy yards of comfortable small towns, and in the fields and woods of the wider countryside.

Gary Snyder, for example, grew up in the Pacific Northwest, in the forested country north of Seattle. His parents kept milk cows, and a flock of chickens, as well as some ducks and geese. They had a kitchen garden, and an orchard of ten or twelve fruit trees. There were several acres of fenced-in pasture land, and a stretch of second-growth forest. As a child, Snyder was assigned regular chores. He was expected to feed the chickens, to weed the garden, to milk the cows and stack the firewood. But he also spent a considerable amount of time wandering on his own across the hills, hunting small animals, gathering plants.

"The childhood landscape is learned on foot," he wrote years later, "and a map is inscribed in the mind—trails and pathways and groves—the mean dog, the cranky old man's house, the pasture with a bull in it—going out wider and farther." He believes that all of us possess clear memories of that early terrain. "You can almost totally recall the place you walked, played, biked, swam."

The naturalist Robert Michael Pyle has just such an allegiance to the High Line Canal, a weedy ditch on "the wrong side of Denver." This was his place of exhilaration and discovery, where he caught his first butterflies, and once, in a storm, ducked inside his "thunder tree" to hide from hail the size of walnuts. Pyle believes that "most people seem to have a ditch somewhere"—a creek or a meadow, a woodlot or marsh. For him, "these are places of initiation, where the borders between ourselves and other creatures break down, where the earth gets under our nails and a sense of place gets under our skin."

Given the chance, most children do their best to seek out such wild and half-wild places where they can run and play without supervision. They show a special fondness for trees, which can after all be climbed, made into forts and dens and treehouses, and drawn into elaborate private games. They like the ragged edges of public parks, jungly tangles of shrubbery, straw bales to climb and jump from, long grass or corn in which to hide. Such adventures are especially crucial between the ages of eight and eleven, the so-called "earth period" of middle childhood. When a child heads out of the door in search of freedom, he is, in a sense, building the foundations for his own independent identity. As Kim Stafford writes, in his own autobiographical essay, his parents' house was "privacy from the street, from the nation, from the rain":

> But I did not make that house, or find it, or earn it with my own money. It was given to me. My separate hearth had to be invented by me, kindled, sustained, and held secret by my own soul as a rehearsal for departure.

NATURE DEFICIT DISORDER

"It takes a universe to raise a child," says the self-described "geologian" Thomas Berry. "The star-filled sky, meadows in bloom, tumbling rivers, soaring raven songs." But opportunities to explore that universe are shrinking fast, and a contemporary Seamus Heaney—or Kim Stafford or John Muir—would be hard-pressed to find a wild place to call his own. Many communities now do their best to abolish free outdoor play entirely, preferring organized sports or indoor "for profit" play centers, where young people can be closely supervised. A recent study of three generations of nine-year-olds found that between 1970 and 2000, the typical "home habitat" (the space in which they were allowed to roam alone) had shrunk by as much as 90 percent. By fall of 2004, each child under twelve was said to have no more than 2.3 square meters of play space—the size of the average kitchen table.

Nor are matters any easier at school. Since 1977, more than 40 percent of American schools have abolished recess. The authorities are afraid of violence on the playground, and of lawsuits if a child is hurt or injured, or (the most frequent explanation), they quite simply view such respite as a "waste of time." Instead, they prefer what they see as "enrichment opportunities," both mental and physical, often provided by professionally trained adults. The result, at least for middle class and wealthy children, is a calendar crammed with worthy extra-curricular activities (with dance and Spanish classes, baseball, extra math) plus a huge drift (across all demographic classes) away from the outdoors.

According to a recent survey, most American children spent only half an hour a week playing out of doors, out of a possible total of some fifty leisure hours. The writer Richard Louv quotes a fourth-grader called Paul. "I like to play indoors better," he said. "'Cause that's where all the electrical outlets are." It comes as no surprise that most children spend more than five hours a day hunched over some form of non-print media, and a quarter of that time are using more than one screen, dial, or channel. Such habits have real and potent consequences, not least what Louv describes as "nature deficit disorder," including "diminished use of the senses, attention difficulties, and higher rates of physical and emotional illness."

Most of these, alas, are all too easy to track.

Between 1989 and 1999 the number of overweight American children increased by more than a third. Two out of ten are now classified as clinically obese. Such obesity is associated not only with juvenile diabetes and depression, but with attention deficit disorder, mood swings, and aggression. 80 percent of obese adolescents will remain obese throughout their lives, and their health will be compromised as a result. Other, lesser ailments have also emerged, like "Nintendo Thumb," an inflammation at the base of the thumb caused by prolonged use of the video game controller. This can lead to swelling, redness, and considerable pain. It can also give rise to more chronic conditions, such as tennis elbow and carpal tunnel syndrome.

Meanwhile, teachers continue to pride themselves on their access to the new technologies, encouraging their students to surf the web for homework assignments, or download images to illustrate their reports. Children are eager to comply. But this glut of heady, fact-filled data can make ordinary life seem "boring" by comparison, as the educator Lowell Monke explains:

> Having watched Discovery Channel and worked with computer simulations that severely compress both time and space, children are typically disappointed when they first approach a pond or stream: the fish aren't jumping, the frogs

aren't croaking . . . and the raccoons (not to mention bears) aren't fishing.

All too soon, the modest details of our daily lives become, in Bill McKibben's poignant phrase, "missing information." The younger generation no longer breathes in, as if by osmosis, the skills and knowledge of their ancestors. Zonked out in front of the screen, they miss the coyote loping across the winter field, the changing colors in the sunset sky. They recognize more than one thousand corporate logos, but less than a dozen native plants and animals. "What is that thing over there on that stuff?" asked a poet friend of mine, on her first visit out of New York City. Did she mean the robin in the maple tree, or the sheep in the field, or the morning glory stretching its long tendrils up a nearby fence? It was impossible to tell. She literally did not know the words.

In 2009, the editors at Oxford University Press removed a swathe of nature-related words from their latest *Junior Dictionary*. Childhood favorites like *gerbil* and *hamster, goldfish* and *guinea pig* were excised. The familiar names of flowers and trees and birds and fish and animals vanished from the page. *Primrose* and *dandelion, hazel* and *walnut* were replaced by terms like *blog* and *voicemail. BlackBerry* supplanted *blackberry.* The *heron* and the *kingfisher*, the *magpie* and the *raven*, even the tiny *wren* flapped their ancient wings and flew away. Vineeta Gupta, head of children's dictionaries at Oxford University Press, seemed unembarrassed. She blamed the world itself for the edits that had been made. "Nowadays," she said, "the environment has changed."

AN EDUCATION OF CRAM

We tend to think of the crazy-busy, over-scheduled, rushed and frantic life as a predominantly American phenomenon. And certainly that urge to accelerate lies deep in our culture. When the French psychologist Jean Piaget went on tour across the United States, giving lectures on children's cognitive development, his audiences applauded his insight and erudition. They were fascinated by his account of the different cognitive stages. But again and again he would be asked what he came to think of as "the American question." *What might we do, Dr. Piaget, to speed our children through a little faster?*

It takes time to write a poem or to plant a garden, as it takes time, perhaps a lifetime, to raise a child. Here in the States, we're surely culpable if we imagine otherwise. But in fact we are by no means the first to put such pressure on our children. Even allowing for the exigencies of child labor (many children in the early nineteenth century started work as young as six, as some do in the Third World to this day), there are numerous other examples of the theft and compression of child time. One of the best documented is the story of the philosopher John Stuart Mill.

Mill was forced by his ambitious father to turn himself into an infant prodigy, learning Greek at the age of three and Latin at eight, as well as making his way through a mind-boggling list of classic texts. By the time he was nine, he had read Herodotus, Xenophon, Plato, and Homer in the original. Between eight and twelve, he mastered Virgil, Horace, Ovid, Lucretius, Sophocles, Euripides, and Aristophanes, as well as studying algebra, calculus, geometry, and Roman history. Years later, he defended his father's program. "Mine," he said, "was not an education of cram." The sympathetic reader may well beg to disagree.

Mill admitted that his father demanded of him "not only the utmost that I could do, but much that I could by no possibility have done." He was permitted scarcely any toys or children's books, and had no friends of his own age. Although he grew up fit and healthy, he lacked most of the usual physical and manual skills. As he said himself, his education was "much more fitted for training me to *know* than to *do.*"

In time, Mill became famous as a leader of the empirical school in England. He wrote on a number of literary and political topics, and was elected to Parliament. But that relentless education had its consequences. In his early twenties, he suffered a serious mental breakdown. "I was in a dull state of nerves . . . unsusceptible to enjoyment or pleasurable excitement." He found this difficult to bear; it was neither "interesting" nor in some crucial way "respectable." It was then that he first read Marmontel's *Memoirs* (which moved him to tears, and provided some measure of relief), followed, not long after, by the poetry of Wordsworth. He had picked up the book out of curiosity, not expecting much, and was astonished by the consolation it provided.

> What made Wordsworth's poems a medicine for my state of mind, was that they expressed, not mere outward beauty, but states of feeling, and of thought colored by feeling, under the excitement of beauty. . . . In them I seemed to draw from a source of inward joy, of sympathetic and imaginative pleasure, which could be shared in by all human beings.

It helped that Wordsworth had had similar experiences to his own, and that so many of the poems focused on "rural objects and natural scenery." Mill realized then what before he had always doubted, "that the habit of analysis has the tendency to wear away the feelings," and that "passive susceptibilities" need to be cultivated as much as active ones. He learned, in other words, that he had indeed endured "an education of cram," and that the right books could act as antidote, both dissolving his habitual melancholy, and returning him, for solace, to the green fields and wildflowers he had first known as a small boy in North London.

WORLD ENOUGH & TIME

One day, I was walking in the Brooklyn Botanical Gardens when a couple of children came racing across the grass. There was a boy of about six and his younger sister, who was maybe four. They were chasing each other down a slope towards the lilac trees. Next thing I knew, the boy had stumbled over a root, and fallen sprawling to the ground. He got up slowly, feeling himself for bruises. "It's fun to fall on the grass!" he said in astonishment. "It's fun to fall on the grass!"

For the next ten minutes, he and his little sister practiced falling. They dashed across the grass and flung themselves down on it, lay there for a moment, overcome with giggles, then picked themselves up and started all over again. I watched them for a long time, both enchanted and appalled. The experience was clearly new to them. For these children, "ground" meant asphalt or concrete or macadam. That springy turf came as a complete surprise. They had never imagined that the earth could be so generous.

Adults tend to think of nature in terms of "the great outdoors." They crave distant, glittering vistas, snow-capped mountains, broad, far-reaching valleys. Children are less particular. A hedge, a ditch, a tiny knoll will give them all the countryside they need. Audre Lorde spoke passionately about a little park in Harlem, close to where she had lived as a child. "*That* place, the green, the trees, and the water, formed my forest of Arden." It was the only green place she'd ever seen.

> I will never forget, after my first book, some students said, "Miss Lorde, would you call yourself a nature poet?" And I thought, "What? Me?" And then I realized how wedded to these images I was. And they came from this pocket park. I would fantasize about sun on a red brick roof. It was the shards of sun against the wall. . . . And that became entrenched in my mind as beauty. The sun on a red brick roof. And a rose trellis.

Such places may look like nothing to the casual passerby. But for the ardent child, they make a whole enchanting world. "Look, Mama!" cried the little boy across the aisle, as our bus drew level with the fenced-off territory that constituted Tompkins Square Park in Lower Manhattan. "Look, Mama! It's the *forest!*"

You can see the forest in a handful of scraggly winter trees, as you can see heaven in a wildflower, but to do so, you need both world enough and time, or, in Emily Dickinson's terms, "revery."

To make a prairie it takes a clover and one bee,
One clover, and a bee,
And revery.

The revery alone will do,
If bees are few.

We have the clover and the bee, at least for now. But time for revery is shrinking by the minute. One tends to assume that the burden of this falls mainly on adult shoulders, and perhaps on school-age children. But in New York, at least, the language of haste and deprivation has reached even the youngest among us.

Olivia is just three years old. She lives in Manhattan with her parents and her older brother, Luke, and spends most of her time at home, playing and taking naps, with the occasional visit to the Central Park Zoo. Her father is the writer Adam Gopnik. In *Through the Children's Gate,* he writes about Olivia and her imaginary friend, who goes by the name of Charlie Ravioli. Although he is only seven and a half, Ravioli already has a lively independent life. He lives on "Madison and Lexington," goes to the beach in the summer, and, according to Olivia, has been "working on a show." But (and this is the quintessentially New York part of the tale), *he is always too busy to play with her.*

> [Olivia] holds up her toy cell phone to her ear, and we hear her talk into it: "Ravioli? It's Olivia. . . . It's Olivia. Come and play? Okay. Call me. Bye." Then she snaps it shut and shakes her head. "I always get his machine," she says. Or she will say, "I spoke to Ravioli today." "Did you have fun?" my wife and I ask. "No, he was busy working."

On a good day, Olivia "bumps into" her invisible friend and they go to a coffee shop. "'I bumped into Charlie Ravioli today,' she says. 'He was working.' Then she adds brightly, 'But we hopped into a taxi.' What happened then? we ask. 'We grabbed lunch,' she says."

Olivia is a bright, impressionable child, and the world she is describing mimics the one she sees around her. Most of the adults she knows are busy urban professionals, and "the language of busyness" dominates their conversation. As her father explains, "Busyness is our art form, our usual ritual, our way of being us." What is actually remarkable is that Olivia should manage to triumph over such unprepossessing material, making out of stress and disconnection an opportunity to hone her own inventiveness, and, yes, indulge her capacity for revery.

TIME WITH CHILDREN

In *Of Woman Born: Motherhood as Experience and Institution,* Adrienne Rich describes an idyllic summer at a friend's house in Vermont. Her husband was abroad for several weeks, leaving her and her three sons (then aged nine, seven, and five) to spend most of their time by themselves. Without a male adult in the house, they fell into what she experienced as a "delicious and sinful rhythm." It was a stretch of unusually hot, bright weather, and they ate almost all their meals out of doors, staying up late to watch bats and stars and fireflies, living "like castaways on some island of mothers and children." At night the children fell asleep without a murmur, and Rich stayed up until the early morning hours, reading and writing as she had when she was a student. "I remember thinking: *This is what living with children could be—without school hours, fixed routines, naps, the conflict of being both mother and wife with no room for being, simply, myself.*"

I love this passage, not just for its joyous lyricism, but because it reminds us all, so simply and insistently, of *what is possible.* Children have no power to rearrange their schedules; they are at our mercy. But most of us, as adults, have at least some choices. We do not have to drive ourselves into the ground with overwork, or fritter away our evenings watching mediocre television. We have the power to stop, to alter the shape of our days and weeks and years, to give ourselves over, at least occasionally, to what Thoreau called "the bloom of the present moment."

And yet, the fact is that we almost never do. In the past half century, the time adults spend with children has consistently declined. "We spend, on average, six hours per week shopping," writes the environmentalist David Orr, "but only forty minutes playing with our children." Only rarely do we take the time to mentor them, or to teach them practical skills. Meanwhile, children's own unstructured time has diminished by some sixteen hours a month, and the omnipresent screen (TV, video, computer) has become, perforce, the bland-faced babysitter for the entire family.

Parents have come to believe, perhaps, that this is necessary: that without early exposure to technology, their children will be unable to keep up with their peers. In practical terms, this is incorrect: young people need just one year of computer class to learn sufficient skills for work and college. But in terms of their social lives such access has become, quite simply, indispensable. Today's teenagers are busy texting (tweeting, blogging, updating their notes on Facebook or Myspace, talking on their cell phones) almost every waking minute. It has become as hard for them to submit to the shapeless vagaries of ordinary life as for many of their parents. Only the smallest (and most protected) still inhabit what we might rightly call "child time."

The scholar Stephen Mitchell has a salutary parable to tell in this regard. When his daughter was about two, he wanted very much to go for walks with her, but soon found them "agonizingly slow." His idea of a walk entailed *momentum*: "brisk [forward] movement along a road or path." His daughter had rather different ideas. She wanted to pause and investigate whatever they encountered. One day, they came upon a fallen tree by the side of the road, only twenty yards from their front door. The rest of the "walk" was spent exploring the insects and toadstools on, under, and around the tree. It wasn't easy for Mitchell to give up his own clenched notion of what a "real walk" should be. Only when he allowed himself to adapt to his daughter's rhythm (to surrender, in other words, to "child time") was he finally able to enjoy himself.

The philosopher William James made a useful distinction between "directed attention" (what we use when we drive a car or follow a recipe) and what he called "fascination." At two years old, Mitchell's daughter was guided entirely by fascination. When adults and children spend this kind of time together, it gives them both a chance to slow down, to move away from the *me-me-me* of human-centered life, and (in David Abram's lovely phrase) to "fall in love outwards" with a particular place and its native denizens. Such "education" (and the word of course derives from *educare*: "to lead out," or "to draw forth") reaches far back into the distant past. Here, for example, the anthropologist Dorothy Lee describes how children used to be raised by the Oglala Sioux.

"From infancy on, they were taught to use their senses to the utmost, to sit still and listen to that which they could not hear, to smell and see and become aware of that which was not obvious to the senses." A mother would take her baby outside long before the little one could talk, gently drawing his or her attention to different animals and birds. Only later would she supply the names. As they grew older, children would be sent outside on their own to listen and observe, and then helped to interpret their findings on return.

There was, in other words, a broad margin left for the child's own response: a margin between the noticing and the naming, between the observation and the conclusions. "Fascination" could take its own slow time. The children were not rushed or energetically encouraged. From early on, they learned the power of patience: a calm, attentive, "drinking in" of their surroundings.

The traditions of the American Southwest seem very similar, at least as understood by Robert Coles. In *The Spiritual Life of Children*, he describes his work with Natalie, an eight-year-old Hopi girl from New Mexico. School officials had dismissed her as an "average student," and one who was inclined to be moody. But the more Coles came to know her, the more he was astonished by her depth of character. He came to realize what a serious naturalist she was, and how utterly absorbed she could become, "so engrossed was she with the land and sky, the sun, moon, and stars, the flowers her mother grew, the animals, the changes of light that came with clouds."

I think of the two Aboriginal girls I saw, aged six and eight, "dancing the kangaroo" at the City Lore Poetry Festival in New York City. They were dressed in orange cloth, with white paint daubed along their burnished arms. I watched them as they held their hands up, leaf-shaped, to their heads, "listening" with an animal alertness, then bounded across the stage as if they too possessed the heavy haunches and long muscular tail of a kangaroo. When I complimented their mother afterwards, she told me they had done very little professional dancing. But clearly they had done a lot of looking. They knew what it was to be engrossed. Their brother too, aged sixteen, seemed to melt effortlessly into the body of the animal, as if there were simply no distinction between its fluent movements and his own.

NO CHILD LEFT INSIDE

It is easy to idealize the knowledge of native peoples, Sioux or Hopi or Native Australians, as if our own children could never hope for such a gentle, expansive relationship to the natural world. But this is not necessarily true. There are, in fact, numerous organizations devoted to healing or alleviating nature-deficit disorder, from ordinary public schools with an emphasis on "place-based education" to Outward Bound programs and old-fashioned summer camps. I have included a list of such resources at the back of this book, but parents and teachers should certainly investigate the Center for Ecoliteracy, the Ecopsychology Institute, and "Learning in the Real World," and encourage their children to submit poems to Robert Hass's annual competition, "River of Words."

"Much has been made of 'No Child Left Behind,'" says the nature writer John Elder. "But what we actually want is 'No Child Left Inside.'" Clare Walker Leslie agrees. As one who has taught natural history and journal-keeping for more than half a lifetime, she knows the power of the simple question, the utterly modest assignment. "Who are your neighbors?" she asks her second graders. "They're not just people, they're also salamanders, chipmunks, rabbits, great blue herons." Again and again she leads her students out into the schoolyard, out into the local park. After the usual noisy babble of the classroom,

"We all go out in silence, and just listen." John Tallmadge concurs. Another freelance educator, with many years of college teaching behind him, he emphasizes how a twenty-foot strip of grass between the street and the sidewalk can engage the children's interest. "Starlings, burdocks; the cardinal is a blaze of wonder. The city becomes a huge museum without walls."

Every winter, when I teach at Williams College in western Massachusetts, I ask the students to adopt a particular spot on campus, and to return to it again and again. I ask them to visit that spot at sunrise and sunset, and under the white light of the full moon, in wind and rain and boring slushy daytime, in heavy driving snow. They do not see the point of this at first. The requirement seems empty and repetitive. But little by little, the stories begin to accumulate—the call of a barred owl through the midnight branches, the humped tunnels of the meadow voles revealed under the crusted snow, the snow fleas leaping in the bright sun—and suddenly they too are giddy with enthusiasm. "I have found much joy wandering round campus with my friends," wrote one student, "pointing out some of the little things I have been noticing over the last few months." And another noted, "Once I reached my plot, the snow changed from being a nuisance to a miracle."

There are many such assignments one can give. When Janet Fout's daughter was a little girl, the two of them used to spend time together out of doors, playing and inventing nature games. My own favorite was *listening for the sounds they could not hear*, which Fout called "The Sounds of a Creature Not Stirring." Examples might include: *sap rising, snowflakes forming and falling, sunrise, moonrise, feathers, dew on the grass, a seed germinating, an earthworm moving through the soil, an apple ripening, wood petrifying, a spider weaving its web, a leaf changing colors, a salmon spawning.*

Janet Fout is an environmental activist, as John Elder and John Tallmadge are committed nature writers, and Clare Walker Leslie is a lifelong artist and keeper of nature journals. But making space for "child time" does not demand any special credentials. Any interested adult can provide practical help: a ride to a local park, a guide book to birds, cheerful encouragement to go outside and play.

Eleanor Roosevelt was famously unhappy as a child. Her parents and younger brother all died before she turned nine. She was seen as sour and sullen, moody and rebellious. In fact, she was such an odd, old-fashioned child that she was always known as "Granny." But on occasion, "Granny" was able to persuade one of her young aunts to get up before dawn, so that they could walk through the woods to the Hudson River, row down to the village of Tivoli to get the mail, and row back before the family was at breakfast. It was, she said long afterwards, her greatest pleasure.

The geneticist Barbara McClintock was the youngest of three girls, and her father raised her as a boy, allowing her a large measure of privacy and independence. As a little girl, in the early 1900s, she persuaded her parents to have bloomers made for her, "so that I could do anything I wanted. I could play baseball, I could play football, I could climb trees, I could just have a completely free time, the same kind of a free time that my brother had." Years later, she won a Nobel Prize for her discovery that genes "jump" from one chromosome to another. "As you look at these things, they become part of you. And you forget yourself. The main thing is you forget yourself."

Such ease and self-forgetfulness are especially important to girls. *Don't run so fast! You'll fall and hurt yourself. Don't get wet! Don't dirty your nice dress!* Again and again grown women report the fussy anxious voices that held them back as children, and in some cases still haunt them as adults. For myself, I still remember the aged nun peering up into the branches, as I climbed ever higher towards the clear blue sky. "Come down!" she cried. "Come down, tree climber!" and angrily, obediently, I made my descent. At home in Scotland I spent hours climbing trees and building treehouses, catching fish with my hands, or wandering alone across the moors. But there at school I could do nothing but submit.

NATURE WRITING

Not all children are given the gift of time, or the support of interested adult mentors. Sometimes guidance and inspiration come in the form of the natural world itself: a tree, an animal, a particular patch of ground. Sometimes (perhaps more often than you might expect) they reveal themselves through books.

When Kim Stafford was eight and nine and ten, playing in "The Woods" outside Portland, his grandmother presented him with a book called *Ishi* about the last California Indian. This grandmother was a "small, genteel woman," the widow of a minister. But it was she who gave Kim that crucial book, and sewed him a fringed buckskin shirt, she who asked each day that crucial question, *"What did you find today?"* and listened while he told her his discoveries.

As a child, I read and reread *Wind in the Willows,* along with Jean Craighead George's classic, *My Side of the Mountain,* and a couple of books by Denys Watkins-Pitchford, published under the sporting pseudonym of BB. *The Little Grey Men* and *Down the Bright Stream* told the story of four ancient gnomes, detailing their adventures in a toy sailing boat. Pitchford, an avid naturalist, took every opportunity to enliven his simple tale: birds and fish, animals and insects were all precisely observed, all deliciously and lyrically described.

When I was ten or eleven, my mother gave me a copy of *A Girl of the Limberlost* by Gene Stratton Porter. I had never heard of Porter, could not even tell if the author were a man or a woman. I knew nothing of moths or birds or the natural history of Indiana. But I knew passion when I encountered it, and courage and injustice, and the story of Elnora Comstock drew me back again and again. Thirty years later, I stumbled on a book of Stratton Porter's nature writings, edited by Sydney Landon Plum. Here were the memories of her childhood, her love of birds. Here, above all, was an account of the beneficent freedom in which she had grown up.

From the time she could walk, Geneva (her given name) was a devoted ornithologist. All day long, from breakfast until lunch, and from lunch to supper time, she made the rounds of the local nests, watching the birds as they went about their business, and championing their cause against cats and snakes and squirrels, as well as her numerous older siblings. After an astonishing scene in which she defended a male hawk against her preacher father (armed with a rifle), he presented her, formally, with the ownership of every single bird on his land. It was a magical present, and the child was overwhelmed.

> [E]ven while he was talking to me I was making a flashing mental inventory of *my property*, for now I owned the hummingbirds, dressed in green satin with ruby jewels on their throats; the plucky little wren that sang by the hour to his mate . . . the green warbler, nesting in a magnificent specimen of wild sweetbriar . . . the song sparrow in the ground cedar beside the fence.

From then on, she chose sixty nests to visit daily, imitating the birds' calls and offering grain and berries, until by the end of the season, most of her brood trusted her completely. Warblers, phoebes, sparrows, and finches swarmed all over her, perching on her head and hands and shoulders, while she stood beside their nests, feeding their young chicks.

With such a heritage, it comes as no surprise that Gene Stratton Porter should have grown up to be a writer and a naturalist and a well-known nature photographer, nor that she should have written her first book (she published more than twenty) in the voice of a cardinal. As Edith Cobb has argued, and others have confirmed, many creative people (writers, poets, artists, environmentalists) return again and again to their early experiences in nature. It becomes, in fact, a prime source for their imaginative work as adults.

SEARCHING & DREAMING

When Theodore Roosevelt was a boy in the 1860s, he spent his days building wigwams in the woods, gathering hickory nuts and apples, and hunting frogs. E.O. Wilson had similar memories. "Most children have a bug period, and I never outgrew mine. Hands-on experience at the critical time, not systematic knowledge, is what counts in the making of a naturalist. Better to be an untutored savage for a while, not to know the names or anatomical detail. Better to spend long stretches of time just searching and dreaming."

It is an attitude Thoreau would have applauded. As he notes in his journals, "Sometimes, in a summer morning, having taken my accustomed bath, I sat in my sunny doorway from sunrise till noon, rapt in a reverie, amidst the pines and hickories and sumacs, in undisturbed solitude and stillness, while the birds sang around. I grew in those seasons like corn in the night, and they were far better than any work of the hands would have been. They were not time subtracted from my life, but so much over and above my usual allowance."

From sunrise to noon is a considerable stretch of time, especially at the height of the summer. One cannot imagine a contemporary writer squandering even a fraction of those hours. But Thoreau had a tremendous capacity for patience, as his friend Emerson understood. "He knew how to sit immovable, a part of the rock he rested on, until the bird, the reptile, the fish, which had retired from him, should come back and resume its habits, nay, moved by curiosity, should come to him and watch him."

Thoreau knew too what contemporary thinkers are only just beginning to understand—that the human mind is not some isolated little manikin inside our heads; rather it is fed and nourished by every sight and smell and sound that we encounter, from the movement of the clouds to the shrill of birds outside our morning window. "I sit for a long time and watch one thing," says writer Barry Lopez. "If you don't do that homework, you don't make yourself vulnerable enough to a place, and it never releases itself into you." He keeps his study window open always. His notes get rained on and sun-stroked, "But I don't ever want that window closed."

Without that "window," the life, the soul, will suffer. With it open, there is always the possibility of surprise. In this context, I like to remember the words of the great ornithologist Roger Tory Peterson. By the time I met him, he was well into his eighties. But a few months earlier, he had seen something that took his breath away: a flock of swallows—a massive congregation—spiraling down like a tornado against the orange blaze of sunset, tens of thousands of them at one time. It was, he said, the most remarkable thing he'd ever witnessed.

For all the stress and overwhelm in which we live, there is no end to such daily miracles. The Beat poet Gary Snyder has made a life honed by such knowledge, and in relation to "child time," his advice is well worth taking. Here then, in conclusion, is his poem, "For the Children":

> *The rising hills, the slopes,*
> *of statistics*
> *lie before us,*
> *the steep climb*
> *of everything, going up,*
> *up, as we all*
> *go down.*
>
> *In the next century*
> *or the one beyond that,*
> *they say,*
> *are valleys, pastures,*
> *we can meet there in peace*
> *if we make it.*
>
> *To climb these coming crests*
> *one word to you, to*
> *you and your children:*
>
> *stay together*
> *learn the flowers*
> *go light.*

Tactics

↭ Go for a walk at the pace of a small child. Saunter, wander, loiter, look around; allow yourself to pause and to digress.

↭ Buy a microscope or a telescope or a pair of binoculars, and share them with your children, or with the children of your friends.

↭ *Consider the following quotations:*
"Common sense and a sense of humor are the same thing moving at different speeds. A sense of humor is just common sense dancing."

WILLIAM JAMES

"One of the very best things about the world is that so little of it is me."

ANDREW GREIG

CHAPTER FOUR

In Praise of Walking

*I only went out for a walk, and finally concluded
to stay out till sundown; for going out,
I found, was really going in.*

JOHN MUIR

Lost & Found

As a teenager, I used to go off on long boisterous walks across the moors, a book in one pocket and an apple in the other. Often I came home soaking wet, my boots squelching, my hair damp and tangled. Not that I cared. The walk was what mattered: the springy tussocks of heather underfoot, the blue flanks of the hills. In the winter, there'd be the geese rising from the loch, hundreds of them, beating their dark V across the sky. However long it took, I always came home happy (happy and ravenous!), my book a little battered, the apple long since eaten, down to its bony core.

I walked at night too, for the simple pleasure of it, along known roads, between familiar hedges, guided from above by the great whispering basket-work of trees. Sometimes there'd be a moon, or at least a piece of one; sometimes not. But I was never frightened. I knew the road, the muffled sound of the sheep shifting behind the gates, the icy bars of the cattle grid. And when cars came, screaming out of the darkness, there was plenty of time to get to the side. Sometimes the drivers would stop, startled to catch sight of anyone out walking at that hour, let alone a gawky, half-grown girl.

"Want a lift?"

The flare of a man's face in the half-light of the car, the smell of cigarettes and petrol, the tiny private life behind the wheel.

"No. No, thank you. No."

Years later, in my early thirties, I took off across Ireland, on marvelous makeshift journeys involving buses and trains and rented bicycles, plus some hitching and the usual lengthy walks. I visited the Burren and the Dingle Peninsula, and spent several weeks on Aran, guided by Tim Robinson's book, *Pilgrimage,* and his brilliantly detailed maps. I hung over the edge of cliffs where the waves beat up across the wild Atlantic, and photographed holy stones and ancient chapels. But mostly I walked.

I would set out early in the morning, carrying the most minimal of baggage: a map and notebook, a rain mac, a bar of chocolate, a little cash. My troubles unraveled on the road behind me. In their place came sudden bursts of ecstasy: joy at the sheer beauty of the land, love and affection for my far-off friends. I walked as if an angel strode behind me with great green radiant wings.

"Things come toward you when you walk," writes William Stafford. "You blow a little whistle—/And a world begins under the map." Walking and writing, getting lost and being found, are perhaps more alike than we might think.

LINGER, SAUNTER, DAUNDER

A recent issue of the Scottish PEN newsletter advertised a "Sponsored Daunder" in the Pentland Hills. "Daunder" is the Scots word for "stroll" or "amble," which in this case was to be combined with pleasant company and conversation. It is not easy to imagine a similar advertisement on the part of PEN International in New York City. Words like *linger, saunter, stroll,* and *amble* have all but disappeared from our vocabulary, along with casual synonyms like *stray, range, roam, ramble,* and *wander.* "Why has the pleasure of slowness disappeared?" asks the writer Milan Kundera. "Ah, where have they gone, the amblers of yesteryear? Where have they gone, those loafing heroes of folksong, those vagabonds who roam from one mill to another and bed down under the stars?"

There is a blunt answer to this, which is that such straying and strolling, rambling and roaming is now seen as boring, even suspect, across much of the western world. Ray Bradbury has a terrific story set in the year 2052 called "The Pedestrian," in which a lone walker is stopped by the police (or rather, in that futuristic universe, an empty car). "What are you doing out?" asks an iron voice. Leonard Mead attempts to explain. He is out walking, he says, "just walking."

> "Walking, just walking, walking?"
> "Yes, sir."
> "Walking where? For what?"
> "Walking for air. Walking to *see*."

But the explanation isn't good enough, and Mead is carried off to "the Psychiatric Center for Research on Regressive Tendencies." It is perhaps not accidental that he calls himself a writer, which the metallic voice immediately defines as "No profession."

For many of us, walking has come to seem an odd, old-fashioned pleasure, modest and invisible, easily dismissed. People pay lip service to its health benefits, but there is an underlying impatience; few choose voluntarily to loaf or linger. Walking *per se* has been reduced to exercise; wind and birdsong replaced by our own personalized soundtrack, interrupted at short intervals by the ubiquitous cell phone. Pedestrians worldwide now walk 10 percent faster than we did in 1995; in China and Singapore, the percentage has increased by as much as 20 to 30 percent. It is as if speed had become a good in and of itself, with driving the expected norm, and the ordinary human trudge excruciatingly slow. "The poetry of motion!" cries the children's book character Mr. Toad, in praise of his brand-new motor car. "The *real* way to travel! The *only* way to travel! Here today—in next week tomorrow! Villages skipped, towns and cities jumped—always somebody else's horizon!"

No surprise then, that so many of us spend so much of our time crouched behind the wheels of our cars, struggling with the dial of the FM radio, and swearing at the oncoming traffic. The average U.S. citizen drives twice as much as the average European or Japanese: a total of more than twelve thousand miles a year. He or she spends as much as seventy-two minutes per day on the road (more in rural areas), and this in turn devours yet more time, for example, the weeks and months needed to earn the money to pay for gas and car insurance, let alone to repair and ultimately replace the car itself.

In 2006, an award for America's longest commute was given to a man in California, who traveled 372 miles a day from his home in the Sierra foothills to his workplace in San José and back: a total of seven hours. Seven hours is astonishing, but four hours, alas, is not. One in six U.S. workers now commutes more than forty-five minutes each way. Three and a half million travel more than ninety minutes each way: so called "extreme commuters." These are the people who eat almost every meal in transit, for whom the road to work is more familiar than the faces of their family and friends or the daylight view outside their kitchen window.

The sad fact is that such commuting makes us miserable. Yes, it pays for the beautiful new house in the suburbs, the pricey gadgets and designer clothes. But those of us who have an hour-long commute must make at least 40 percent more money if we are to feel as satisfied as a non-commuter, and this we rarely do. It is anyway difficult to make informed comparisons between the clear advantages of "more cash" and other crucial imponderables like rest and leisure and companionship. Commuting can be devastating in its disregard of just such things: its casual erasure of long slow mornings, dreamy afternoons and evenings, and all too often, of the longed-for weekend, which becomes a mini work-week of its own, splintered into chores and stores and insistently consoling entertainment.

If commuting by car gives rise to one form of "hurry sickness," then airplane travel (and the accompanying jetlag) ratchets that sickness upwards into fever pitch. Days are squandered in the stale air of parking lots and airport terminals, amid a lurching sense of loss and unreality. Pico Iyer describes his private discombobulation, following a series of intercontinental flights back and forth to Japan. "My words have not caught up with me," he writes. "It's as if they are pieces of luggage that the airline has misplaced and sent on by a later flight—and it is only slowly, day by day, that I come back into focus." Scientists confirm that such a response is all too predictable: one's attention drops 500 percent immediately after a long distance flight, and there are other, more lasting consequences too, ranging from mild depression to cataracts and high-frequency hearing loss.

The advantage of course is moving *fast:* a poignant word, and a revealing one. In the sense of "swift" it derives from the Old English *faest* (meaning "firm"), as in "keeping close to that which is pursued." But *faest* is also related to the Old English *faestan*, "to fast or abstain." To jet around the globe, to "live life in the fast lane," is also in some sense to abstain, to deny oneself the pleasures of a slower, more expansive way of being.

For years, many of us have been ready to tolerate such losses. But the deprivations, both personal and environmental, have come to seem increasingly acute. Offered a choice between more free time and higher pay, most Americans now claim they'd choose free time. Once again, the current recession may prove to be a blessing in disguise. People are hungry for the chance to slow down, to savor and luxuriate, and walking offers them the opportunity for all these things. As Edward Abbey wrote back in the 1970s, "Walking takes longer than any other form of locomotion except crawling. Thus, it stretches time and prolongs life. Walking makes the world much bigger, and therefore more interesting. You have time to observe the details."

SOLVITUR AMBULANDO

Abbey and Kundera are not the first writers to protest against the frenzy of the outer world, or to find clarity and sustenance in walking. *Solvitur ambulando* goes the Latin tag: "You can sort it out by walking." Among the best-known literary walkers are the brother and sister William and Dorothy Wordsworth. Much has been made of their unprepossessing appearance—both stooped when they walked, and William, apparently, "walked like a cade," which is to say, in a strange and sideways fashion. But their work was none the worse for that. Dorothy's exquisite journals and William's tremendous output as a poet both testify to the long focus walking gave to their lives.

The Wordsworths were born in the English Lake District, children of a local land agent. Their mother died when they were still small, and Dorothy was sent away to live with relatives, while William was boarded with a retired carpenter and his wife in the little town of

Hawkshead. From then on, he was free to roam about the country-side, hunting birds' eggs, trapping birds, going for walks both alone and in company, both by night and by day. His long autobiographical poem, "The Prelude," draws on these memories, perhaps most vividly in the section entitled "Childhood and School Time":

> *Well I call to mind*
> *('Twas at an early age, ere I had seen*
> *Nine summers) when upon the mountain slope*
> *The frost, and breath of frosty wind, had snapped*
> *The last autumnal crocus, 'twas my joy*
> *To wander half the night among the cliffs*
> *And the smooth hollows, where the woodcocks ran*
> *Along the open turf.*

The boy was open to more tranquil pleasures too: walking home through gray November days, "When vapours, rolling down the val-leys, made/A lonely scene more lonesome; among woods/At noon, and 'mid the calm of summer nights."

Such walks continued far into old age. In his *Recollections of the Lakes and the Lake Poets,* De Quincey estimates that Wordsworth must have covered between 175,000 and 180,000 miles over the course of his lifetime. At twenty, he completed a 2,000-mile journey with a friend, walking across France and over the Alps into Switzerland, averaging thirty miles a day for more than three months. Back in the British Isles, he continued to climb mountains, walk the streets of London, and go out for daily constitutionals with Dorothy and other friends.

One of his first published poems was called "An Evening Walk," and many others with similar subject matter were to follow, some-times culminating in an encounter with another human being, sometimes in a more personal epiphany. In "Resolution and Inde-pendence," the narrator finds himself upon a lonely moor, where he comes upon an aged leech-gatherer, and is inspired by his courage. In "The Solitary Reaper," he watches a "solitary Highland Lass" singing to herself as she bends over her sickle, and pursues his climb alone, still haunted by her music. In "Daffodils" too (now, alas, grown empty and insipid through its very fame), he carries away the image of the golden petals fluttering in their thousands by the lake, an image which will continue to "flash upon [his] inward eye" many long years hence.

It is clear that Wordsworth enjoyed walking for its own sake. But its primary purpose for him was as a means of composition. He walked in order to write, pacing out his lines as he went, either in some favored spot out of doors or on the terrace in front of his house. He did not like to be watched while he was doing this. But inevitably, there were times when he was overheard. One of the Grasmere locals described the bard at work:

> He would set his head a bit forrad, and put his hands be-
> hint his back. And then he would start a bumming, and it
> was *bum, bum, bum, stop*; then *bum, bum bum*, reet down till
> t'other end; and then he'd set down and git a bit o' paper and
> write a bit.

Some of the local children, running across him unexpectedly, would be frightened almost to death when they heard that great voice "a groanin' and mutterin' and thunderin' of a still evening." No wonder that Wordsworth's maid, when asked to indicate the master's study, said that his library was over there. "But his study is out of doors."

In the Welsh language, the word for "song" or "poem," *cerwid*, can also be applied to a walk or longer journey. The walk gives rise to the song, and the song gives energy and gusto to the walk. Wordsworth's younger contemporary, Keats, spent four months tramping though Scotland and the north of England, intent, he said, on a kind of poetic apprenticeship. Keats was no slouch: he and his friends would get up at five each morning, and walk for twenty miles before dinner. One tends to think of him as a touch grandiose, at least in his stated aims, but in fact he was sweetly self-mocking about his aspirations.

> I have been *werry* romantic indeed among these Mountains
> and Lakes. I have got wet through, day after day—eaten oat-
> cake and drank Whiskey—walked up to my knees in Bog—

got a sore throat—gone to see Icolmkill and Staffa; met with wholesome food here and there as it happened. . . . Sometimes when I am rather tired I lean rather languishingly on a rock, and long for some famous Beauty to get down from her Palfrey in passing, approach me, with—her saddle-bags, and give me—a dozen or two capital roast beef Sandwiches.

By the time he returned home, he and his companions had completed some four hundred miles on horseback, and walked more than six hundred. He had done what he set out to do, and could rightly claim that he had managed to "clamber through the Clouds and exist."

RAMBLING MEN

There is a mass of prose writers too, on both sides of the Atlantic, for whom walking has been both subject and inspiration, among them Boswell and Johnson, Walter Scott, Dickens, and Carlyle. Those most often quoted belong to the nineteenth century. I think especially of Hazlitt's essay, "On Going a Journey," Thoreau's "Walking," Emerson's "Notes on Walking," and Robert Louis Stevenson's "Walking Tours."

The essayist William Hazlitt was inspired to write by meeting Wordsworth and Coleridge at the age of nineteen. He became, in many ways, the obstreperous younger brother of the Romantics, though with more energy and grit and (a favorite word) *gusto*, than one associates with any of them. Like Wordsworth, he preferred his own company. For him, nature was companion enough, and the entertainment of his own good brain. "Give me the clear blue sky over my head, and the green turf beneath my feet, a winding road before me, and a three hours' march till dinner—and then to thinking!" It is clear that his thinking was both frolicksome and fertile; indeed, he describes himself as laughing and running and leaping for joy: a gorgeous picture of middle-aged abandon. But unlike Coleridge, he was unable to speak easily and extemporaneously in such a state, nor did he wish to match phrases with another person. "I can make nothing on the spot," he wrote. "I must have time to collect myself."

Thoreau's walks were clearly undertaken in a very different spirit. Walking for him was not so much a pleasant pastime as a moral imperative. He liked to spend at least four hours of every day out of doors. He had "no walks to throw away on company," he said. Walking for him had nothing to do with taking exercise. "[It] is itself the enterprise and adventure of the day."

"Walking," written in 1851, is itself a "rambling" essay, and covers lots of interesting ground, beginning with the origin of the word "saunter" (whether derived from those who roamed about the country and asked charity on pretext of going to *la Sainte Terre,* the holy land, or from those who were without a home, and therefore, *sans terre).* Thoreau himself preferred the first of these derivations, since for him the holy land was to be found underfoot at any time. Indeed, he cherished the fact that "Two or three hours' walking will carry me to as strange a country as I expect ever to see."

The difficulty now in reading Thoreau's essay is that it has been so quoted and misquoted over the years as to seem curiously uneven, at one moment packed like pemmican with overly familiar maxims ("In Wildness is the preservation of the World," "I believe in the forest and in the meadow, and in the night in which the corn grows") and at another startlingly fresh and unfamiliar. I myself was especially drawn by his reference to *Gramatica parda,* the "tawny grammar" of the out of doors, which he felt every child should have a chance to learn.

But orderly as he was in his own excursions (carrying an old music book under his arm in which to press plant specimens, and cramming his pockets with diary and pencils, spy glass, microscope, pocket knife and twine), Thoreau was also wary of too much conscientious accuracy. "I must walk more with free senses," he wrote in his journal. "It is as bad to *study* stars and clouds as flowers and stones. I must let my senses wander as my thoughts, my eyes see without seeing. . . . What I need is not to look at all, but a true sauntering of the eye."

Such "sauntering" shows up most lyrically in his account of the sunset lighting up the pines at Spaulding's Farm. It was, he says, "as if some ancient and altogether admirable and shining family" had come to settle there. The *joie de vivre* with which he enters into that image and the ease with which he elaborates it (seeing them "recline on sunbeams," and persuading himself that he can overhear the "sweet musical hum" of their thought) shows us a playful and imaginative Thoreau, very different from the youthful pontificator who has come down to us over the years.

Thoreau's mentor was, of course, Emerson, one of the great essayists, though even more of a preacher than Thoreau himself. It is easy to bridle at his assertions, as if one were being force-fed slabs of wholesome whole-wheat bread. But it would be hard to disagree with his qualifications for a walk, which he defines as "endurance, plain clothes, old shoes, an eye for Nature" (capitalized!), along with "good speech, good silence, and nothing too much." That his ideal companions on such a jaunt should be an artist, "that is, [one] who has an eye for beauty," and a naturalist, from whom one can learn the elements of geology, botany, ornithology, etc., seems like obvious good sense, with the added pleasure of a private thumbnail portrait of Thoreau.

Both the gusto and the faint taint of home-spun righteousness continue with Robert Louis Stevenson, whose essay "Walking Tours" first appeared in 1876. Like Hazlitt (whom he admired enormously), Stevenson felt that walking should be embarked upon alone. There should, he writes, "be no cackle of voices at your elbow, to jar on the meditative silence of the morning." Rather, "you must be open to all impressions and let your thoughts take colour from what you see."

Stevenson died at the age of forty-four, having written a surprising number of books in his short life: adult novels and children's books, poetry and essays and plays, as well as several volumes of letters. Nonetheless, one of his most heartfelt pleas was in favor of moderation (even, at times, idleness), which he saw as a woefully underrated virtue. Fiercely, he castigated what he called "your over-walker" who returns "to his inn at night, with a sort of frost on his five wits, and a starless night of darkness in his spirit." He himself preferred a far gentler, more temperate form of exercise, in which the emphasis on clock-time fell away.

It is almost as if the millennium were arrived, when we shall throw our clocks and watches over the housetop, and remember time and seasons no more. . . . You have no idea, unless you have tried it, how endlessly long is a summer day.

LUNCH POEMS

From Wordsworth on, the list of "walking poets" is a long and honorable one. One thinks of Wallace Stevens striding back and forth to work each day, of e. e. cummings painting in Washington Square Park, then strolling home to Patchin Place, of Allen Ginsberg, loitering round Boulder, Colorado, always ready to stop, to listen and observe, his notebook open in his hand. The poet Frank O'Hara (graceful, gay, light-hearted, tender, camp) worked at the Museum of Modern Art in New York City and spent most of his lunch breaks walking the nearby streets. The inhabitants of Manhattan are devoted walkers (even now, two-thirds of the trips around Midtown and Lower Manhattan are made on foot) and O'Hara was no exception. His day was framed by walking, given form by it, as were many of his poems. Among his publications are *Lunch Poems* and *Second Avenue*, as well as the essay collection *Standing Still and Walking in New York*. One of his poems, entitled, simply, "Poem," opens with these words:

> *Let's take a walk, you*
> *and I in spite of the*
> *weather if it rains hard*
> > *on our toes*
>
> *we'll stroll like poodles*
> *and be washed down a*
> *gigantic scenic gutter*
> > *that will be*
>
> *exciting!*

The invitation, the zany, cartoon-like analogy, the ebullience of the exclamation mark, are all quintessential O'Hara, as are the poignant lines which surprise the reader at the end:

> *And the landscape will do*
> *us some strange favor when*
> *we look back at each other*
> *   anxiously*

O'Hara wrote hundreds of other walking poems during his short life (he died in 1966, just past his fortieth birthday). Among my favorites are "The Day Lady Died," written as an elegy to Billie Holiday, "In Memory of My Feelings," dedicated to his friend Grace Hartigan, and "Avenue A" with its moon "gliding broken-faced over the bridges." But the one I love the most is a page-length poem called "A Step Away From Them." It begins easily, unselfconsciously, without any fanfare:

> *It's my lunch hour, so I go*
> *for a walk among the hum-colored*
> *cabs*

and saunters on,

> *   First, down the sidewalk*
> *where the laborers feed their dirty*
> *glistening torsos sandwiches*
> *and Coca-Cola . . .*
> *   Then onto the*
> *avenue where skirts are flipping*
> *above heels and blow up over*
> *grates.*

The precise enumeration is delicious, especially matched with the quirky observations: *hum*-colored cabs, feeding the *torsos* sandwiches? It is as if the summer heat has blurred the phrasing somehow, or (more accurately) as if the ordinary way of saying things had been transformed by its passage through O'Hara's very particular sensibility. He ambles on, glancing at bargains in wrist-watches, the illuminated advertisements in Times Square, a black man "languorously agitating" his toothpick, a blonde chorus girl. He stops to eat; buys himself a cheeseburger and a chocolate malted. Briefly, he mourns the dead: his friend Bunny, John Latouche, Jackson Pollock, then strolls off into the early afternoon.

> *A glass of papaya juice*
> *and back to work. My heart is in my*
> *pocket, it is* Poems *by Pierre Reverdy.*

What is it that is so wonderful about this? The tenderness and humor, the sense that every encounter, however trivial or unexpected, can somehow be made welcome; that there is a place in the poem (in O'Hara's arena of enjoyment) for the grimy workmen with their yellow helmets, for his dead friends, for the cats frolicking among the sawdust. In this, O'Hara is, I think, a true heir to Whitman and his ecstatic catalogues of praise.

WORKS! WORKS!

I moved to New York City in the early eighties, and I remember for myself the pleasures of life on the Lower East Side: the beautiful lithe poplars in the empty lot on Houston Street, Economy Candy with its biscuits and dried fruit, its velvety chocolate smell. I made a list of "Things to be glad of in NYC," which included "the names of the subway stops, Bleecker and Astor and Spring, Kate's pink door, the short walks and the long ones, the busyness of snow." More than anything I liked what my friend Rosie and I called "going on a wander"—down to the East River to watch the tugs and barges passing by, off through Chinatown for soup in the Mayflower Café, and on to Bayard Street for delicious ices flavored with mango or ginger or green tea.

But the city by then had come to seem a very different place. O'Hara's ease and lyricism, his sunny sense of entitlement, had gone. Anxiety was rife, the price of real estate was rising; this was the era of drugs, disaffection, danger.

My first apartment was on Avenue B, opposite a well-known heroin hotel. You could stand at the kitchen window and watch the junkies shooting up: a bizarre kind of puppet show. Down on the street, there were often as many as fifty people circling and prowling. "Toilet!" they yelled. "Mr. C—*Co*-caine! Red Devil! Blue Tips! White Horse! Excalibur!" These were the brand names of different drugs, mostly heroin, which at that time went for ten dollars a deck (enough for one shot). "Fly with me, fool!" read the mural on East Sixth Street, a beautiful painted eagle dangling a syringe in its gold claws.

My journal of that time is tense with noticings, mind stretching to accommodate extraordinary new facts: "The fear of walking two blocks to the bank. The screams on the street. 'Works! Works!' The couple handcuffed on Houston. The kids throwing rocks at the streetlamps." Dealers and junkies lounged against broken furniture and burnt-out cars, took over the sidewalks and the stoops of houses. I learned to be firm and matter-of-fact approaching my front door, key tight-clenched inside my fist. "Excuse me, could you let me through please?" And then the sharp slam shut, so that no one would push in behind me, the utter silence leaning up against the wall, belly slack, heart thumping with relief.

I had been a lively, talkative child, "a clever girl," but years before, at college, I'd realized, *Inside I am slow.* My default mode was dreamy, self-absorbed. I was drawn to the kind of walking Stevenson describes, where one's thoughts take their color from the surrounding atmosphere and merge imperceptibly with birds, sky, wind, and leaves. This simply was not possible in my new neighborhood. One afternoon, I paused on the curb to take a photograph, and a strange woman came hurtling across the street, knocking my camera from my hands. I'd been hoping to record a recent starburst of graffiti, but she was sure my camera had been aimed at her.

I remember too, one winter evening, trying to find a corner on the sidewalk from which to look up at the sky. The moon was out, the so-called "blue moon," and all I wanted was to stand and stare. But the moon was only visible from two or three strategic points, and none was especially welcoming. If I stood outside the Gap store on Eighth Street, people thought I was a hooker. Seventh Street was bustling and loud. Next to the lamppost on First, a homeless man was digging in the garbage.

I walked down Third Avenue like a madwoman, head tilted to the distant sky, staring up at the moon's bald face. I wanted to take my time, to converse with it somehow, drink in its blue-green radiance. Other pedestrians eyed me curiously, and backed away. Such self-forgetfulness could easily lead to an unpleasant interchange, if not a car crash or a mugging. "What the *fuck* d'you think you're doing?"

Years later, I came across a journal entry by Walt Whitman, taken from his book *Specimen Days*. It was written during the Civil War, when he was volunteering his services among the wounded soldiers at the hospital. Even now, I find myself envying his unselfconscious ease.

> October 20th, 1863: Tonight, after leaving the hospital at 10 o'clock (I had been on self imposed duty some five hours, pretty closely confined), I wandered a long time around Washington. The night was sweet, very clear, sufficiently cool, a voluptuous half-moon, slightly golden, the space near it of a transparent blue-gray tinge. I walked up Pennsylvania Avenue, and then to Seventh Street, and a long while around the Patent Office. Somehow it looked rebukefully strong, majestic, there in the delicate moonlight. The sky, the planets, the constellations all so bright, so calm, so expressively silent, so soothing, after those hospital scenes. I wandered to and fro till the moist moon set, long after midnight.

SHAKESPEARE'S SISTER

In her magnificent book *Wanderlust: A History of Walking*, Rebecca Solnit describes walking as "the something [that is] closest to doing nothing." She spells out "the delicate balance between walking and idling . . . being and doing," when the mind and body fall into comfortable alignment, and thoughts are free to wander at their leisure. "The mind is also a landscape of sorts," she writes, "and walking is one way to traverse it."

When a friend of Solnit's had her truck stolen, it actually came as something of a relief, forcing her to slow down to the "stately pace" of walking, or to travel by public transport, both of which resulted in a stronger sense of place. Suddenly she found herself living in "the whole world," not just in a series of interiors.

Solnit quotes this approvingly, pointing out how the recent multiplication of technologies has eradicated the "in-between time," the all-important limbo in which wool-gathering and cloud-gazing can occur. It is just this kind of time that allows one to brood and muse and reflect and dream, and also, of course, *to encounter something new*—Wordsworth's leech-gatherer, Thoreau's "shining family," O'Hara's "hum-colored cabs." This is the place where walking intersects most obviously with creativity.

For centuries, men have been free to walk the streets, both by day and by night, finding what they need by way of inspiration. Their work testifies to the value of such excursions. I think of Steele's "Twenty Four Hours in London," of Dickens's tremendous night walks, and of Joyce, who wrote his own perambulations into *Ulysses,* transformed into the slow trudge of Mr. Leopold Bloom around Dublin. "Chance furnishes me what I need," he wrote. "I am like a man who stumbles along; my foot strikes something. I bend over, and it is exactly what I need."

But what if you are not permitted to go out? What if (like the New York City teenagers I once worked with) you are forbidden even to walk three or four blocks to your local park? Whitman's city of "orgies, walks and joys" is not always so joyful for the female pedestrian. Our vocabulary reflects this: "a streetwalker" is a prostitute, whereas "a man of the streets" is just another citizen. Women (young women in particular) still face almost certain insult each time they leave the house. Denise Levertov writes with sad accuracy about "Those groans men use / passing a woman on the street / or on the steps of the subway / to tell her she is a female / and their flesh knows it." The listener wants to discard this ugly compliment, but can't.

> *it goes on buzzing in her ear,*
> *it changes the pace of her walk,*
> *the torn posters in echoing corridors*
>
> *spell it out, it*
> *quakes and gnashes as the train comes in.*

During my first years in the Lower East Side, I had my head shaved to a blue-white dome, all except a ragged spiky fringe. I wore jeans and monkey-boots and a thick black baseball jacket with tarnished silver sleeves. I was edgy and skittish as a teenage boy, and you couldn't tell my gender without a second glance—which was exactly how I wanted it.

I did not know the statistics then—that women are still the primary target of sexualized violence, that two-thirds of American women are afraid to walk at night in their own neighborhoods. But I understood, viscerally, that being a woman meant I was not safe. Except in the calm center of the day, I skulked or scurried through my neighborhood, rather than strolled or sauntered. I was ashamed of that timidity, and blamed myself, my cowardice, realizing only much later, and with rage, how rare it is for women to feel safe and unselfconscious out of doors.

Such experiences have, alas, a long, familiar history. When Dorothy Wordsworth first walked through the Lake District with her brother, her aunt chided her for "rambling about the country on foot." Dorothy did her best to defend herself: she had made good use of her native strength, and saved at least thirty shillings besides. But the rebuke struck home nonetheless. A gentle, local stroll was an acceptable pastime, as Jane Austen makes plain in *Pride and Prejudice*, but a deliberate hike, a purposeful excursion, was something else altogether. Women of a certain class were not supposed to roam about outdoors. As Virginia Woolf asked rhetorically about Shakespeare's imaginary sister, Judith, "Could she even get her dinner in a tavern or roam the streets at midnight?"

Woolf herself never walked the streets at midnight—at least not unaccompanied by her husband. Nonetheless, her essay, "Street Haunting," written in 1930, provides a glowing example of the successful female pedestrian. She is going out, she says, to buy a pencil, but really, she's in search of immeasurably greater spoils, indulging in "the greatest pleasure of town life in winter—rambling the streets of London."

> As we step out of the house on a fine evening between four and six, we shed the self our friends know us by and become part of that vast republican army of anonymous trampers, whose society is so agreeable after the solitude of one's own room. . . . The shell-like covering which our souls have excreted to house themselves . . . is broken, and there is left of all these wrinkles and roughnesses a central oyster of perceptiveness, an enormous eye. How beautiful a street is in winter!

By the time Woolf returns home at seven or eight, the lamps have been lit, and the road is "of hammered silver." Woolf herself is filled to the brim with images and encounters, some real and some invented. Like her old friend and rival, Katherine Mansfield, she has succeeded in "going out and looking at a tree and coming back *plus* the tree." She recapitulates for herself the encounter with the dwarf in the shoe shop, the vision of the Mayfair mansion, the quarrel in the stationer's where she has finally bought her pencil. "In each of these lives one would penetrate a little way, far enough to give oneself the illusion that one is not tethered to a single mind, but can put on briefly the bodies and minds of others. One could become a washerwoman, a publican, a street singer." As a female reader, one heaves a small sigh of relief. Woolf has not been held hostage to her gendered self. The city has liberated and inspired her. As with a thousand male writers before her, it has answered precisely to her needs.

THE GREEN DREAM

Tibetans use the phrase *gadrii nombor shulen jongu,* which translates "to give a green answer to a blue question." The literal meaning has to do with not being given the kind of answer you expect: you ask the price of fish, and the clerk informs you it's a miserable day. But sometimes, more interestingly, the question itself is what's at fault. You're thinking sky, and the answer's in the trees. You're thinking blues, a smoky basement bar, and the solution is to leave the city altogether.

Long ago, at the very beginning of the twentieth century, John Girdner wrote a book called *Newyorkitis,* in which he identified a new disease, a precursor of Larry Dossey's hurry sickness. This was a kind of inflammation caused by living in big cities (at that time, specifically New York), and was identified by "rapidity and nervousness and lack of deliberation in all [one's] movements."

I loved Manhattan, but after ten years of living there, there's no question I was suffering from newyorkitis. My nerves were shot; I was tired and edgy and impatient. Few things felt truly satisfying. I remember my rage as I stood on the sidewalk, waiting for the light to change, how I would hurl myself up the subway stairs, exasperated by the simple presence of my fellow passengers, their garish backpacks and sad, raincoated shoulders. Each day became a series of escalating emergencies, in which I walked or ran or raced down ugly streets, hastening always to the next appointment, aching to be off and on my way. I was one of those people, described by singer-songwriter Suzanne Vega, for whom not even instant gratification is fast enough. I had become, in other words, a true New Yorker.

Meanwhile, I was teaching poetry and oral history in the New York City public schools, and courses in autobiography and nature writing at the college level. I was asking my students to write about childhood, to take the time to interview their family elders, to read Rilke and Rukeyser and Wallace Stevens, to eat an apple very, very slowly. I was accompanying them to the Central Park Zoo, and the Bronx Botanical Gardens, urging them to slow down and pay attention, trying to provide them with a sense of spaciousness that I myself had lost.

I was working on a novel at the time, and my favorite character was a child called Duncan, a dreamy, intuitive little boy. I would sit at my table every weekend and do my best to summon him, to hear his voice, my own slow tendrils reaching out and out. And then I would go back into the frenzy, back into the racket of the streets, and it was as if Duncan were being vaporized right in front of me.

How do people manage it? I asked myself. I could string a few words together, organize a class, a presentation. I could turn out reputable reviews for the *Nation* and *The Village Voice*. But the dreamy child in me could not keep up. *What on earth was one supposed to do?*

Years later, I read an interview with the scientist Antonio Damasio, in which he spoke of the neurological effects of urban life. The cognitive part of our brains works very fast, he said. "So you can do a lot of reasoning, a lot of recognition of objects, remembering names in just a few hundredths of a second." But the emotional part of our brains works very differently, and there is precious little evidence that that is going to change. Because it is a body regulatory system, the chances are that it will continue to work very slowly, with timescales of a second or more. Tasks that have to do with empathy and imagination, with slow-growing qualities like love and fidelity and ethics, will continue to develop in their own sweet time.

Back in the early nineties, I had no words for any of this. But then, one morning, early in the fall of 1992, I woke up from the following dream.

I was walking downtown on Second Avenue when I chanced upon a gently sloping hill. It looked like a Dürer painting, lush and green, with a small reedy pond at its foot. Beavers were playing in the water, their dark heads wet and sleek, and wolves were cavorting round about, elegant gray wolves with a white flourish to their tails. As I watched them, a crowd gathered, till there were twenty or thirty of us standing there, silently united in relief and gratitude.

"We need this green—" someone said.

It was as if the green were somehow symbolic of a deeper truth, glimpsed just beneath the chaos of the working day: a hidden pulse of pleasure and delight. *This too is possible*, I told myself as I woke up. *This too.*

The answer had arrived: the green answer to my blue question. Eighteen months later, I left New York for good.

IN PRAISE OF WALKING

The Scottish poet Thomas A. Clark was born in Greenock, on the River Clyde. This is (and was) a raw industrial town. But Greenock has magnificent views off towards the Highlands and Argyll, and "that sense of hills and water" was always a presence in Clark's life. By his late teens, he had begun to take off on long solitary walks. He valued this enormously, "Just that ability to walk up a hill and not only leave behind where you came from, but to move, gradually, into a wider and wider view."

Clark left school at fifteen and worked in factories, and also as a laborer. At twenty-three he "retired," and became "a kind of itinerant poet." Over the next ten years, he educated himself in the avant-garde literature of the time, starting with concrete poets like Ian Hamilton Finlay and Dom Sylvester Houedard, and moving on to American writers like Robert Creeley and Lorine Niedecker. He also apprenticed himself to the early Celtic nature poets, and to Japanese haiku-masters like Basho and Santoko.

Back in Scotland, after a long sojourn in the south, Clark seems well satisfied with what he has accomplished. He has published a host of small editions —note-cards, postcards, tiny books—as well as several volumes of poetry, among them *Tormentil and Bleached Bones,* and a more recent volume entitled *The Hundred Thousand Places*. Both books include a number of poem sequences drawn from long walks he has taken, in Southern Italy, in Portugal, in France and Andalucia, as well as in the Scottish Highlands and Islands.

There is a particular quality to these poems: an emphasis on nouns, proper nouns, and the defining adjective, combined with close, attentive looking. In "Coire Fhionn Lochan," for instance, a poem about a small loch, he simply lists the shimmering changes on the surface of the water:

> *lapping of the little waves*
> *breaking of the little waves*
> *spreading of the little waves*
> *idling of the little waves*

That effort to look, to "pour out the intelligence through the eyes," (Clark's phrase) is at the core of his intentions as a poet. Walking is very much part of this for him, especially walking *away*—"not only from the culturally predominant modes, but also from your own habitual obsessions, your habits of mind, your assumptions, *towards* something else."

Clark clearly enjoys walking; he has the rugged, relaxed look of one who is at home in his own skin. But his emphasis on walking is not dictated solely by private preference or aesthetics. He is powerfully conscious of the speed that dominates so much of contemporary life, and of the distraction, and (his term) "bewilderment" this brings in its train. In response to this, he says, "the obvious tactic is one of slowness. . . . The more displaced and harried people are, the easier it is to control them. The easier it is to sell them things, actually. And to walk away from that is literally a way of recovering your wits, of coming back to your senses, in both meanings of that word."

Clark carries a little notebook with him at all times. He stops for a moment to scribble in his notebook, to look around, and turns aside to examine things that interest him. "Though the word 'walking' occurs a lot, one could say that standing and sitting are as common for me as walking, and as important." An early book of his was called, not surprisingly, *Pauses & Digressions*.

That emphasis on "the pause" or "the delay" shows up in his work, as Clark moves from the small notebook to the computer, and on to the printed page. From his point of view, "One of the advantages of poetry is that it's got a lot of pauses in it. So there's a pause at the end of the line, before you move into the next line, and there are pauses, tiny little pauses, internal to the line." When he writes, he does his best to slow things down, to register each word and syllable: *to give them a material presence on the page.* Perhaps because his poems have so much to do with quiet and reflection, he is especially interested in the use of white space. Here, for example, is a one-line poem, what is known as a "monostich."

A ripple from the little loch of the trout.

Such a line gives you a moment of breathing space. Printed on a postcard, it slows you down a little. As Clark himself says, "It is a modest object, but with a large ambition."

Readers in general have been very receptive to this, partly because Clark's poems are so plain and comprehensible, partly because of his emphasis on perception. So many contemporary poems are, he says, "like a sort of higher crossword puzzle, where you have to work it all out." His own work does not demand such exegesis. Also, as he says, "In the thirst I have for space and clarity and time, I'm not alone."

Nonetheless, Clark's poems (most of them printed by his wife and himself at their Moschatel Press in Pittenweem) can at times seem almost bald in their minimalism. *One Hundred Scottish Places* (printed in the Netherlands in 1999, and bound in the soft purple of blooming heather) contains nothing but the names of different places, translated from their original language (Norse or Gaelic or Pictish) back into English. Each phrase lies alone on its own page, as if the reader were walking towards it across a desolate moor. Many carry violent or tragic overtones: *hill of the wild cat, hill of the slaughter, streamlet of blood,* though the book ends, encouragingly, with a kind of homecoming: *township of the hollow, cape of the standing stones, cairn of the blessing, slope of brightness.*

Like Whitman, Clark wants both to share "the aroma" of his own life and to encourage his readers to seek out such experiences for themselves. As he explains, "Typically, with poetry, you're sitting in a chair, and in imagination you are walking on a hillside." If the speed of contemporary culture is one major problem, "the other is its increasing self-reference." It is as if the natural world had no real existence except as temporary decoration. "I know many people who are committed green activists, but they couldn't name you a single wild flower. They're committed to the planet, but they don't know anything about nature. They've lost all sense of its details."

"Le bon Dieu est dans le détail," said Flaubert: *God lives in the details*, and Clark urges us to be alert to them. Meanwhile, as he writes in "In Praise of Walking,"

> *That something exists outside ourselves and our preoccupations, so near, so readily available, is our greatest blessing.*

> . . .

> *Early one morning, any morning, we can set out, with the least possible baggage, and discover the world.*

Tactics

↦ Go for a daily walk, however brief. Pay attention to what catches your eye.

↦ Visit somewhere you've never been before, and allow yourself to get thoroughly and happily lost. (Be sure to bring along a map to refer to should you need it!)

↦ *Consider the following quotations:*
"I found the poems in the fields / And only wrote them down . . ."

JOHN CLARE

"The geographical pilgrimage is the symbolic acting out of an inner journey. . . . One can have one without the other. It is best to have both."

THOMAS MERTON

CHAPTER FIVE

The Art of Looking

Stare. Educate the eye.
Die knowing something.
You are not here long.
WALKER EVANS

Seeing New

Jon Kabat-Zinn lives in western Massachusetts, not far from a beautiful hilly field. He passes this field each time he walks his dog, spring and summer, fall and winter, and always he finds something else to notice. The field, he says, enhances his ability to see. Gazing at it, he feels somehow changed, "recalibrated, more finely tuned to both inner and outer landscapes."

One hot July morning, he paused for a moment in the shade, drinking in the abundance of daisies, the lacy dragonflies. He noticed the trees, the color of the sky, the brown and gold of the field itself, and little by little, he began to relax. On his way home, the colors looked brighter and more vivid. There seemed to be more dragonflies than there'd been before; the swallows too (which at first he had barely noticed) were now swooping and flitting over the long grass. He sensed a welcome, an enveloping luxuriance. One moment he was separate from the surrounding countryside, the next, there was no "scene," no verbal commentary, only being there, "only seeing."

Kabat-Zinn is not alone in experiences like these. His is an ordinary field, one might even say an "ordinary" entrancement. The human eye is easily delighted: a pair of cardinals on a snowy bough, a ripple of sunlight on an empty wall, will give it all the satisfaction it requires. And yet our ability to see, *really see*, has never been more compromised. There is so much to see, and it passes by so fast, on the tiny screens of our digital cameras and the larger ones of our personal computers, on TVs and videos and flashing billboards, let alone the giddy speed-linked frames of what are rightly called "the movies." One moment we are staring at the close-up of a sunflower, the next at an infant starving in Darfur. We are greedy for novelty, and at the same time we're exhausted, easily bored. Inevitably, in self-protection, we close down. We look, but we do not see. We see, but we do not remember. Did we "really see" that sunflower, or was it just some passing ad? Like the inhabitants of Plato's cave, we are mesmerized by the flickering shadows on the wall (or the super-size TV) while the real world unfurls invisibly outside our door.

At times it seems impossible to pull free from such entanglements, and simply look at what is there in front of us, to see, and to relax into the seeing. And yet we hunger for that respite, that gentle, quiet immersion, those moments of attentive revelation. The writer Terry Tempest Williams is a case in point. In her "Ode to Slowness," she asks wistfully whether it might be possible to make a living "simply by watching light".

> Monet did. Vermeer did. . . . Perhaps that is what I desire most, to sit and watch the shifting shadows cross the cliff face of sandstone or simply walk parallel with a path of liquid light called the Colorado River.

She and her husband were comfortable with their busy city routine, but nonetheless:

> The speed of my life in Salt Lake City was its own form of pathology: drive here, meet there, talk, eat, talk, listen, look at my watch, run to work, teach, more meetings, talk, listen, talk, listen, run to the health club, run some errands, shop, buy, load the car, drive the car, car in traffic, too much traffic, speed, brake, speed, brake, red light, green light, hurry home, almost home, pick up mail, pick up phone, call, talk, call, talk, time for dinner, go out for dinner, drive to dinner, eat, talk, drive, return home, bathe, read, sleep, wake, eat, dress, drive, drive to work, work, work—and the next day moved right on schedule.

They wanted more, she says. They wanted less. They wanted more time, and fewer distractions. More time to write, to breathe, just to be conscious of their lives. And so they moved to a little village in the desert, where they could build their days "as a ceremony around s l o w n e s s, an homage to tortoises and snakes." Their priorities are different now. Williams is not as easily seduced by speed as she once was. "To see how much I can get done in a day does not impress me any more." She is becoming the one she used to dream of being, "a caretaker of silence, a connoisseur of stillness, a listener of wind where each dialect is not only heard but understood."

ASPEN BRANCHES

The poet Stanley Kunitz once heard someone say that he'd rather look at a painting of the sky than at the sky itself—a remark that Kunitz found preposterous. Nonetheless, some kind of "art apprenticeship" can be immensely helpful for anyone who is interested in a more attentive looking. Reading artists' letters and journals, studying their work (whether in books or galleries or museums), learning a little of their lives and daily diligence, are all rich and inspiring practices, especially if one also tries, however clumsily, to draw or doodle, paint or sculpt oneself.

The art critic John Ruskin grew up in a strict Victorian household, with neither friends nor siblings. His mother took excellent, even excessive, care of him. But the rule was that he had to find his own amusement. As a small child, he had only a bunch of keys to play with. Later, he was provided with a cart and a ball, and two boxes of well-cut wooden bricks. But that was all. On one occasion, a well-meaning aunt presented him with a magnificent Punch and Judy, decked out in scarlet and gold. But he was not allowed to keep them. On damp days, he spent much of his time tracing the squares and comparing the colors in his carpet, or examining the knots in his wooden floorboards. When it was fine, he was sent out into the garden, where he devoted himself to "close watching" of the ways of plants.

I had not the smallest taste for growing them, or taking care of them, any more than taking care of the birds or the trees, or the sky, or the sea. My whole time was spent staring at them, or into them.

It was, he said, a "very small, perky, contented, conceited, Cock-Robinson-Crusoe sort of life."

In the nineteenth century, every educated person drew as a matter of course, and Ruskin was no exception. He drew intricate landscapes; he drew trees and clouds. By the time he was twelve, his parents had hired a drawing master for him. Not long after, they took him on his first trip to Europe. Ruskin drew as the carriage went along, and "worked up" his drawings in the evenings. The trip was, from today's perspective, marvelously tranquil and unhurried:

> Between nine and three,—reckoning seven miles an hour, including stoppages, for minimum pace,—we had done our forty to fifty miles of journey, sate down to dinner at four,— and I had two hours of delicious exploring by myself in the evening; ordered in punctually at seven to tea, and finishing my sketches till half-past nine,—bedtime.

Some ten years later, at Fontainebleau, Ruskin found himself lying on a sandy bank, with nothing in sight but a little aspen tree. He had been awake with a fever all night, and felt too ill to travel the next day. But he put his sketchbook in his pocket, and tottered out, lying down by the roadside to see if he could sleep. It was then he saw the branches of the aspen against the clear blue of the sky.

> Languidly, but not idly, I began to draw it; and as I drew, the languor passed away: the beautiful lines insisted on being traced,—without weariness. More and more beautiful they became, as each rose out of the rest, and took its place in the air. With wonder increasing every instant, I saw that they "composed" themselves, by finer laws than any known

of men. At last, the tree was there, and everything that I had thought before about trees, nowhere.

Ruskin drew off and on for the rest of his life: landscapes, architectural studies, sketches of trees and birds and flowers. These sketches are well worth looking at even now. I think, for example, of his "Study of a Velvet Crab" (all opalescent shell and snapping claws), or his series of "dawn studies" painted in rich blues and oranges on blue and blue-gray paper. They were intended as models for his students, to inspire them to make such studies for themselves. But unlike most artists, Ruskin valued the seeing more than the doing. "The sight is more important than the drawing," he said. "I would rather teach drawing that my pupils may learn to love nature, than teach them looking at nature that they may learn to draw." And again, "The greatest thing a human being ever does in this world is to SEE something, and tell what he saw in a plain way. Hundreds of people can talk for one who can think, but thousands of people can think for one who can see. To see clearly is poetry, prophecy and religion—all in one."

LEARNING TO SEE

When I was small, I thought that all grownups could draw, certainly all grown-up men. My uncle Rory painted leaves and flowers and roots, less botanical illustrations than portraits of each individual plant. His pinks and carnations hung in the drawing room, brilliant in scarlet and soft rose. My uncle Jamie painted birds with equal skill. When I asked, at ten or twelve, if he would contribute something to my autograph album, he sent me a beautiful hand-painted hummingbird, with jeweled head and slim, snow-spattered wings. My father's specialty was the swift, incisive sketch, an almost cartoonish likeness appearing with startling speed under his hand. Once or twice, when the local fête was held at our house, he set up an easel on the grass, offering his artistic services for 2/6 (two shillings, sixpence or about fifty cents). Sketches of the six of us, in faded felt-pen, still adorn my mother's bathroom walls.

I used to wish that I could draw and paint myself. But when I look at my early efforts—a lone piper, a sad little line-up of smudgy watercolor thistles—I can see that I was right to stick to words. I kept a diary from the age of eleven, and wrote quantities of poems and stories, as well as the obligatory school essays. But by my late teens I also spent much of my time *just looking*. I had another uncle to thank for this, my uncle Johnny, then just starting out as an art critic in London. We would eat lunch in some pub, and then wander together round the big museums and galleries, strolling and looking and pointing things out to each other. Perhaps it was this that gave me the courage to go to Paris, walking, as I saw it, in the footsteps of Rilke and Gwen John.

I'd been reading Rilke's poems for a couple of years by then. I knew he had acted as a secretary for the sculptor Rodin, and that it was Rodin who had advised him to visit the Jardin des Plantes to teach himself to see. Gwen John, the English painter, was also part of Rodin's entourage. They became lovers in 1904, soon after she moved to Paris, and she also posed for him, modeling for his "Monument to Whistler" (never finished). She and Rilke knew each other well, and continued to correspond in the decade after Rodin's death.

In the fall of 1977, I made my way to the Musée Rodin: a large, mild house with gleaming parquet floors. A violet-tinted chandelier hung overhead, and the wooden paneling was edged in gold. I was struck by the green and white of the marble mantelpieces, "strange spinach-colored jewels," I noted. But it was the sculptures themselves that I was trying to befriend: the little orphan from Alsace with her clear, bold gaze, her bald head swathed in its clumsy veils; the "Old Man with the Broken Nose"; the lovely Juliet. I wandered among them, light-hearted and ardent, making spiky notes in my black notebook. "The coolness of the rooms and their *fraîcheur*, airiness. Shadows on the floor. The slow noises of people walking and pausing. Outside in the garden, old ladies in a row."

I did my best to draw Balzac with his great potbelly, and Nijinsky too, caught in the whirl of his dance. Like Rilke, I was overwhelmed by the sheer magnitude of Rodin's accomplishment. At the same time, the sculptures seemed very real to me, humanly and sensuously real. "There's so much more to love in the human body than the inside of a woman's thigh. Rodin's *Orphée*—the space between waist and hip, the tender stomach."

What did it mean to write in this way, to try to draw and notice and observe? I wasn't sure. I found a bench in the garden, and let my eyes fall on the limetrees and the chestnuts, the prim pink roses and clipped triangular yews, then turned back to gaze at the house itself, its pale yellow walls and gray roof, its arched windows with their creamy frames, hoping to paint in words what I could not paint on the page.

A couple of years later, I came upon a book that helped me understand what I was doing. *A Life of One's Own* is still in print even now, though it was originally published in 1936. It was written by a British psychoanalyst called Marion Milner, under the pseudonym of Joanna Field. In it she outlines, in gentle unpretentious language, that same "apprenticeship in looking" I'd been trying to pursue, something she achieved, in part, by keeping a diary.

Milner had always been drawn to pictures, in a general way. But she had felt uncomfortable too, because so often she could not explain what she admired. Then one day, she happened to stop in front of a Cézanne painting: green apples, a white plate, a rumpled cloth. Because she was tired and restless, and distracted by the crowds of Sunday sightseers, she simply sat and looked at it, without bothering to interrogate her own response.

> Slowly then I became aware that something was pulling me out of my vacant stare and the colors were coming alive, gripping my gaze till I was soaking myself in their vitality. Gradually a great delight filled me, dispelling all boredom and doubts about what I ought to like. . . . Yet it had all happened by just sitting still and waiting. If I had merely given a cursory glance, said, "Isn't that a nice Cézanne," and drifted on with the crowd, I would have missed it all.

Scientists testify that anxiety and fear (both highly primitive emotions) actually help improve one's visual focus—a fact that would have served our long-ago survival. Given the weight of our contemporary neuroses, this can be turned to our advantage even now. Certainly Milner's encounter with Cézanne came to seem like a parable to me. It taught me to be patient, not to try too hard, taught me, above all, the power of the pause, of receptivity. Suspending one's judgment, that was the key, learning (that tender phrase, so frequently abused) "to take one's own sweet time."

THE ART OF LOOKING

Bernard Berenson once said that he had never really enjoyed any work of art, whether verbal, visual or musical, without sinking his identity into it and somehow "becoming it." Gazing at the leafy scrolls on the doorjambs of a church outside Spoleto, he felt as if every stem, tendril, and curl of foliage had become alive, and he himself had finally emerged into the light after a long groping in the darkness. He felt "as one illumined," transported into a world in which every edge and outline was now in sensuous relationship to himself, "and not, as hitherto, in a merely cognitive one."

Such revelations do not happen casually. As Milner knew, to see like this takes time. One has to know how to stop: to let go of one's usual worries and preoccupations and simply *be there* for the leafy foliage (or the poem or the painting or the piece of music) for however long it takes. This is one thing with books or music, both of which can be enjoyed in solitude. It is something else entirely with a piece of visual art. Most are on display in public galleries and museums, and always there are the crowds with their whispering head-sets, let alone the voices of the guides, the printed commentary, the racket of the gift store and the café. It is not easy in such circumstances simply to allow oneself to wait.

In 1902, when the poet Rilke was not yet thirty, he visited Paris for the first time. For years, he had looked at paintings as so many writers look, concentrating on their lyrical or narrative qualities. But at the artists' colony in Worpswede, he'd met the painter Paula Moder-sohn-Becker, as well as the sculptor Clara Westoff, who later became his wife, and the two women had taught him to see in a new way. From them he learned what he called "this daily attentiveness . . . this thousand-fold looking . . . this being-only-eye." Because of them, he also encountered the work of Rodin and Cézanne, which was, quite literally, to change his life.

Clara Westoff had been a student of Rodin in 1900, and Paula too was well acquainted with his work. When Rilke arrived at Rodin's house, the rapport was immediate. "He was kind and gentle," Rilke reported back to his wife. "And it seemed to me that I had always known him." At times, the two men would sit together in the garden, musing, dreaming, neither of them saying a word. After a couple of hours, Rodin would get up and rub his hands.

"We *have* done a lot of work this morning!" he would say.

The remark was not intended to be ironic; on the contrary. Work, for Rodin, could take many forms. He could withdraw into himself, said Rilke, becoming "blunt and hard towards the unimportant." But he could also be wholly open and receptive.

> [W]hat he gazes at and surrounds with gazing is always the only thing, the world in which everything happens; when he fashions a hand, it is alone in space, and there is nothing besides a hand.

Rodin's work, the clarity and concentration of his gaze, were for Rilke tremendously inspiring. It was because of Rodin that he wrote "The Panther," the first of the so-called "thing-poems" (*Ding-Gedichte*), poems about people and animals and works of art, where the emphasis is less on feeling than on observation, less on the observer than the thing observed. Through Rodin's example, he came to feel that he too had "patience for centuries," and could live as though his time were "very large."

In the years that followed, Rilke wrote two essays on Rodin, and made him the subject of several lecture tours. He never met Cézanne, who died in 1906, but he was equally inspired by his work, which he first saw at a memorial exhibition held at the *Salon d'Automne* in Paris. Writing to Clara back in Worpswede, Rilke was brimful of admiration at what the artist had accomplished. He described how Cézanne had used his old drawings as models, piecing together the subjects of his paintings from whatever he could find: apples and wine bottles and some borrowed bed covers.

> And (like van Gogh) [he] makes his "saints" out of such things; and forces them—*forces them*—to be beautiful, to stand for the whole world and all joy and all glory, and doesn't know whether he has persuaded them to do it for him. And sits in the garden like an old dog, the dog of this work that is calling him again and that beats him and lets him go hungry.

Rilke returned again and again to the exhibit, pausing for as much as two hours in front of a few pictures. Like Marion Milner, he hadn't known how to look at them at first. He felt puzzled and insecure. And then, "suddenly one has the right eyes." Standing on the threshold between the two rooms full of pictures, he felt the power of their combined presence. "The good conscience of these reds, these blues, their simple truthfulness, it educates you," he wrote. It was "as if these colors could heal one of indecision once and for all."

Rilke was not the only one to be inspired in this way. Matisse bought Cézanne's *Three Bathers* (now in the Petit Palais, Paris) when he himself had almost no money. The picture shows two chunky nudes reclining on the grass by an idyllic pond, while a third woman stands upright, next to a swaying birch tree. The painting helped Matisse and gave him confidence. "It sustained me morally in the critical moments of my venture as an artist," he wrote years later. "I have drawn from it my faith and perseverance."

One might imagine that such earnest concentrated looking had fallen out of fashion. But not at all. When writer Lawrence Weschler was covering the Yugoslav war-crimes tribunal at The Hague, he returned over and over to the nearby Mauritshuis, to commune with the three Vermeers that were on display: *Diana and Her Companions*, the *Girl with a Pearl Earring*, and the *View of Delft*. Jangled as he was from the long days of painful testimony, he marveled at the "centered serenity" he felt in their presence, as if it were something that the paintings themselves had the power to bestow.

Festina lente, says the Latin tag. "Make haste slowly." Or in relationship to looking: *look again*.

A TINY STONE, A FISH

When I spoke with Thomas Clark at his home in Pittenweem, I asked if there were any assignment, any special "homework" he might propose for an apprentice poet of today. His answer startled me.

"I would ask the young poet to choose some simple task, something very ordinary and non-utilitarian, and ask them to repeat it at regular intervals. For example, one might climb a hill, pick up a stone, carry it back down, and then take it back up the hill the following day."

The task would be pointless in and of itself. But doing it would create what Clark called "a continuum," a context in which small events could resonate: a counter-story to the larger, public one.

Clark's response sounded a little crazy to me at first. But the more I considered it, the more I came to see it as a kind of koan, one of those wise, unsettling conundrums from which, with luck and diligence, a certain striking revelation may emerge. "To learn something new," said the naturalist John Burroughs, "take the path today that you took yesterday." All professions have need of such devoted practitioners, willing to push past their own boredom, their own comfortable familiarity, in order to arrive at something new. As Proust once said, "The true voyage of discovery consists not in seeking new landscapes, but in having fresh eyes."

One thinks of Goethe, who trained himself to watch leaves as they grew, remembering each stage with such clarity that he could actually "see" their metamorphosis. One thinks of Denise Levertov, in her last years, addressing poem after poem to the peak of Mount Rainier, just visible above the rooftops of Seattle. Above all, perhaps, one thinks of the Swiss zoologist Louis Agassiz, and the extraordinary assignment he once gave a student.

In 1859, when Nathaniel Shaler applied to study at the Harvard laboratories, he was sent to Agassiz for an entrance exam. The first part of this had to do with languages and scientific classification, and Shaler passed with flying colors. He also trounced Agassiz in an impromptu fencing match. The second half of the exam was both simpler and more complicated. It focused on a certain preserved fish.

"I want you to examine this," said Agassiz, presenting him with the fish in a tin pan. "I'd like you to find out everything you can, without damaging the specimen."

Obediently, Shaler set to work. He expected Agassiz to return within a couple of hours. But Agassiz did not come back. Not that day, nor even that same week. Shaler kept on patiently, studying the fish, and on the seventh day, Agassiz finally put in an appearance.

"Well?" he asked.

Shaler pointed to all the details he had learned about the fish: its teeth, its jaws, its fins and scales and so on. Agassiz listened carefully. "That's not right," he said. And once again he vanished for an entire week.

Shaler returned, disconsolate, to his tin pan. *Was Agassiz completely crazy? Perhaps he should have let him win that fencing match?* But even while he puzzled over the professor's methods, Shaler began to recognize how much he was benefiting from them. Each day he was learning more and more about that fish, a hundred times more than had originally seemed possible. And by the time he was accepted at Harvard (after a further two months of disentangling a box of mixed fish bones, and reassembling them into their different species) no one could have said that he was not truly qualified.

THE ANCIENT ONES

Agassiz trained Nathaniel Shaler in what one might call "deep looking." Most of the others I've referred to here, writers and poets, painters and psychoanalysts, have been obliged to train themselves. But all have testified to the joy and sustenance of that extended gaze. Ruskin, as the only artist-educator among them, was perhaps the most fervent, recommending daily studies to his students as a way to "calm and purify" their thoughts. Drawing had its scientific uses, but ultimately he saw it as an act of worship.

Human beings are the only animals that draw. The horses, bison, lions, and panthers on the walls of the Chauvet Cave in France are at least thirty-two thousand years old, while the first known human portrait (an ivory and clay statue of a woman from what is now the Czech Republic) dates back to 26,000 BCE. For thousands of years, art-making has been something that we do: anonymous, ubiquitous—and, more often than you might expect, entirely beautiful.

I turn the pages of a glossy library book, marveling at a cave bear's curious snout, a small rhinoceros with laughing mouth and upward-swirling horn. Here is a tumult, a brotherhood of lions lunging at the bison cowering across the page; here, an elegant little ibex painted in charcoal on a creamy-yellow wall. "They've invented everything," Picasso said, after his first visit to a Paleolithic cave. And he was right. To look at these paintings, even in reproduction, is to begin to understand, viscerally, something about the long attentive cherishing of the human eye, and its alliance with the busy working hand. It is to share the hard-won accuracy of the hunter-gatherer, the vision of the original artist/shaman, and the gratitude and admiration of all those who have benefited from their skill.

Some three hundred Paleolithic sites have been identified, most of them in southern France and northern Spain. They range in age from thirty-seven thousand to eleven thousand years: more than a thousand human generations. The experts can explain how such paintings came to be made, using embers of Scotch pine to make a rich black charcoal, and crushed hematite to achieve a blackish red. They can tell you precisely which animals have been portrayed, and in what numbers. They can spell out what is absent: sun and moon and stars, trees and rivers, a firm horizon line, even human beings themselves, of whom only about twenty are fully represented.

Who made this work? And for what purposes? Again, the archeologists are chock-a-block with information and statistics, a palimpsest of different explanations, ranging from "art for art's sake" to shamanism, hunting magic, and fertility rituals. But the truth is that no one explanation can ever hope to be sufficient. Just as any ordinary room may be used and re-used, its identity shifting over the years, now a parlor, now a borning-room, now a teenage hangout, so the caves will have served a myriad different purposes over the course of their long lives.

What is clear is that the paintings in those early caves were made by people who had grown up watching animals, and lived with them in daily intimacy. The wild horses with their long grave faces, lips and nostrils flaring, the rumpled bison with his curly head, the hungry lions: these were deeply familiar. To know animals in this way is to be alert to them always, both in their presence and their absence. It is to crouch in the damp reeds, waiting for the geese, learning as much about the moon and the stars and the chilly darkness as one ever learns about the birds themselves. It is to duck behind a rock, atlatl at the ready, hoping for a herd of aurochs, a capricious goat, however bored or hungry one might be, however frightened or exhausted. This was the double knowledge that was carried down into the caves and represented on those painted walls: the electric presence of the animals, in looming flank and playful silhouette, and their equally potent and unsettling absence.

Who knows where it began? Perhaps there was a thunderstorm, an especially fearsome winter, and a small band of people found shelter in a cave, sleeping there at night, exploring by day. Perhaps they were inspired by a particular rocky outcropping: the bulge that defines a haunch or outstretched neck, the knot or nodule that provides an eye. Thus at Altxerri, in the Spanish Basque country, a stone cut-out of a bird emerges from a ledge, its eye and beak incised by some witty Stone Age artist, while at the Niaux caves in France, a long oval hole has been transformed into a stag, its antlers bristling on the walls to either side. Some bold inventive soul would make such marks, and then elaborate upon them, using crushed grit of a contrasting color, or charcoal left behind from last night's fire. Later, in the flickering light given by the grease lamps (a plant wick, set in animal fat inside a hollow stone), the images would pulse and tremble on the walls, as if the animals themselves were moving. A drumbeat would provide the thunder of their hooves.

Some caves are thick with images: claw-marks, scrapings, charcoal drawings, layered one upon another; others, strangely blank. Smaller, more isolated corners may have been used for meditation and retreat, something equivalent to the Native American vision quest. Larger spaces would most likely have been communal, serving the purpose of a local cinema, an art gallery, a dance hall, even a cathedral. Hundreds may have gathered to dream and marvel, to commune with the ancestors. Many of the caves are marked with palmprints and hand stencils, and what are called "finger flutings" (long sinuous marks, made with two or more fingers), as if in touching the walls, the participants were in some way reaching past the painted images to the world of vision and imagination, a world in which such animals might come alive.

There are times when nothing seems impossible.

W. B. Yeats tells the story of a Japanese artist who painted horses on a temple wall. Her work was so vivid, so complete, that one of the horses slipped down in the night and galloped off across a neighbor's rice field. Next morning, a pilgrim came very early to the temple, and was startled by a shower of water drops. Looking up, he saw the horse still wet with dew, still "trembling into stillness."

That shift between the real and the imagined, that magical vivacity, is what inspires us to return to those ancient paintings, nourishing our fretful, anxious spirits, steadying our gaze. "It is our slowness I love," says the poet Jorie Graham, "growing slower, tapping the paintbrush against the visible, tapping the mind."

SEEING/DRAWING

When the painter Emily Carr was a little girl, she wanted to draw a dog. She sought out Carlow, the family pet, and settled herself down beside his kennel. For a long time, she just stared at him. Then she fetched a charred stick from the grate, split open a brown paper bag, and began to draw. That bag was found years later among her father's papers. He had written on it, "By Emily, aged eight."

In drawing with a charred stick on a rough uneven surface, in choosing to draw an animal, Carr linked herself, unwittingly, with a long and honorable tradition. There was a certain gravity about her work: *she really took the time to look at Carlow.* Such focus has become increasingly rare. The average child starts to draw about the age of three, and stops, abruptly, at the age of eight or nine. In those five short years, he or she will draw a person (a circle with a dot inside it, and a multitude of arms), then gradually a house, a cat, and so on. But such drawings tend to be schematic. There is rarely much "real looking" involved. A five-year-old asked to draw two apples will draw them side by side, even if one is slightly in front of the other. She will draw what she knows, not what she actually sees.

Soon, she may refuse to draw at all, because as my students tell me, plaintively, "The computer can do it so much better." Instead of illustrating their own poems, many of them prefer to press a button, to choose an icon from some fail-safe image bank. They have lost the art of drawing: the shift from eyes to hand to breathing body, and back into the slowly roaming gaze. They have lost the pleasures of a brand-new pencil, the crunch of charcoal on the page, the smudge of Prussian blue. Above all, they have lost that sweep of unselfconscious attention (from the Latin, *ad tendere*: "to stretch towards"), the dreamy, joyful, mindful receptivity that is rightly known as "flow."

It isn't easy for any of us, child or adult, to set aside the sturdy competence of our workaday left brain and surrender to the flounderings of the right. Perfectionism is hard to jettison. No less an artist than Jan van Eyck framed his portrait in the words of his own self-judgment: ALS ICH KAN, he wrote. "As well as I can." But effort, in the sense of earnest striving, is not what matters here. As Henry Moore once said, "Drawing itself is a part of learning: learning to use one's eyes more intensely. To encourage everybody to draw is not to turn people into artists, just as you don't teach grammar to turn them all into Shakespeares."

In recent years, Frederick Franck has been a potent voice for what he calls "Seeing/Drawing," understanding this as a kind of meditation, a way of getting in touch with the visible world around us, and also with ourselves. His many books, among them *The Zen of Seeing*, repay close attention, and can serve as guide and encouragement for those who find themselves without a teacher.

Franck feels strongly that most of us are constantly bombarded with undifferentiated noise and visual stimuli, and that Seeing/Drawing can act as an antidote to this, establishing "an island of silence" in which it is possible to restore ourselves and come to focus. His instructions to his students read as follows:

> 1) to find a spot at least six feet away from the next person, and to sit down comfortably and let yourself relax.
> 2) to let your eyes fall on whatever happens to be in front of you: a plant, a bush, a tree, or perhaps some grass, and then to close your eyes for five minutes.
> 3) to open your eyes again, and look at that plant or leaf until you feel it looking back at you, until you are alone with it on the earth.
> 4) to keep on looking, and to let the pencil follow what the eye perceives. To feel as if you are caressing the contours, the whole circumference of that leaf. Not to let your eyes wander, nor to lift your pencil from the paper.

"Above all," he says, "don't try too hard, don't 'think' about what you are drawing, just let the hand follow what the eye sees. Let it caress."

There is something very comforting about the extreme simplicity of these instructions, not least, perhaps, that they run so entirely counter to our usual behavior. To stop rushing around, to sit down quietly, simply to allow oneself to see, is, as Franck says, "an unforgettable experience." The eye relaxes, the heart expands, and "curiosity is dissolved in wonder." Drawing the landscape, one in a sense "becomes" it. Jon Kabat-Zinn spoke in similar terms, as did Bernard Berenson. But in the artist's case, every patch of light and shade, every dot and line and curlicue, has passed through his entire organism. Or, as Franck says, "I have learned that what I have not drawn I have never really seen, and that when I start drawing an ordinary thing I realize how extraordinary it is, sheer miracle."

THE LIFE OF THE HAND

My friend Barbara Bash is a naturalist, and an artist too: a gentle woman with the lithe body of a dancer, and a mass of dusty autumn-colored hair. When she was a little girl, she invented her own script, a mysterious and powerful language she would scrawl along the margins of her books. As she grew older, she began to draw. But always she had a fascination with the forms of letters in and of themselves. From very early on, her words had pictures in them, and her pictures were interspersed with words. She was helped by seeing traditional Chinese scrolls, in which painting and calligraphy complement each other, as well as by contemporary American artists like Ben Shahn. Her teachers too were encouraging. In high school, she volunteered to make all the public signs and posters, exhilarated by the massive shift of scale.

"To watch someone writing big characters a foot high. Ah, is this not happiness?" wrote the seventeenth-century critic Chin Shengt'an. Certainly it was happiness for her.

At college, Bash had a stint with a wonderful art teacher who taught her close looking in the traditional nineteenth-century style. She made "very delicate renderings of three pebbles," magnified to the point where every single little pockmark could be seen. She also studied pottery and dance, delighting in their fullness and fluidity. But it was not until later, when she began to study broad-edged pen calligraphy, that at last she felt she had "come home." She remembers sitting down with the model sheets, and feeling, "I know how to do this," as if it were in some crucial way familiar.

By 1976, Bash was living in Colorado, and taking classes at the Naropa Institute. She was also studying meditation with the Buddhist teacher Chögyam Trungpa. She came to see calligraphy and religion as very much entwined, whether in the Buddhist sutras, the medieval manuscripts, or the Islamic calligraphic and pictorial traditions. Training one's hand and eye led naturally and inevitably into training one's mind, and slowing down was at the heart of it.

> It's just not possible to do a calligraphic stroke in a hurry. It is like it has a powerful self-protective guardian around it. You rush around and do lots of things, and then you get to that place of sitting down and working. . . . And it's as *if the only doorway is through slowness.*

There were days when Bash felt as if she had lost that doorway, or as if it had become overgrown with vines. But time after time, she would find her way back again. As a child, she had studied the piano, and when it came time to do the recitals, her mind would "just kind of melt" on her. But with calligraphy she was somehow able to remain centered, "in touch, you know . . . and in no hurry, steady," however large the audience.

In the years that followed, Bash began to decorate her work. It was as if she herself were following the path of the medieval scribes—first the pure unadorned field of words, then the letters themselves beginning to leaf and sprout. (Curiously enough, the word "page" itself derives from *pagina,* which means "vineyard" in Latin, on account of those illuminated vines.) Not long afterwards, she saw an exhibit of botanical art at the Morgan Library in New York City. These images amazed her. "It wasn't just a neat and tidy art form," she told me. "It was bold. There would be a huge leaf bending across the page, and then this enormous flower. . . . It was really outrageous and strong." She began to paint similar images of her own, combining them with calligraphy, starting with leeks and chives and turban squash, and gradually adding birds and other creatures.

> When you go outside to draw you're not walking, you're not hiking, you're not talking, you're just sitting. Just through the

physics of the act, you're somewhat still. Out of this quiet, the world starts to emerge. The birds are curious and come closer. That's always been this sweet aspect of doing it. It slows me down so that the world can open up. I begin to hear and see in a different way.

Bash teaches now, and has published several books. *True Nature: An Illustrated Journal of Four Seasons in Solitude* appeared in 2004. In it, she brings together her long-time Buddhist practice with the wise eye of the trained artist. A brown-and-yellow snake slithers across the breadth of two large pages. A thistle spills its silvery stars onto her tabletop. Sounds are translated into invented letter-forms: a soft blotchy gray for the mourning dove, italic scarlet for the cardinal, the ur-script of her childhood revived with adult skill.

"It's a delicate thread," she told me, "the life of the hand." These days, she practices "slow blogging," posting new images each month, intercut with her own haiku-like commentary. She sees drawing as a form of dharma practice, following the moving line that keeps meandering through her life. "The hand is directly connecting us to the pathways of the heart. What we make with our hands keeps those pathways humming. And that motion with the computer mouse won't do it."

FOLLOWING THE LINE

In *The Shape of a Pocket*, John Berger recounts a dream in which he is a curious kind of dealer, "a dealer in looks and appearances." In the dream he has discovered a secret, how to get inside whatever he is looking at—a bucket of water, a cow, the city of Toledo—and once inside, to rearrange its appearance for the better.

> Better did not mean making the thing more beautiful or more harmonious. . . . It simply meant making it more itself so that the cow or the city or the bucket became more evidently unique.

I love this dream. John Berger is an art critic and a novelist, but he is also a practicing artist. And one feels that his dream could be the dream of any maker: to see the outside world so clearly that in some sense one does "get inside it," and so make it more alluringly alive. I wanted to teach my students this kind of immersion, but I wasn't clear how I should go about it. Then, one bright fall day, my friend Barbara Bash came to teach in the little elementary school near where I lived. I sat in the back and listened, working alongside the children, and in the course of this I learned a little about what was meant by "following the line."

I learned that it is very much worth drawing, even if you are convinced you cannot draw; that you can divide the page into many different sections, filling each one with a different image; that you can change the scale of your picture, as if you were working with a zoom lens, shifting from large to small to microscopic, and then back again. I learned that it is possible to write or paint in color, and to use invented shapes to record sound: the delicate rustle of a single leaf, the roar of an airplane, the call of a chickadee outside the window. But most of all, I learned the practice of blind contour, a simple yet extremely powerful drawing exercise, and one which is, perhaps, the epitome of close looking.

"Choose a stone or shell or leafy twig," Bash told the children. "And hold it in your non-drawing hand. Scoot round, so you are sitting at an angle to your desk. And then for one whole minute, I'd like you to draw. Don't look down at your page, however much you're tempted. Just keep looking at the object you are holding, and try to trace its outline on your page. It's as if your pencil were a tiny creature—an ant perhaps—following the edge of that object. Keep on drawing, slowly and patiently. But don't peek. And don't lift your pencil from the paper."

The children finished their blind contour drawings (one long minute), and burst out laughing as they saw what they had done. Bash gave them time to enjoy the absurdities (this is not an easy exercise for a perfectionist!) and asked them to write a little poem, placing it very carefully on the page. Then she guided them in a second blind contour drawing (this time for two minutes, with one peek halfway through), and then a third (for three minutes, with two chances to peek), again with a little poem in between. The alternation between the writing and the drawing kept the children spry, and helped distract them from their own self-judgment.

The following spring, I tried a similar exercise at the Scottish Poetry Library in Edinburgh, working with a group of twelve-year-olds. Between drawings, I read them a poem by the Japanese haiku-master, Basho:

> *A crow*
> *has settled on a bare branch.*
> *Autumn evening.*

And the children wrote their own poems in response:

> *The cat*
> *cleaning itself beautifully.*
> *Monday morning.*

> *A young pet rat*
> *nestles in my hair*
> *while watching Saturday morning TV.*

> *Winter deer*
> *tasting snow.*
> *Christmas morning.*

Blind contour is not easy. The desire to peek can at times seem overwhelming. And always there is the battle with the voice inside, the judging voice that disapproves of everything you do. But little by little one learns to relax, as the children had done, to keep the line courageous and alive.

THE BIG DRAW

The year 2000 was the centennial of John Ruskin's death. In his honor, the Guild of St. George created a nationwide celebration with one marvelously simple aim: "to get everybody drawing," and in the process, "to teach people to see." The Big Draw has since become an annual event at most museums and art galleries across the United Kingdom, as well as at numerous schools, libraries, churches, and community centers.

"If you can draw, even a little bit, you can express all kinds of ideas that might otherwise be lost," says the painter David Hockney. "Everywhere you look there's something interesting to draw."

Most of us know how to draw, however clumsily, with a pencil or a fine ink pen. But one can also draw using charcoal, clay, birch twigs, sand, wire, and digital imagery. Recent Big Draw projects have included murals, mosaics, mazes, cartoons and charts, even smoke and vapor trails. At one venue, participants wandered round a twelfth-century cathedral in search of angels, dragons, and green men, drawing as they went; at another, they abandoned the London guidebook to draw maps of their own neighborhood; at a third, they made an especially large line drawing on a local beach, using sawdust, which was then sprayed with paraffin and set alight. Clearly there's no limit to the possibilities.

"With the Big Draw we seem to have struck something in the national consciousness," says the children's book illustrator Quentin Blake. "It's as though everybody had just been waiting to be told that they are allowed to draw."

When I teach poetry to adults, I often begin by asking them to draw a memory map—a map of a special childhood place—an assignment borrowed from artist Hannah Hinchman. I encourage everyone to shut their eyes for a while, to allow the images to drift back into focus. Sometimes I play a little background music: Chopin nocturnes, Celtic harp. Always, I encourage them to include not just precise physical details (the wild strawberries hiding in the long soft grass, the broken gate), but the imaginary ones as well.

"What frightened you?" I ask. "What gave you pleasure? Did every rainbow have its pot of fairy gold? Let in those other kinds of truth as well."

The students hunch over their maps for thirty or forty minutes, sketching them in pencil, filling in the color and the details. No other assignment generates this level of concentration. Inevitably, one or two of them begin to cry. Their grandmother is dead now. The summer cottage has long since been sold. They find themselves astonished by the rush of memories. "This is a good thing," I tell them. "Don't be worried or embarrassed. This shows that you are definitely on to something. You'll have lots to write about."

And in fact, this is true: the poems they write next, for which the map acts as a warm-up, are inevitably some of their richest and most detailed. Drawing is a powerful force for clarity and focus: it helps to stimulate memories, and also to shape and order them; when necessary it can also act as a kind of exorcism.

After the genocide in the Sudan, researchers from Human Rights Watch traveled to neighboring Chad to speak with refugees who had fled across the border. While they were talking to the adults, they gave the children paper and crayons to keep them busy. When the interviews were finished, the researchers glanced at the children's pictures. There, in the notebooks, were pictures of the Janjaweed, the Arab militia who had terrorized Darfur. There were the burning villages, the brutal rapes, the soldiers with Kalashnikovs, the falling bombs. A thirteen-year-old boy called Mahmoud explained what he had drawn.

"These men are taking the women and the girls. They are forcing them to be wife. The houses are on fire. This is a helicopter. These here, at the bottom of the page, these are dead people."

Physician Bernie Siegel wishes that all doctors would keep a box of crayons in their consulting rooms, not just for children, but for adults too. The ancient Greeks and Romans believed that the images one made actually passed into the blood, affecting one's physical well-being. Jim Smyth, who has taught art for twenty years, believes that the drawing process can produce serotonin and endorphins in certain individuals. "I see people who are not aware of their arthritis pain when they are drawing," he says. "When they are not drawing, it comes back." The Swiss psychiatrist Carl Gustav Jung created his own drawings and paintings, and believed strongly that "our hands know how to solve a problem with which the intellect has struggled in vain."

Sometimes the solution arrives almost instantaneously, sometimes not. Drawing can take all the time in the world, and it can take no time at all. It is worth remembering the story of Chuang-tzu.

Chuang-tzu was a Taoist philosopher, but he was also an artist of great skill. One day, the Emperor asked him to draw a crab. "Very well," said Chuang-tzu. He would be happy to do it. But first he needed a country house and twelve servants, as well as five uninterrupted years. Five years later, the Emperor returned for his drawing. But Chuang-tzu had not even started work. "I need another five years," he told the Emperor. And once again, the Emperor agreed.

At the end of that time, Chuang-tzu picked up his brush, and in a single stroke, he drew the perfect crab.

Tactics

↬ Every morning, when you get out of bed, take a moment to look up the sky. Buy yourself a drawing book and crayons, and try to draw something of what you see.

↬ Play with "found art" in your home habitat, making small arrangements of the things that cross your path. Write a note on a leaf, and let it blow off into the wind.

↬ *Consider the following quotations:*
"Modern art spreads joy around by its color, which calms us."

HENRI MATISSE

"One day I discovered an entirely new joy. Suddenly, at the age of forty, I began to paint. Not that I considered myself a painter or intended to become one. But painting is marvelous; it makes you happier and more patient. Afterwards you do not have black fingers as with writing, but blue and red ones."

HERMANN HESSE

CHAPTER SIX

The Intensest Rendezvous

Only one hour of the normal day is more pleasurable than the hour spent in bed with a book before going to sleep and that is the hour spent in bed with a book after being called in the morning.

ROSE MACAULAY

The Joy of Reading

Long ago, when I was a little girl in London, my mother made up stories about Wiggly-Wiggly the Snail and Herbert the Caterpillar, and read to me from *The Oxford Book of Nursery Rhymes*. By the time I was five or six, my head was crammed with riddles and tonguetwisters, skipping songs and counting songs, ballads and carols and half-remembered lullabies. They entered me as easily as breathing, till I hardly knew when I was thinking my own thoughts, and when I was riding the images and rhythms of times long past.

Soon after I turned eight, my parents moved to Scotland, and I was sent to weekly boarding school. I hated it. School was an agony with its forced gregariousness, days sliced apart by bells. In a world where "home" had been reduced to half a dresser-top (just enough room for a framed photograph of your parents and a plastic statue of the Virgin Mary), books were the only luxury that remained. I carried one in my satchel at all times, so I could snatch a few paragraphs between lessons. I did not read in church or during meals, but I read in the car on the way home from school; I read on the loo or in the bath; I read perched on the fireguard in the nursery, and underneath the bedclothes with a torch. There was a windowseat behind the curtains in my bedroom, and I used to crouch there in the dark, reading by moonlight, making out one small word at a time.

Ordinary life was bumpy and tumultuous, full of questions and admonitions, of "Darling, *please!*" and "Silence, girls!" and "Who can remember the names of the Scottish coalfields?" Books were a blessed antidote to all of that: joy and consolation and escape. I *infinitely* preferred them to real life. Why should I care if the other girls disliked me, if I couldn't turn proper cartwheels, or make sense of French or Latin or geometry? My friends were Sara Crewe and Pippi Longstocking. I was hiding under the floorboards with Arietty, watching Tom Sawyer as he managed *not* to paint that fence, or slipping down the bright stream with Dodder and Baldmoney, Cloudberry and Sneezewort, the last gnomes in all of England.

THE LITTLE GREY MEN

The Little Grey Men and its sequel, *Down the Bright Stream,* are a pair of classic boys' adventure stories, written in Britain in the 1940s. Their author, BB (*aka* Denys Watkins Pitchford), was, above all, a passionate naturalist, blessed with a robust imagination and an easy, lyrical storytelling style. A sickly boy, he had spent much of his childhood on his own, wandering the woods and fields of his native Northamptonshire. Writing about the gnomes allowed him to describe, in exquisite detail, a world he deeply loved, and which he already understood was being lost.

For BB, the little grey men are "the most English things in England, the oldest beings alive." They have a house under a gnarled old oak tree at the edge of the Folly Brook, and live by their wits as they have always done, sewing coats and breeches out of mouse and moleskin, building coracles out of frogskin, and fishing for minnows with horsehair casts and beautifully fashioned bone hooks. Like Mary Norton's "Borrowers," they seize every opportunity for creative scavenging. Thus Oak Pool House has a door made from a discarded soap box, and a scrubbing brush that was once the head of an old toothbrush. Baldmoney carries a hunting knife made of hammered iron, part of an old hinge. Copper caps sliced from the ends of three or four cartridge cases make "splendid little frying-pans."

My sister Kate and I would have liked nothing better than to toast our toes around a blazing fire, over a shell of Dodder's elderberry wine. We envied the gnomes their beechnut griddle cakes and kippered minnows, their stewed crab apple, sweetened with peppermint cream. We wanted to *be* those little grey men, to face their perils, and rejoice in their extraordinary lives. We shivered with Baldmoney and Sneezewort as they crouched in the moorhen's nest, sharing their terror at Stoat's "cruel flat head, sharp muzzle, and primrose-yellow chest," and drowsed happily with them in the meadow, the buttercup heads like "miniature golden bowls" suspended overhead.

We read those books over and over, and gained from them a mass of inimitable country lore, as well as an exhilarating glossary of brand new words: *coppice* and *spinney, holt* and *drey,* along with the individual names of trees and plants and birds. But beyond the explanatory asides, and the pleasure of a working vocabulary, was something else: a gift for ardor, for gusto, which lifts BB out of the ranks of competent children's writers and into another realm entirely. The gnome books taught us how to love the world in all its myriad beauties: how to relish it, how to exult. BB models that exultation over and over, sometimes in a casual sentence, sometimes in a longer passage:

> How pleasant it was to lie in your bunk and listen to the reed warblers all a-singing, to hear the sweet bell-like voice of the cuckoo sounding across those spacious evening meads. Sometimes oak woods, bluebell floored, came right down to the river's brim, and in those soft summer evenings, delicious with the scent of hayfields and meadowsweet, they watched the big river bats hawking to and fro.

Contemporary child readers may never have heard the cuckoo, never have smelt the scent of hayfields or meadowsweet, never have seen oak woods "bluebell floored." But the images gather strength as the pages turn, and, for those who are able to listen, BB's singing memories become their own.

THE INTENSEST RENDEZVOUS

The Chinese author Lin Yutang (1895-1976) writes beautifully about the joy of reading, seeing it as a great privilege "to be able to live two hours out of twelve in a different world." There is, for him, no such thing as a classic, no books that everyone should feel obliged to read. Instead, we should seek out an author whose spirit is akin to our own. "It is like love at first sight.... The author is just right ... his style, his taste, his point of view. ... And then the reader proceeds to devour every word and every line that the author writes, and because there is a spiritual affinity, he absorbs and readily digests everything. The author has cast a spell over him, and he is glad to be under the spell."

The real scholar scarcely knows what "study" means, since reading provides such rich uncomplicated pleasure. Lin Yutang describes the scholar Ku Ch'ienli (1770-1839), remembered for reading Confucian classics naked on steamy summer days, and the literary critic Chin Shengt'an (1608-1661), who liked nothing better than reading a banned book behind closed doors on a snowy night. Absorbed in their books, such dedicated readers may appear to be doing nothing at all. An eye blinks, a muscle shifts, a hand reaches up to turn the page. But such focused concentration is also highly active. "To read a story well," says the novelist Ursula le Guin, "is to follow it, to act it, to feel it, to become it." Few writers have given the feeling of this absorption with greater tenderness and lucidity than the American poet Wallace Stevens:

> *The house was quiet and the world was calm.*
> *The reader became the book; and summer night*
>
> *Was like the conscious being of the book.*
> *The house was quiet and the world was calm.*
>
> *The words were spoken as if there was no book,*
> *Except that the reader leaned above the page,*
>
> *Wanted to lean, wanted much to be*
> *The scholar to whom his book is true, to whom*
>
> *The summer night is like a perfection of thought.*
> *The house was quiet because it had to be.*

The poem draws you in, its hypnotic repetition of such words as "quiet" and "calm" and "house" and "night" creating the very atmosphere that it describes. Once, when I was a student at Cambridge, some friends and I stayed up till dawn reading Stevens aloud to each other. I remember the sky brightening behind the glass, the room swirling with his words like colored smoke. We ended with the last poem in the book, "Final Soliloquy of the Interior Paramour," with lines that seemed to have been written just for us:

> *This is, therefore, the intensest rendezvous,*
> *It is in that thought that we collect ourselves,*
> *Out of all the indifferences, into one thing:*
>
> . . .
>
> *Here, now, we forget each other and ourselves.*
> *We feel the obscurity of an order, a whole,*
> *A knowledge, that which arranged the rendezvous,*
>
> . . .
>
> *Out of this same light, out of the central mind,*
> *We make a dwelling in the evening air,*
> *In which being there together is enough.*

LECTIO DIVINA

Next time you're in New York, make your way to the Asian section of the Metropolitan Museum, and look for a scroll called *Reading the Sutras by Moonlight* (painter unknown). You'll find a little figure in a loose robe sitting under the branches of a wispy pine tree, holding a book in one hand, while he pulls at his bushy eyebrow with the other. He has a gorgeous, intent, humorous face.

> *In the early morning sun I*

143

mend my ragged clothes;

In the moonlight I read my
sutra assignment

writes the Song poet, Wang Fenchen, and there, in the moonlight, the monk is getting down to work.

In the West too, monks have a long tradition of what they call *lectio divina*, reading at set intervals from their sacred liturgy or *Book of Hours*. They muse, they ponder, they practice *ruminatio*, mulling over the text through prayer and meditation. For the remainder of the day, as they go about their business in the monastery, cooking, gardening, dealing with office work, they are nourished by the slow, contemplative practice of "divine reading."

In the *Confessions* of Saint Augustine, written around 397 AD, the first nine chapters describe his worldly activities, and the remaining four the life of his mind: the books he read, his concentrated study of *Genesis*. Such literary communing can come to seem more real even than reality, as conversations open up between the past and the present, the dead or distant author and the living reader. The Renaissance scholar Machiavelli (an unlikely candidate!) went so far as to dress up in special clothing in order to be worthy of his imagined interlocutors. Every evening, he would pause on the threshold of his study, pull off his everyday clothes, and replace them with what he called "royal and courtly garments." Only then, suitably attired, did he feel able to enter into converse with the beloved dead.

"There, without shame, I speak with them and ask them about the reason for their actions; and they in their humanity respond to me."

In Martin Buber's terms, the text itself had "become a Thou."

READING & REREADING

Compared to drawing and carving, the making of pots, and the weaving of baskets, reading is a relatively recent human accomplishment, dating back no more than fifty-five hundred years. Unlike speech, which is acquired by easy osmosis, reading is not something that comes naturally to most of us. Instead, it must be learned, slowly and painstakingly, by each successive generation. The eye works its way across the page in little jumps, known technically as "saccades," pausing at intervals like a frog on a lilypad, in order to ingest the next new word. As science writer Simon Ings explains, "The eyes literally cannot see stationary objects; they must tremble constantly in order to bring them into view." Whereas listening is relatively fast (one needs only a hundredth of a second between sounds in order to distinguish them), looking takes far longer (one needs at least a tenth of a second between two images if they are not to blur), and reading takes longest of all, requiring a full quarter second for each individual word.

Reading, then, involves a considerable amount of work. Literate Greeks and Romans preferred to have their books read aloud to them by slaves, and Saint Augustine was actually startled when he first saw Ambrose, the Bishop of Milan, reading to himself in silence. "When he read, his eyes scanned the page and his heart explored the meaning, but his voice was silent, and his tongue was still." Such "deep reading" was not usual among the European aristocracy until the fifteenth century, and it would be another 250 years before it became common among the lower classes, fueled by a new explosion of books and newspapers, and by the gradual development of coffeehouses, lending libraries, and reading societies. More widespread schooling helped as well, at least for male children. But even then, more people *listened* to a book than read one to themselves. By the early nineteenth century, and in some cases, well into the twentieth, many families would gather round the fireside, three and sometimes four generations, and read a book together. Much of Dickens was read in this way, in gripping installments, night after night. Rereading *A Portrait of the Artist as a Young Man* or *Tess of the D'Urbervilles*, I still hear my father's warm, dry voice as he read aloud to us, his cranky teenage children.

Such reading is especially effective in the case of poetry, which by its nature has much to do with slowing down. The poet Mark Strand writes of the pleasure of "reading the same thing again and again, really savoring it, living inside the poem." Because there's no rush to find out what actually happens, the reader can luxuriate in the texture of the words themselves. As Strand explains, "It's really about feeling one syllable rubbing up against another, one word giving way to another, and sensing the justice of that relationship between one word, the next, the next, the next."

The poet Muriel Rukeyser used to ask an entire class to read the same poem, one after another, all around the room. Tedious as this sounds, her students enjoyed it, and her friend Denise Levertov also found it surprisingly helpful, seeing the process as a kind of alchemy, a "filtering, refining and intensification of understanding" that was far more effective (and indeed more moving) than the usual verbal analysis.

Levertov herself proposed "an unthinking, sensuous, dreamy, or drowsy rereading" of poems that were already familiar to the reader, suggesting that this too might result in many unexpected clarities. Returning again and again to the same piece of writing not only deepens our knowledge of the text, but also resonates with changes in ourselves. We notice words and images we may have missed the first time around, as well as moments that confirm or contradict our own experience. In some cases, it may take almost half a lifetime to know a work in depth. The Italian novelist Umberto Eco has a lovely example of the treasures to be found in such "slow reading."

Eco is a great admirer of a novella called *Sylvie* by the nineteenth-century French poet Gérard de Nerval, which he first read in Paris back in 1952. In subsequent years, he read the book again and again, perhaps as many as forty-nine or fifty times. But it was not until he decided to translate it that he discovered something new: within the text, which is prose, there were hidden verses! Eco had never noticed them before, because in all his years of reading and rereading *Sylvie*, he had never taken the time to read the book aloud.

If we are fortunate in our choice of text (and in our lives) such discoveries continue to accumulate. As Chang Ch'ao remarked, back in the mid-seventeenth century,

Reading books in one's youth is like looking at the moon through a crevice; reading books in middle age is like looking at the moon in one's courtyard; and reading books in old age is like looking at the moon on an open terrace.

Finally, at seventy-five or eighty, the full moon blazes forth in all its glory.

LEARNING BY HEART

One Christmas, I joined a friend and her mother at a local church. The mother had Alzheimer's, and could scarcely find her way to the front pew. But she sang, flawlessly, without a prompt, all the words to all the different carols. She had learned them by heart, years before, and they rose up in her, a towering cathedral, when all else lay in ruins round about.

Hymns and carols, work-songs, ballads, there was a time when everybody used to know such things, along with a casual smattering of folk songs, pop songs, country and westerns, jokes and limericks and children's jump-rope rhymes. As a child in Scotland, in the '60s and early '70s, I remember the tail end of rowdy parties, where huge grown-up men would sway back and forth on their polished heels, reciting verse after verse of their favorite "party piece," usually some lugubrious Victorian ballad, dark with blood and melodrama and unrequited love, and glittering with sexual innuendo.

My friend, the Scottish poet and translator Alastair Reid, carries a lifetime's worth of poems—an entire small library—in his head. "Do you memorize them?" someone asked him once. "No," he answered gravely. "I *remember* them." Reading for him is not distinct from re-reading; the poems he returns to, those he's fondest of, become, perforce, part of the furniture of his mind. But in the hurly-burly of the new millennium, such unselfconscious garnering has grown increasingly rare. Kindergarten children no longer repeat nursery rhymes, middle-school children are no longer asked to recite poems, adults no longer reach to cap their speech with a punchy apothegm or prized quotation. There is, alas, small surprise in any of this. Writers and critics, publishers and pundits, journalists and academics are all agreed on one thing: *fewer and fewer people are finding time to read.*

Indeed, some experts have come to believe that the Internet is restructuring the very process of our thought. The writer Nicholas Carr used to find it easy to immerse himself in a book or lengthy article. Now his concentration starts to wane after only a couple of pages. "I get fidgety," he says, "[and] lose the thread, begin looking for something else to do. . . . The deep reading that used to come naturally has become a struggle." Nor is Carr alone. In his book, *The Shallows,* he quotes the web consultant Jakob Nielsen, who monitored readers as they surfed the web, tracking their eye movements with a tiny camera. Apparently, most of us read in an "F" shape—along the first line or two, and then down, and halfway across a few more lines. "F" reported Nielsen, "is for *fast.* That's how users read your precious content."

As the habits of the Internet are transferred beyond the screen, books come to seem increasingly "dull" and "difficult." Four out of ten American adults do not read a book—any book—from one year's end to the other. Fiction is especially unpopular. More than half the adults in the United States now read no fiction at all. They take the time to scan their email, or trawl the web for crucial bits of information. They glance at the occasional bestseller by Stephen King or J. K. Rowling. But for the rest, they're just not interested. They are bent over their iPods and iPhones, they are puzzling over another set of instructions for another brand new gadget, and their books are lying untouched on their shelves.

THE TROUBLE WITH POETRY

When the poet Charles Simic was a student in the fifties, a recent immigrant from war-torn Yugoslavia, the public library was the best place in town. Forty years later, he marveled at its munificence. "Incredibly, they'd let you take those thick art books home so you could sit in your kitchen, eat your hot dogs and beans, and study the paintings of Giotto and Rembrandt." Simic took full advantage of such generosity. "I read riding to work; I read while pretending to shuffle papers on my desk; I read in bed and fell asleep with the lights still on."

Such greedy reading would be a mystery to my adult students, many of whom seem to find it painful even now: a kind of tiny calisthenics of the eye. Poetry is particularly suspect. But, following in the footsteps of Rukeyser and Levertov, I try to guide them, very gently, to explore its pleasures. William Stafford has a poem, entitled, simply, "Poetry":

> Its door opens near. It's a shrine
> by the road, it's a flower in the parking lot
> of The Pentagon, it says, "Look around,
> listen. Feel the air." It interrupts
> international telephone lines with a tune.
> When traffic lines jam, it gets out
> and dances on the bridge. If great people
> get distracted by fame they forget
> this essential kind of breathing
> and they die inside their gold shell . . .

When I teach, I like to read that poem aloud, throwing out different lines: poetry as "a shrine by the road," as "a flower in the parking lot," poetry as "an essential kind of breathing." We take the time to brood and muse over the words, to allow the images to resonate. Keats, in one of his letters, spoke very highly of this practice:

I have an idea that a Man might pass a very pleasant life in this manner—let him on any certain day read a certain Page of full Poesy or distilled Prose and let him wander with it, and muse upon it, and reflect from it, and bring home to it, and prophesy upon it, and dream upon it. . . . How happy is such a "voyage of conception," what delicious diligent Indolence!

"Delicious diligent Indolence!"—the phrase alone returns us to the nineteenth century. But by now it should be clear that these casual, leisurely, apparently aimless ways of knowing are just as "intelligent" as our usual speedy ones.

> *It is difficult*
> *to get the news from poems*

writes William Carlos Williams,

> *yet men die miserably every day*
> *for lack*
> *of what is found there.*

"So what *is* found there?" I ask my students. *"What is that news? And do you really believe it can be found in poetry?"* Most of them don't, at least not to begin with. They think of poetry as an unpleasant kind of conundrum, which only specially trained or sensitive readers can hope to understand. For them, poetry is "a school thing, a skirt thing, a church thing," to borrow a handful of phrases from Saul Bellow. "What is the poet *trying to say?*" they ask, as if the poet were someone with a speech impediment, and it were my job, as teacher, to translate his or her vatic utterances back into ordinary prose.

"What do *you* think?" my own professors used to respond, infuriatingly.

But as a teacher, I am perhaps a little less ferociously Socratic. If I can help someone to understand a poem with a casual gloss, then I will do that. I want very much that my students should "get the news from poems," and so I try to undo the fallacies that hamper them: that poetry has to rhyme, that it is essentially "very hard." I do my best to reassure them, to help them see that there are lots of poetries, and to demonstrate what some of these might be.

At the same time, I do emphasize that poetry is a genre in and of itself; not just a page or two of richly textured prose which some clever charlatan has chopped up into lines. There is, after all, a difference between the two, as poet James Tate explains:

> While most prose is a kind of continuous chatter, describing, naming, explaining, poetry speaks against an essential backdrop of silence. . . . There is a prayerful, haunted silence between words, between phrases, between images, ideas, and lines. This is one reason why good poems can be read over and over. The reader, perhaps without knowing it, instinctively desires to peer between the cracks into the other world where the unspoken rests in darkness.

Not all poetry has this "prayerful, haunted silence." But the poems that interest me, that I am eager to reread, do indeed possess the qualities that Tate describes. After 9/11, thousands of people turned to poetry in search of consolation. When fear and chaos have us in their grip, and the TV shows only replays of the anguished people, the collapsing buildings, it is then we turn to Williams for his "difficult" news, or to Stafford for his "essential kind of breathing." It is then we peer between the lines for what Yeats called "the condition of quiet that is the condition of vision."

"What use is poetry?" Sam Hamill asks.

I sat down September twelfth,
two thousand-one in the Common Era
and read Rumi and kissed the ground.

WHAT IS FOUND THERE

The writer Jacques Lusseyran, best known for his autobiography, *And There Was Light,* was blinded in an accident at the age of eight. Despite his disability, he became one of the founders of the Youth Resistance in France. Later he was captured by the Nazis and sent to a concentration camp. In his essay, "Poetry in Buchenwald," he describes what happened when his friend Saint-Jean suddenly began to recite some verses by Apollinaire. "It was as though he came bearing news—good news that was going to brighten our wretched lives."

Then Lusseyran himself began to recite. He chose verses at random, any he could think of. In a plain, undramatic voice he recited Baudelaire, Rimbaud. Little by little, another voice joined in, and then another:

> Voices had timidly joined in behind me, and in front of me.
> . . . Without even intending to, I began to recite more slowly.
> [Then] more men came. They formed a circle. They echoed
> the words. At the end of each stanza there rose a great hum
> of the last syllables.

By the time he paused to catch his breath, there were fifty men surrounding him, leaning towards him, swaying, crying out. Some of them were Russian, some German, some Hungarians. Most of the Hungarians were Jews, waiting for what the SS called "transfer to the sky." None of them spoke French, not even a little, but listening to someone recite poetry, they threw themselves upon it "as if it were food."

"I learned then," said Lusseyran, "that poetry is an act, an incantation, a kiss of peace, a medicine . . . one of the rare, very rare things in the world which can prevail over cold and hatred. No one had taught me this." In the weeks that followed, he gave himself over to a daily poetry campaign. He would stand on a bench at midday, just stand there and recite poems. Passersby would stop, press in around him. He could feel their breathing, the relaxation of their muscles. And "for several minutes there was harmony, there was almost happiness."

P-O-N-D, R-I-P-P-L-E, WORDS-WORTH

When Stanley Kunitz was a little boy, he was in love with words, their sound and resonance. Each day he would search the family dictionary for gorgeous words, then run outside and shout them into the trees. "I considered it my duty to give my new words to the elements, to scatter them." The woods were for him the perfect audience.

When Adrienne Rich was four or five years old, her father asked her to copy a few lines of poetry every day.

A thing of beauty is a joy forever . . .

Tyger, tyger, burning bright,
In the forests of the night

The lines were intended as a lesson in handwriting. But what stayed with her was the rhythmic power of the words. It was that "rhythm meshed with language" which got her started as a poet. Later, she read Keats and Blake on her own account. But at the beginning, poetry was for her a physical thing, "an elemental force that [was] *with* her, like the wind at her back as she [ran] across a field."

Such practices have fallen out of fashion in recent years. Few children now copy poems in their best, most elegant handwriting. It is the rare adult who still keeps a commonplace book to record her favorite quotations. Instead we have scanners and digital printers, a brand new copyshop on every corner. Poems may be preserved like this, but they are not necessarily remembered. They have been seen by the eyes, but they have not been enlivened by their passage through breath and body and working hand. In ancient China, when someone studied calligraphy, he did not simply copy the original. Instead, he spread out the scroll against the wall, and stared at it for a long time. Only when he had, as it were, incorporated it completely, did he finally pick up his brush and begin to work.

Robert Pinsky suggests that young writers should apprentice themselves in a similar way to the poets they admire, not by buying every copy of their books, or by attending every reading, but by typing out their poems for themselves (or, even better, by copying them out longhand). This, he feels, will teach them *what a poem is made of*—word and breath and line and image—as nothing else can do.

The artist Paulus Berensohn often practices *lectio divina*, which he defines as "reading any book as if it were *the* book." When he first encountered David Abram's book *The Spell of the Sensuous,* he conceived a tremendous admiration for its last chapter, "The Forgetting and Remembering of the Air." Since Berensohn is himself a practicing bookmaker, he made a special journal to contain it: cutting windows on the left side, and gluing Abram's pages into them. Then he rewrote the chapter very slowly, defining the words, looking them up in the dictionary, and rephrasing them in his own language, "so it got into my body." On the right-hand page, he would doodle in response to Abram's text.

"Doodling has been an incredible teacher for me. The slower I doodle, the more story rises out of it, always."

Poems inspire other poems, words give birth to words, sometimes in the most unlikely way. Jimmy Santiago Baca grew up poor, taught to despise his own language. In jail at twenty, he stole a textbook from a desk attendant, and read it at night under the covers.

> Slowly I enunciated the words . . . p-o-n-d, r-i-p-p-l-e . . .
> Even as I tried to convince myself that I was merely curious,
> I became so absorbed in how the sounds created music in
> me, and happiness, I forgot where I was. . . . I stumblingly
> repeated the author's name as I fell asleep, saying it over and
> over in the dark: Words-worth.
>
> Words-worth.
>
> Days later, with a stub pencil I whittled sharp with my teeth, I
> propped a Red Chief notebook on my knees and wrote my first
> words. From that moment, a hunger for poetry possessed me.

A MATTER OF INFLUENCE

"Every book is worth reading which puts the reader in a working mood," writes Emerson. But no one can tell in advance what such a book might be. Some books are daunting in their sheer achievement: reading Proust almost silenced Virginia Woolf forever. Woolf was thrown by Katherine Mansfield's work as well. She felt there was a certain understanding between them, "a queer sense of being 'like'— not only about literature," but was jealous of her too, happy, she said, to hear her work abused. And yet, when Mansfield died, Woolf felt strangely lonely. Suddenly she had no company, no competition.

Woolf and Mansfield were almost too alike: their strengths and sensibilities uncomfortably (at times provokingly) close. The same could be said of Anne Sexton and Sylvia Plath, at least during their early years in Cambridge. Sexton's poem "My Friend, My Friend," carries strong echoes of Plath's poem, "Daddy." Other writers—other books—are just too different from ourselves to be of use. As a young man in Chicago, Charles Simic read Thoreau and Emerson and Robert Lowell, Sartre and Camus. For a while he was tempted to imitate the Eastern literary establishment, to put on "English tweeds with leather elbow patches and smoke a pipe." But his friends wouldn't let him. "Remember where you came from, kid," they told him. And Simic listened. He was already a wild brew of different ethnicities— Yugoslav, American, Jewish, Irish, and Italian—and from his point of view, "the stew wasn't ready yet. There were more things to add to the pot. More identities, more images to cook." He kept on reading, kept on writing, kept on paying attention. It took more than half a century, but in 2007 he was appointed Poet Laureate of the United States.

Male writers are famously said to be especially troubled by "the anxiety of influence" (the title of a book by Harold Bloom), so much so that when Kenneth Koch asserted that he "liked to be influenced," it was treated as a startling piece of news. But in fact every writer, male or female, has to walk a delicate line between originality and inspiration, encouragement and craven imitation. Some material is simply inappropriate for a given writer. The short story writer Grace Paley enjoyed reading Wright Morris's book *The Territory Ahead*. "But if I—the writer—should pay too much attention to him, I would have to think an awful lot about the Mississippi River. I'd have to get my mind off New York." And for her, that was simply not an option. "I always think of New York."

As one who "always" thinks of nature, it is not surprising that

Mary Oliver should find sustenance in the writings of John Muir and Henri Fabre, John James Audubon and Henry Beston, praising them as "Four Companions with a Zest for Life." Similarly, she returns in thought to the Ohio of the 1950s, remembering her first encounters with Walt Whitman. When her high school was seized by a crisis of student delinquency, Oliver took to the woods, lugging a private knapsack full of books. Down by the creek or in the open meadow, she read and reread Whitman, "my brother, my uncle, my best teacher," reveling in his ardor, his enthusiasm, the glorious specificity of his words.

> But first and foremost, I learned from Whitman that the poem is a temple—or a green field—a place to enter, and in which to feel. . . . I learned that the poem was made not just to exist, but to speak—to be company. . . . I remember the delicate, rumpled way into the woods, and the weight of the books in my pack. I remember the rambling, and the loafing—the wonderful days when, with Whitman, I tucked my trowser-ends in my boots and went and had a good time.

Tactics

↔ The Canadian writer Carol Shields said that learning to read was the central experience of her early life. Choose a book you loved as a child, and reread it as an adult.

↔ *Lectio divina* is not the same as scholarly or analytical reading. Instead one is asked to brood and ruminate and ponder, to live with the text as one might do with a koan. Allow yourself time to read a book in this way.

↔ *Consider the following quotations:*

> *To read a book of poetry*
> *from back to front,*
> *there is the cure for certain kinds of sadness.*

> *A person has only to choose.*
> *What doesn't matter; just that —*

> JANE HIRSHFIELD

"It's funny, you read someone like T. H. White for an hour in the early morning, and your mind grooves on him and you find your-self writing away downhill as if guided and balanced by his invisible hand at your elbow. You don't have to even think about a thing. Just push off and freewheel."

ROGER DEAKIN

CHAPTER SEVEN

A Feast of Words

Take notes on the spot, a note is worth a cart-load of recollections.

EMERSON

Isle Ornsay

THE SUMMER I WAS NINE, MY FAMILY stayed for two weeks on Isle Ornsay, a tidal island off the coast of Skye. It was a beautiful windswept place, with a tall whitewashed lighthouse, two converted cottages, and a walled garden filled with brambles and wild roses. Soon after we arrived, our mother presented each of us with a cardboard-covered scrapbook filled with cloudy gray-blue pages.

"You can write in this," she said, "or draw, or stick in postcards. I'll show you how to press some flowers if you'd like."

The scrapbook has survived, and I turn the pages slowly, smiling at the shriveled corpses of *Thrift* and *English Stonecrop, Ragged Robin, Tormentil*, each one carefully labeled in an earnest, girlish hand. There are postcards too, bought with my weekly pocket money: postcards of Isle Ornsay and Skye and "the ferry we came in," plus a solitary Highland cow standing stolid and melancholy against a luridly tinted meadow. We had seen Highland cattle on our long drive from the Borders, our first ever.

Isle Ornsay was a lot of "firsts" for me, and I tried valiantly to contain it, to pick it, count it, catalogue, record. Exasperated by my clumsy artwork, I pestered my father to draw a lobster for me (which he did, skillfully), and then a crab in swift electric green. Meanwhile I did my best to keep track of everything I thought might be important: the twenty-nine cars lined up ahead of us as we waited for the ferry, the twelve waterfalls we counted on the way back. I wrote about my brother and sisters and the games we played, how we had made a house among the rocks, and kept two shops where we sold stones and shells and colored glass, how my sister had found a sea urchin and it was "quite rare," how she also found a starfish and a baby prawn. I took my crayons and made a picture of the rockpool, with its bulgy pink sea anemones and sea urchins and crabs, titling it in bright fluorescent letters, "A Rock Pool By the Sea."

"I never thought it would be so nice," I wrote. "But it was lovely."

Without the scrapbook, I would remember none of this. I would have forgotten the hermit crabs, with their strange bunched claws, and the bits of broken china we found washed up on the strand, water-thumbed and fumbled, their edges soft as chalk. I would have no record of the old boat we liked to play in, or the mussel soup my mother made, with its tiny iridescent grayish pearls. People say that a child comes into his or her identity at eight or maybe nine. As for me, I know exactly when it happened. I was standing in the garden one windy afternoon, alive to everything I saw around me: the big lumbering sheep with their dung-encrusted tails, the rush and thrust of the encroaching sea, the seagulls crying just above my head. I had a pocket full of sea glass and colored shells, and I was as happy as I've ever been before or since.

GLEANINGS FROM THE FIELD

My great-grandfather kept a stationery store in Liverpool, England. He died many years before I was born. But I have always wondered if my own love of journals and notebooks and tiny pocket "seedbooks" has not been inherited from him. I have kept a diary now for more than forty years, beginning at eleven or twelve with child-sized diaries, and graduating to sturdy British sketchbooks in scarlet and black, and American composition books in speckled black-and-white. Keeping a journal has helped me stand my ground: made a refuge for my cranky private self, a place to plant my thoughts and noticings.

Such tactics are surprisingly recent. Human language has been in existence for some fifty to seventy thousand years. But writing was invented less than five and a half thousand years ago, by the farmers and shepherds of ancient Mesopotamia, the area lying between the Tigris and the Euphrates that is now Iraq. At first its uses were extremely prosaic, consisting of little more than detailed agricultural records, listing sacks of grain and heads of cattle. Over time, however, such memoranda developed into a way of recording actual speech, and finally, into what we now call literature: the accumulated legacy of poems, songs, prophecies and stories, incised on clay or carved on stone, inked onto papyrus or paper, and honored as a priceless cultural heritage.

In the three or four millennia that followed, writing remained a practical or public act. Only rarely does one stumble across the traces of a singular sensibility, for example in the notations of two Irish monks, writing about a thousand years ago. One pauses in his work to note the sunlight flickering along the margins of his manuscript; the other shivers and laments his solitude. "I am very cold without fire or covering. . . . The robin is singing gloriously, but though its red breast is beautiful, I am all alone. Oh God, be gracious to my soul and grant me a better handwriting."

The heart jumps in sympathetic recognition, but the monks remain anonymous; diaries as such did not exist until the 1600s. Gilbert White, a curate in Selborne, Hampshire, kept a journal from the age of fifteen. But he is best known for his "Garden Kalender" (begun in 1750 at the age of thirty), and for the "naturalist's journal" he kept thereafter, and that was, incidentally, one of Thoreau's favorite books. Writing every day about his garden, his neighbors, and quiet rural events, White's modest diligence often flowers into something close to poetry:

23rd June 1783. Vast honey-dew; hot & hazey; misty. The blades of wheat in several fields are turned yellow, & look as if scorched with the frost. Wheat comes into ear. Red even: thro' the haze. Sheep are shorn.

13th July 1783. Five great white sea-gulls flew over the village toward the forest.

17th July [1783]. The jasmine, now covered with bloom, is very beautiful. The jasmine [i]s so sweet that I am obliged to quit my chamber.

The same dedicated attention can be found the following century, in the diaries kept by Samuel Taylor Coleridge, Henry David Thoreau, and Gerard Manley Hopkins. All three were passionate observers, filling their journals with detailed images from nature, as well as quotes and conversation, and private moments of exhilaration and delight. Coleridge took notes much as an artist sketches, as part of his own literary apprenticeship.

My walks were almost daily on top Quantock, and among its sloping combes. With my pencil and memorandum book in my hand, I was making studies, as the artists call them, and often moulding my thoughts into verse, with the objects and imagery immediately before my senses.

Over the course of forty years (1794-1834), he kept a total of sixty-seven notebooks, jotting such things as addresses, appointments, and laundry lists on the inside covers, and saving the actual pages for his personal and literary endeavors. He wrote wherever he found himself, in bed and in the dark, on hillsides and mountaintops, over the rumble of a moving stagecoach. Sometimes he was sober, sometimes drunk or under the influence of opium. In their anxiety and precision, their slap-dash intelligence, his writings feel astonishingly modern even now.

Here, for example, he muses upon the exigencies of married life:

April-June 1803. A man who marries for Love a Frog who leaps into a well—he has plenty of water, but he cannot get out again/—

Why we two made to be a Joy to each other, should for so

many years constitute each other's melancholy—O! but the melancholy is Joy—

And here, provides a touching sketch of fatherhood:

Hartley fell down and hurt himself—I caught him up crying & screaming—& ran out of doors with him.—The Moon caught his eye—he ceased crying immediately—and his eyes & the tears in them, how they glittered in the Moonlight!

Here, in more poetic mode, is his description of a winter sky:

November 1803. The Sky black Clouds, two or three dim untwinkling Stars, like full stops of damp paper—& large Stains and Spreads of sullen White, like a tunic of white Wool seen here & there thro' a torn & tattered Cloak of Black.—Whence do these Stains of White proceed—all over the Sky—so long after Sunset—and from their indifference of place in the Sky seemingly unaffected by the West?

Whereas Coleridge's journals were meant, at least initially, as sourcebooks for his poems, Thoreau's journal soon became an end in itself. He started it in 1837, when he was only twenty, and kept scribbling for the next quarter century, a total of thirty-nine notebooks and two million words. As one of a family of pencil makers (in his day, John Thoreau & Co. pencils were considered the best in America), it comes as no surprise that his first notes, written out of doors, were made in pencil, which he later transcribed and expanded on in ink. "My Journal," he writes on 8th February 1841, "is that of me which would else spill over and run to waste, gleanings from the field which in action I reap. I must not live for it, but in it for the gods. They are my correspondent, to whom daily I send off this sheet postpaid."

Thoreau's confidence in the gods (small g) was considerable. Perhaps it was this that allowed him to pontificate with such authority. Again and again, his journal entries crystallize into compact little sermons, remarkable in their brilliance and concision. Here, for example, he comments on the importance of enthusiasm in a writer:

> We cannot write well or truly but what we write with gusto. The body, the senses, must conspire with the mind. . . . A writer, a man writing, is the scribe of all nature; he is the corn and the grass and the atmosphere writing.

and here on the value of a certain ease and leisure:

> A broad margin of leisure is as beautiful in a man's life as in a book. Haste makes waste, no less in life than in housekeeping. . . . We live too fast and coarsely, just as we eat too fast, and do not know the true savor of our food.

Gerard Manley Hopkins found such faith more difficult to muster. He had been ordained as a Jesuit in his early thirties, and there were times when his God seemed to require of him the sacrifice of everything he valued most: his writing, his privacy, his searing originality. He was primarily a poet (though a tormented one), and his diaries are crammed with luscious and original observations, ranging from urbane art criticism to Irish folklore and etymology. Like Coleridge and Thoreau, he also had a keen eye for natural history. Here, for example, he describes a walk with a friend:

> 5th May 1866. Walk with Urquhart to Wood Eaton. Saw a gull flying. Fumitory graceful plant. Vetch growing richly. Some beeches fully out in pale silky fur when held against the light on the edge.

And again,

> 20th May 1866. Beautiful blackness and definition of elm tree branches in evening light (from behind). Cuckoos calling and answering to each other, and the calls being not

equally timed they overlapped, making the triple *cuckoo*, and crossed.

Hopkins was a writer who also liked to draw (a surprisingly numerous group, which includes Franz Kafka, Sylvia Plath, and Derek Walcott, along with more familiar names such as William Blake, John Ruskin, and John Berger). His tight-sprung verse reads very differently from Mary Oliver's plain, transparent lines, but in their passionate love of nature, their yearning for epiphany, their work chimes back and forth across the centuries.

A PLAIN & FRAGRANT OBJECT

Mary Oliver's day starts at five each morning, when she sets off on a long, solitary, attentive walk. "What I write begins and ends with the act of noticing and cherishing, and it neither begins nor ends with the human world. . . . I am forever just going out for a walk and tripping over the root, or the petal, of some trivia, then seeing it as if in a second sight, as emblematic."

Like Coleridge, who scribbled words and phrases while he was out in the field, Mary Oliver likes to use a pocket notebook, "small, three inches by five inches, and hand-sewn." She doesn't draft whole poems in these books, but she does write down words and phrases as they occur to her. The entries are made at random, interrupted by recipes and addresses, shopping lists and quotations, and the writing is blurred and disorderly, since it is almost always done out of doors. But behind such surface casualness lies tremendous precision, as Oliver herself explains:

> What I write down is extremely exact in terms of phrasing and of cadence. In an old notebook I can find, "look the trees / are turning / their own bodies /into pillars of light.

> . . .

Sometimes what is written down is not generally understandable at all, but is a kind of private shorthand. The entry "6/8/92 woof!" records for me that on this day, and with this very doggy sound, I first came upon coyotes in the Provincelands.

"The words do not take me to the reason I made the entry," she writes, "but back to the felt experience." And again, "It is the instant I try to catch in the notebooks, not the comment, not the thought."

Little myrtle warblers
kissing the air

The cry of the killdeer / like a tiny sickle.

The things that we attend to reverberate in our lives; to notice and describe is also, in some important way, to cherish. Kim Stafford is a committed writer, author of several collections of poetry and essays. He too is a special fan of the pocket notebook, which he prefers to make for himself, using two full sheets of paper, brown cover stock, and black thread flavored with beeswax. For him, this "plain and fragrant object" feels like riches. He writes in it faithfully. Every few months he sits down to glean the best stories, thoughts, and sayings from his latest stash, filing them with his current works in progress. Whenever an editor gives him some new writing assignment, he leafs through those same small notebooks, to be reminded of the many "rich beginnings."

The question then is not "What shall I write?" but rather, "Which, of the many beauties in my notebooks, do I want to carry forward?" The writer thus sits down to a feast every time, and never to an empty bowl.

EARLY MORNING

Kim Stafford's father was the West Coast poet William Stafford, a man whose "rich beginnings" lay in the calm and quiet of his own sleeping house. Every morning for more than forty years, he would get up at 4 a.m., at least two hours before the rest of his family, and settle down to work. Stafford himself described his practice in terms of "just plain receptivity."

> When I write, I like to have an interval before me when I am not likely to be interrupted. For me, this usually means the early morning, before others are awake. I get pen and paper, take a glance out of the window (often it is dark out there), and wait. It is like fishing. But I do not wait very long, for there is always a nibble—and this is where receptivity comes in. To get started I will accept anything that occurs to me.

Years later, Kim Stafford wrote a memoir about his father entitled *Early Morning*. He described William's steady practice as a "symposium with the self." A particular day's writing might include images from a recent dream, news of the family and the world at large—and a couple of poems. Often, these first drafts didn't seem to amount to very much. Stafford himself said that they were "often so colorless, so apparently random, so *homeless* and unaccountable," that most people wouldn't have bothered to work with them. But by making time for them, by lending "faith and attention" to what he called those "waifs of thought," a total of more than sixty books made their slow way into print.

"A good life is partly a matter of luck," wrote William Stafford. "I can look for it and cherish its intervals. But I can't control it." Still, he could choose to set aside that time: to protect those early mornings. "To get up in the cold, then make a warm place, have paper, pen, books to hand, look out at the gleaming rain, shadows, the streetlight steadfast. You could stay awake all night, not give away those hours."

TONY OWL

When I was six or seven, my father adopted a young owl: a fluffy little bundle of white feathers. It was a tawny owl, he told us, which had fallen from its nest, and been found lying helpless at the foot of a tall tree. Not surprisingly, we called it Tony Owl.

Tony Owl lived on roadkill, augmented by the delicate corpses of white mice, sent at intervals from a pet shop in North London. I watched as he yanked at their stringy intestines, stretching them apart like rubber bands between his beak and sharp gray claws. Couldn't he learn to be more civilized, I wondered?

> *There was a young man who when wee*
> *Taught little owls to drink tea.*
> * 'Cause he said, "It's not nice,*
> * To eat rats and mice."*
> *So he taught little owls to drink tea.*

There were other poems, but that is the first one I remember writing, the first that anyone troubled to record. I wanted to write more. I wanted a study of my own, with lots of books, somewhere the younger children couldn't go. There was nowhere in the house itself. But at the far end of the garden was a black wooden bungalow, and right behind the bungalow there was a shed. It was small and dark and smelled of mold. But for me it was my fortress, my private hermitage. I cadged a brush and swept the dirt floor clean, then hauled out my two white bookcases to stand against the wall. I remember the cloudy window-panes, thick with spiderwebs, and the splintery wooden table at which I first sat down to write. Home at last. Some paper and a pen. It was as if I remembered it from some other life.

KEEPING IN TOUCH

Whether or not we keep a daily journal or a blog, or make time to work on poems or short stories, most of us now sit down to write on a daily basis. Some three-quarters of all Americans spend more than an hour a day reading and responding to email, which has spread its tentacles across the mildest and most uncomplicated schedules, demanding (and often being granted) an almost instantaneous response. Sixteenth-century writers used to scrawl "Haste, haste, haste, for lyfe, for lyfe, haste!" on their most urgent missives. Five hundred years later, every new communication arrives with equal insistence: a true democracy of desperation.

Writing letters was once an easy weekly chore. Most of mine were written (not always legibly) by hand: written, that is to say, in comfortable alignment with the speed of thought. I liked to set aside two or three hours, a Sunday afternoon, perhaps, a Thursday evening, when I could sit down to a stack of unanswered mail, paper and envelopes piled up close to hand. My friend Eleanor Adams, now in her nineties, remembers the precise hierarchies of the stationery drawer: the heavy gray paper with the deckle edges, the plain cream, the headed notepaper with address and phone number engraved across the top. I myself was happy with cheap white typing paper. But I held to the formalities nonetheless. My letters began with "Dear" or "Dearest," and ended with "Yours sincerely" or "All best wishes," "Love" or "Lots of love." Typos were blotted carefully with White-Out, or blithely scribbled in along the margin. In those days, there was one letter, and one letter only. Unless you kept a rough draft, or made a special trip to the copyshop, your recipient got the letter, you had the modest pleasure of accomplishment, and that was that.

All this seems unbelievably long ago.

Most letters have now been replaced by emails or instant messages. Instead of relatively structured, relatively thoughtful epistles, sent to one specific person at one specific address, correspondence has warped into a far brisker and more casual exchange, often sent to several people at a time: something like an eternal (or interminable) game of multi-dimensional table tennis, in which Q&A, confirmation and instruction and expanded commentary are forever ping-ponging back and forth. News proliferates like dust, filling the screen with a daily blitz of information. The body of the text has shrunk to a mere handful of phrases; greetings have become exiguous at best; paragraphs, frequently, are nonexistent. The long, leisurely, expansive screed, full of irony and affection and close-knit observation, has almost entirely disappeared.

Postcards have for the most part vanished too. You can still find them, at exorbitant prices, in big museums and high-end stationery outlets, or (more cheaply) in cut-price tourist emporia, along with baseball caps and snowglobes and keychains and the rest. But many stores have stopped carrying them altogether. The Postcard Distributors Association of North America has dropped the word "postcard" from its name, as the sale of cards continues to decline. Unless you spring for a "souvenir pack" of twelve or twenty cards, no postcards can now be found at the Central Park Zoo in New York City. Visitors prefer to take their own pictures on their cell phones or with disposable cameras; they text their friends right here, right now, as they wander round an exhibit, or call them from the street as they wait for a cab. The pause for thought, for clarity, the quiet limbo between experience and response, has almost entirely disappeared. And the pleasure of a postcard in and of itself: a tiny icon which can be propped on a mantelpiece or a bedside table, attached with magnets to the fridge, slipped into the edge of a mirror, or pasted on the front of a journal, is a loss that no one even seems to mourn.

And yet a postcard—just because it is so cheap, so light, so portable—can be astonishingly resilient and evocative. Who has not opened a book to find a battered postcard thrust between the pages? Who has not puzzled over a date, a smudgy postmark, and reread the message from so long ago, studying the ease or awkwardness of its phrasing, the swirl of a signature, even the number of kisses?

Every time I opened my collected Dickinson, a certain postcard used to flutter out: an image of Virginia Woolf at her most exquisite. A gold heart had been crayoned on the other side, almost obliterated by a barbed-wire tangle of competing words. There were names of drugs like Smack, Red Devil, Mr. C; there were references to life and writing: *Rent, Bookcases, Papa Poems*. There were ugly words like *Fear, Neurosis, Rivalry, Frustration*. The card had no signature, but I had no need of one. It was a Valentine card, postmarked February 1983, and the handwriting belonged to my friend Rosie.

Because of their brevity, and the play between words and image, postcards are perhaps especially potent. But letters have their own intrinsic resonance. The Scottish poet Gerry Cambridge likes to write by hand, using a pen bought in the Fountain Pen Hospital in New York City on his first visit to the United States. This is an heirloom pen, a 520 Waterman Red Ripple, with superflex nib, made circa 1933, and his ink is a brilliant turquoise, unmistakably his own. Artist Barbara Bash uses a fine black felt pen, which arches across the page with a calligrapher's flowing authority. In each case, the writer's character imprints itself upon your eye almost before you have drawn the pages from the envelope. Often there's a distinctive scent as well. My sister Katie's letters used to smell of oil paint; my uncle Patrick's had the tang of pipe tobacco.

Email, on the other hand, is distinguished by little more than its fragmentations and misspellings, its utter transience. Reading it seems to take no time at all. It is as if the message dissolves into the bloodstream instantaneously, leaving only a thin white glitter on the surface of the mind. There are no pages now to muse and ponder over, no handwriting to analyze, no folded envelope to thrust in one's back pocket. Lost in the shuffle is anticipation: the sweet, charged interval between writing a letter to a beloved friend and the satisfaction of his or her reply. Lost too is the hiatus between receiving such a letter and gathering one's own forces in response: the pause for integration and incorporation, the gradual ripening. Gerard Manley Hopkins writes well about such intervals. As a rule, he says, it is best not to respond too promptly. Even if one does decide to indulge the questions put by one's correspondent, a letter should be more than just an answer. "I suppose the right way is to let it sink into you, and reply after a day or two."

That pause, that moment of respite, is entirely foreign to the nature of email, which is predicated above all upon instant gratification, the lightning-strike response. Fortunately, most of us simply can't keep up with the daily waterfall of correspondence, which means that email too has its limbos and longeurs. I'm sure I'm not alone in choosing to print out an especially rich and "letter-like" missive, in order to answer it more carefully at a later time.

When I have an airplane ride ahead of me, I often bring along a batch of just such emails, plus a small leather wallet fat with post-cards, paper, envelopes, and stamps. Wedged between the fold-down table and the padded seat, looking down over the clouds (each cloud, as I recently learned, the weight of one hundred elephants!) I surrender to the pleasures of old-fashioned epistolary friendship: warmed by my friends' kindness, their imagined company, even before I first begin to write.

I realize, of course, that the far-flung buddies whom I conjure up may in reality be as crabby and distracted as my neighbors across the aisle. But as I bring those smiling faces to my mind, I find myself delighted, energized. There is an ease and satisfaction given partly by my imagined interlocutor, partly by my own increasing focus. It is as if the simple act of writing worked like a burning glass, gathering up the accumulated observations, the jokes and memories, the tender questions, and turned them all to vivid, living flame.

AN IDEAL CORRESPONDENT

In daily life, one is not supposed to read another person's letters. One of the joys of published correspondence is that lingering sense of transgression: "This is what Virginia Woolf wrote to her sister Vanessa, or to Katherine Mansfield. This is what E. B. White wrote to Gus Lobrano at the *New Yorker*. This is what Jessica Mitford wrote to her good friend Marge Frantz—*and I am reading it right now!*" But beyond that lies a deeper and more complex pleasure: the God-perspective that comes from viewing the writer across time: as a child and adolescent, in radiant youth and stalwart middle age, and on, if we are lucky, into the faltering older years. At each stage too, a number of different selves come into play, born of love and work and changing circumstances, of particular friendships and family connections, each of them revealing another facet of the writer's personality. This is what makes letters so endlessly fascinating, perhaps especially in comparison to the writer's more polished public voice, or the solid bourgeois narrative of his or her biography.

Virginia Woolf is a case in point. She wrote thousands of letters in her lifetime, of which almost four thousand survive. Bored or edgy, hungry for company, she reached out again and again to the same small coterie, explaining once, to Vita Sackville-West, that "one's friendships are long conversations, perpetually broken off, but always about the same thing with the same person." Thus she wrote to Roger Fry about art, to Lytton Strachey about books, to E. M. Forster about writing, and (oddly, perhaps) to her brother-in-law, Clive Bell, about love. It was as if each new strand of connection acted as an additional guy rope, helping to keep her private tent erect.

Vita was an especially important correspondent. Woolf's letters to her were not necessarily her best, blurred as they were by her sense of Vita's inadequacies as a writer (not quite on a par with herself), and by her own mingled shyness and flirtations. But they gave rise to *Orlando* nonetheless, itself a form of literary epistle, and described by Nigel Nicolson as Woolf's "most elaborate love-letter." It is tempting to trawl literary history for such tales: the fact that Beatrix Potter's stories began as illustrated letters to her friends' children; the long epistolary friendship between Gary Snyder and Allen Ginsberg, and again between Robert Lowell and Elizabeth Bishop: the poems that might not have been published (or even written) without those years of understanding and support. But "productivity" is only one way in which to judge a correspondence. Occasionally one stumbles upon something else: a pair of writers so precisely matched in both their gifts and interests that as a reader, one can only marvel. If I had to pick out one such set of letters, for their ease and urbanity, but also for their keen wit and steady cherishing, I would choose the correspondence between William Maxwell, longtime editor at the *New Yorker*, and the English novelist and short story writer Sylvia Townsend Warner.

Maxwell and Warner met together only four times, including once in 1939 in New York City, and once in 1953 in England. But they were friends for over forty years, and in that time exchanged some thirteen hundred letters. They wrote about books (Goethe, Balzac, Rilke, Yeats). They wrote about art and music and politics. But they also wrote in delicious detail about their own domestic lives (Maxwell's wife, Emmy, and their two daughters, Warner's life companion, Valentine Ackland). There was a practical aspect to their correspondence: paper was scarce in Britain after the Second World War, so Maxwell arranged for the *New Yorker* to make sure Warner was well supplied with envelopes and writing paper. Her letters also include frequent thanks for unexpected treats, a tub of butter, "a magnificent ham." But the core of their friendship had to do with their delighted recognition of each other's sensibility, as writers, as stylists, as human beings. Maxwell says it best, writing to Warner in April 1958:

> I have often thought that we were meant for each other—you to write to me and I to read you . . . every sentence I have ever read of yours gave me immediate intense pleasure—at the world as you saw it, and at how you said what you were saying—the intense pleasure of appreciating a personal style. The influence has long since gone into my bones.

Warner was equally moved by Maxwell's letters, which she said had given her "an unbroken line of pleasure extending back 30 years." Marked by coffee rings, gnawed and clawed by her beloved cats, their empty spaces scrawled with notes and shopping lists, Maxwell's letters were read and reread, treasured, saved, revisited for comfort and for inspiration. Sometimes she wrote to him twice in the same day. "I might die in the night," she told herself. "So I will write to William now."

STARTING FROM SCRATCH

When Katherine Mansfield was a young woman in the South of France, she dreamed of keeping some kind of little notebook, which would afterwards be published. "That is all. No novels, no problem stories, nothing that is not simple, open." The British nature writer Roger Deakin would have agreed wholeheartedly. Much as he enjoyed the exercise of his own literary skill, he claimed he'd often "prefer to be a jotter." It was as if the ease and spontaneity of writing letters and taking notes were somehow truer, more humanly accurate, than a longer and more labored piece of work.

We annotate, observe, we talk, we analyze. But creative writing is something else again. What does it mean to *make something*, to turn that initial flicker of delight and inspiration into a shapely and coherent piece of work? Even if we are lucky enough to have a time and place to call our own—William Stafford's early morning, my small shed—what happens when we first sit down to write?

Every writer—every poet—will have a different answer to that question. For me, the answer has a lot to do with paying attention. Most of us know what it is to be caught (at least momentarily) in a trance of looking, in which ordinary things are suddenly transformed. Anything or nothing can give rise to this: a small bright feather on a sandy path, a half-remembered dream, a piece of music. That moment on Isle Ornsay, on that windy afternoon, was one such an epiphany for me.

But epiphanies alone are not enough. One must also find a way to translate one's experience into words. And that is where the real work comes in, "the deeper listening." Readers tend to imagine that the poet lives in poetry, that he or she is perpetually enchanted and inspired. But this is just not true. Paul Valéry describes a conversation between his friend, the artist Edgar Degas, and the poet Stéphane Mallarmé. Degas had been trying to write poetry, without much satisfaction or success.

"Yours is a hellish craft," he said to Mallarmé. "I can't manage to say what I want, and yet I'm full of ideas . . . "

And Mallarmé answered, "My dear Degas, one does not make poetry with ideas, but with *words*."

Poetry is made out of words, as a painting is made out of paint, or a pot is made out of clay. But those words are meshed in silence, caught in the slow motion of the human heart, the human breath.

Often that throb and pulse precede the actual words. I experienced this for myself, back in the early eighties. My brother and sister had both died the previous year, and I was living in a ramshackle house in central London. I had one room and two big windows, many books. Where was I when it started? At my desk? Scribbling in a notebook? On the bus? I don't remember. Just the sense of something bubbling up from underneath, not words so much as *information:* an ache, a rhythm, an insistent beat.

> *Good and better, good and better. Best.*
> *My father was the best. He had a brain.*
> *He went to Cambridge and he got a First.*

The lines gathered, brutal and inexorable. I scratched them down, let them swirl me into their own dark vortex. I did not want to know what they had to tell me: a heavy, haunted tale of class and Catholicism and loss, told from the point of view of a bewildered child. That child was lonely, desolate, enraged; not at all compassionate or wise. Her anger frightened me. I got down a line or two, some fragments of a later verse.

> *I am so tidy in my clean white tights.*
> *My father's getting better very fast.*

And then the work began, playing that fraught tune over and over in my head, finding the words, acknowledging the feelings. Until finally, after many hours, the poem (the rant, the desperate, repetitive interrogation) had been expelled: was lying in its dark skein on the page.

I was lucky with that piece of work. It had its own insistent form, its own momentum. Students often fear revision, as if to rework a draft were somehow to betray it. Nor are they alone in this. Many of us dream, like Virginia Woolf, of flinging a mass of odds and ends into our journals, and coming back after a year or two to find that they have magically refined themselves and coalesced, becoming "steady, tranquil compounds with the aloofness of a work of art." Like the shoemaker in the fairy story, who laid the leather on his table every night, confident that the elves would sew the shoes for him while he slept, we want to believe that our first heart-scrawl will be sufficient, and that after we can just sit back and wait.

It is true that there are times when our work seems to be given to us, when rhythm and image fly together: a red kite dancing in a clear blue sky. But such transcendence presupposes other times, too often seen as lost or wasted, times of confusion and conscientious drudgery, and times too, when, in Adrienne Rich's words, we were free to "stare into the wood grain of a door, or the trace of bubbles as long as we wanted to . . . times of slowness, of purposelessness."

As Lin Yutang once said, "the art of culture is, essentially, the art of loafing." But who has time for dreaming and loafing now?

A PLACE APART

Changing planes at a crowded airport terminal, I caught a glimpse of a gigantic billboard. "Say YES to Making Just a Getaway Place a Work Place"—an ugly sentence with an even uglier message. I wanted to stand beneath it and shout, "NO!"

Our dreamy intuitive selves have their own sense of time, their own quiet clarity about what they need. We suffer when we are drawn into entrainment with the latest technology, always so much faster and "more efficient" than ourselves. More than a century ago, a contemporary observer decried the effects of the telegraph, which, he said, encouraged short, unambiguous sentences with a minimum of punctuation. "The delicacy, intricacy, nuance of language is endangered by the wires."

Perhaps because that threat was still so new to them, so strange, so visceral, a number of early-twentieth-century writers put time and timelessness at the center of their work. Rilke's *Notebooks of Malte Laurids Brigge* (a quasi-autobiographical novel set in Paris) is worth reading in this context, as is Dorothy Richardson's twelve-volume opus, *Pilgrimage*; Proust's *Remembrance of Things Past*; and much of

Virginia Woolf. All these writers honor quirky, erratic, internal, private time, which dawdles and dallies, shrinks and expands, even reverses itself, in contrast to the steady forward movement of the clock. As Virginia Woolf has Bernard explain in *The Waves*:

> It is a mistake, this extreme precision, this orderly and military progress; a convenience, a lie. There is always deep below it, even when we arrive punctually at the appointed time with our white waistcoats and polite formalities, a rushing stream of broken dreams, nursery rhymes, street cries, half-finished sentences and sights—elm trees, willow trees, gardeners sweeping, women writing . . .

Woolf believed it was the writer's obligation to move beyond "the formal railway line of a sentence. . . . This appalling narrative business of the realist: getting on from lunch to dinner, it is false, unreal, merely conventional." She felt we needed to make room for a more delicate and capricious truth both in literature and life, with plenty of space for idleness and receptivity.

In practical terms, Woolf managed this with great aplomb. She wrote for two or three hours each morning in her garden studio, and went out for walks most afternoons, reading and entertaining in the evening. The simplicity of this schedule served her well. "Creative work needs solitude," writes Mary Oliver. "It needs concentration, without interruptions. It needs the whole sky to fly in, and no eye watching till it comes to that certainty which it aspires to. . . . Privacy, then. A place apart—to pace, to chew pencils, to scribble and erase and scribble again."

In his poem "St. Kevin and the Blackbird," Seamus Heaney describes the saint kneeling in his narrow cell, his arms outstretched in prayer. The cell is so small that "one turned-up palm is out the window," and as he prays, a blackbird lands on it, and builds a nest. Feeling "the warm eggs, the small breast, the tucked / Neat head and claws," St. Kevin is moved to pity, and commits himself to staying put until the young are hatched and flown.

Whether or not the tale is strictly true (Heaney says, "the whole thing's imagined anyhow"), it makes a lovely poem, and for the writer, an especially apt and tender parable. Who has not stayed on, self-forgetful, at the desk, stayed on with sad hunched shoulders and aching neck, praying that those eggs will finally hatch?

"A writer is someone for whom writing is more difficult than it is for other people," said Thomas Mann, without a trace of irony.

Most writers have to find some way to earn a living. We also need to balance the hours spent at our desks with quiet, private rituals of our own. When he worked at the Polish Embassy in Washington, the poet Czeslaw Milosz would return home from the office about seven in the evening, eat supper, take an hour's nap to separate himself from "the day's nonsense"—and then write till two a.m. The novelist Willa Cather, spending the summers in Jaffrey, New Hampshire, worked at her desk all morning, then wandered the woods and trails all afternoon, in search of wildflowers. She told one of her friends that she needed "almost to dissolve into nature daily in order to be reborn to her task."

When the Scottish poet Alastair Reid visited Elizabeth Bishop in Brazil, they went to the local botanical gardens and spent the day together, talking. Reid remembers the exchange as an especially vivid one. "Elizabeth and I sat side by side and talked about what we were looking at. We would look at plants together and notice together." They came up with different words and phrases, imagining how Richard Wilbur might treat what they were looking at, or Howard Moss. It became a marvelous game. They were like children, Reid said later, wandering in the garden, seeing what they could see.

Every writer will develop such tactics for him- or herself. When Dorothy Allison was working on her novel *Cavedweller,* she played the same piece of country music over and over, swaddling herself in its sound. James Baldwin apprenticed himself to Bessie Smith. Sylvia Plath took a surprising number of baths. Balzac slept till midnight, then dressed himself in a white monk's habit, and wrote nonstop, fuelled by fierce black coffee, for as much as fifteen hours at a stretch. Pablo Neruda liked to spend part of each day working in his garden.

When Alice Walker came to write *The Color Purple,* she left Brookyn and retreated to the country, sewing quilts and listening to the trees.

Coffee, yardwork, music, yoga, silence: the specific details are unimportant. What matters is that one honor and protect one's writing time. "I always kept writing uppermost," said the poet Mark van Doren. "In the middle of the night, or even on a train, or going to class . . . if you really want to write something, you're not tired. You know, you can do anything you want to do. . . . You have all the time in the world."

Tactics

↝ Buy a small notebook and carry it about with you at all times. Look and listen, write down what people say.

↝ Next time you visit a big museum, allow yourself the luxury of buying ten or twelve of your favorite postcards. Distribute them around your house or apartment. When they have grown a little too familiar, and you no longer see them and enjoy them, send them off one by one to your most beloved friends and family members.

↝ *Consider the following quotations:*
"The ideal life for a poet is to contemplate the word 'is'."

CZESLAW MILOSZ

"Writing must be done in small amounts. I draft passages in notebooks, revise them, and make the final drafts on the typewriter. My speed is about a paragraph a day."

GUY DAVENPORT

CHAPTER EIGHT

The Space Between

When you are lost, go deeper into the woods.
MAIA

Empty and Alive

IN THE FALL OF 2006, THE CAMPAIGN TO Protect Rural England published a map explaining where to find tranquility. Among its defining categories were the ability to hear bird song and to experience peace and quiet, to see natural landscape (including natural-looking woodland), and to be able to identify the stars at night.

Tranquility belongs to a long list of shadowy essentials to which our culture pays lip service, but to which we are mostly oblivious, among them *rest, sleep, silence, stillness,* and *solitude.* What I am describing is a certain vibrant emptiness, what the Japanese call *ma. Ma* is found in the silences between words, in the white space on a page, in the tacit understanding between two close friends. The Japanese school of Sumi painting says: "If you depict a bird, give it space to fly." That ease, that spaciousness, is *ma.*

The western world is filled with *things,* crammed to bursting point with noise and movement and color and excitement, which to us mean wealth and vigor. From childhood on, we learn to distrust all the varieties of *ma,* and to replace them, as far as possible, with their opposites. We value action over stillness, light over shadow, sounds over silence. But in Asian cultures, such quiet resonance has value in and of itself. It is seen as generative, sustaining, something one can trust. As Lao-tzu wrote in the *Tao Te Ching:*

> *We join spokes together in a wheel,*
> *but it is the center hole*
> *that makes the wagon move.*
> *We shape clay into a pot,*

but it is the emptiness inside
that holds whatever we want.

. . .

We work with being,
but non-being is what we use.

Twenty-five hundred years later, Lin Yutang declared that a room, like a painting, should be *k'ungling,* or "empty and alive," explaining that it is the unused space that makes a room habitable, just as it is our free time that gives our lives their shapeliness and ease. It comes as no surprise that the Chinese character for "leisure" should be made up of "space" and "sunshine"—the pause, the attitude of relaxation, is what creates the gap that lets the sun shine through.

It is easier, perhaps, to write such definitions in one's private notebook, and agree wholeheartedly that they feel right, than to include such luscious emptiness in one's daily life. And yet it is unquestionably true that people are able to work better and more creatively when they are calm, unharried, free of stress, and that this is, at least in part, a matter of choice. "No man will ever unfold the capacities of his intellect who does not at least chequer his life with solitude," wrote Wordsworth's friend De Quincey, and Kafka too has much to say on this: "You don't need to leave your room. Remain sitting at your table and listen. Don't even listen, simply wait. Don't even wait, be quite still and solitary. The world will freely offer itself to you to be unmasked. It has no choice. It will roll in ecstasy at your feet."

MULTITASKING

While I was working on this book, I spent two months at the Mac-Dowell Colony, an artists' retreat center in Peterborough, New Hampshire. I had the use of a live-in studio, with bedroom, bathroom, kitchen, and spacious study, looking out into the snowy woods. Each day was mine to do with as I wished. Lunch was delivered in a basket to my door. At six o'clock, I walked over to the main house for a convivial supper with the other residents.

I loved everything about MacDowell, except for one: the invasion of the laptops.

In the main hall, with its fireplace and three comfortable sofas, people sat side by side, staring at their shimmering silver screens. There were two more sofas over by the door, both similarly occupied. A small table, with portable phone, provided further outlets, and a giant computer squatted opposite, always open and available, its broad face bright with icons, like tiny vivid toys.

I came to Colony Hall to read the newspapers, and to collect my mail. After a long day alone at the desk, I would have welcomed a word or two of conversation. But my comrades, for the most part, were preoccupied. They were checking their email; they were reading the news online. "Hi!" someone would say absently, without looking up or shifting her computer case from the sofa next to her. She *thought* she was being friendly. Surely it was possible to talk to her boyfriend in Seattle, and to me as well. But no.

"Multitasking is going to slow you down, increasing the chances of mistakes," said David E. Mayer, director of the Brain, Cognition, and Action Laboratory at the University of Michigan, in a recent article in the *New York Times*. Other writers and theorists concur. Yes, there is an adrenaline rush of impetus and excitement, at least at the beginning. But only rarely can it be sustained. For almost all of us, competence diminishes with each additional task. The human brain has a hundred billion neurons and hundreds of trillions of synaptic connections. But that does not mean that it can necessarily concentrate on two different things at once.

"Multitasking" is a term drawn from computer technology. It is what a computer does in the tiny flickers of time between keystrokes. Not all machines are equally sophisticated. But some can, in fact, do several things at once: a skill called "parallel processing." And increasingly, human beings have convinced ourselves that we can do the same. It is true that 2.5 percent of the population are what is called "supertaskers"—they really can drive a truck and talk on the phone at the same time without any noticeable decline in their performance. But 2.5 percent is only one in forty. For most of us, "multitasking" is just another word for distraction and inefficiency.

"You see it all the time," says writer Howard Mansfield. "How many tasks, how many multi-tasks, how many things can you do at once? How many bits of information? How much data? And that's just accelerating." It's as if taking things more slowly had somehow become suspect. "You don't even realize what a pace you're going at after a while. It affects people's quality of attention. It affects their dreams. And I think it affects that quiet deep space where people have to maintain solitude or their self or their soul, whatever you want to call it. That is occupied. And I think that's when people start going a little wacko."

A LYTTLE PEECE OF SPUNGE

The last few years have produced a surge of thoughtful books attempting to tackle that "wackiness," among them Maggie Jackson's *Distracted,* Nicholas Carr's *The Shallows,* and William Powers' *Hamlet's BlackBerry.* All three pay tribute to the pleasures and efficiencies of the new media, while at the same time recognizing that something crucial is being lost to us: what Powers describes as "a quiet, spacious place where the mind can wander free."

Some of our difficulties arise from the sheer multiplicity of the data we now have to process. (As Gertrude Stein wonderfully said, "Everybody gets so much information all day long that they lose their common sense.") But the waterfall of data is the least of it. What really matters is the shaping power of the technology itself. The human brain is astonishingly plastic: a fact that can give us tremendous joy, as when we finally learn to ice skate in our fifties, and that can also be a genuine liability, as when we give ourselves over, heart and soul, body and spirit, to the dazzling authority of our screens. As the Internet comes to seem increasingly indispensable (occupying the place of our local cinema, our research library, our post office and radio and daily newspaper), it begins to alter the very character of our minds. Nicholas Carr explains, "If knowing what we know today about the brain's plasticity, you were to set out to invent a medium that would rewire our mental circuits as quickly and thoroughly as possible, you would probably end up designing something that looks and works a lot like the Internet."

The Internet encourages us to do everything at the top possible speed, and at the same time, to keep on changing focus. As Carr says, it is, by its very nature, "an interruption machine." We glide and swoop for small tidbits of information, and then speed off again across the ether. Once interrupted, most of us take about twenty-five minutes to return to our original point of focus, usually attempting at least two other work projects en route. No surprise that as we skim and scroll and surf, our patience and concentration should diminish. What is at issue here is the nature of memory itself.

Computer "memory" is literal and predictable; it does not alter over time. Human memory is considerably more fluid. We need time to muse and dream, to mull, to ruminate, to sort through our own insights and associations. In the words of the philosopher William James, "The connecting *is* the thinking." Without space for that free-floating receptivity, short-term (or primary) memory is not transformed into the long-term (or secondary) kind. Our memories are not consolidated. We mislay the tiny details of our lived experience, the originality and satisfaction of our own opinions.

I experienced this for myself in May 1980, when my father died unexpectedly of a heart attack. I was living in California at the time. Hurled back across the Atlantic for the funeral, beset by immediate practical necessities, inundated by family stories, the few weeks prior to his death melted away like the morning dew. I still don't remember much about that particular spring. My psychic landscape was drenched and splintered, ravaged, rearranged. The short-term memories never did take root.

We need, wherever possible, "a space between," a gap between ourselves and our technology, in which we can, quite literally, recover our core selves. *Hamlet's BlackBerry* was the aide-memoire or seed-book of the day, made of specially coated paper or parchment that could be wiped clean after use. Our minds and psyches also benefit from such erasures. William Powers describes just such a set of "Tables" in the Folger Shakespeare Library in Washington, on display along with their original instructions, "To make cleane your Tables, when they are written on, Take a Lyttle peece of Spunge . . . "

INTO GREAT SILENCE

Back in 1948, the Swiss writer Max Picard published a small book called *The World of Silence*. For him, silence was not "merely negative . . . not the mere absence of speech." Rather, it was a complete world in and of itself. It made things whole again, gave them some of its own holy uselessness, "for that is what silence itself is: holy uselessness."

Without a steady background of silence, it can be difficult (literally) to hear oneself think. Just as a room can be both "empty and alive," so silence too can be restorative, a source of calm and clarity and even wisdom. That we know this on some level, and deeply hunger for it, was shown by the reception given to *Into Great Silence*, a documentary about Carthusian monks, which opened in New York City in the spring of 2007. Scheduled to run for only two weeks, the show was extended indefinitely. Harassed New Yorkers lined up to watch the monks as they went about their daily lives: chanting, praying, gardening, chopping vegetables.

The Carthusian Order was founded by St. Bruno in 1084, at what is now the monastery of La Grande Chartreuse, and includes both choir monks and lay brothers. All live lives of silence, speaking only when it is truly necessary, and for a few hours, recreationally, every Monday. When filmmaker Philip Gröning approached them in 1984, asking if he might make the documentary, they asked for time to consider his request. Sixteen years later, they called him back to say yes. The anecdote has the makings of its own *New Yorker* cartoon. And it is true that the monks are not without humor. One of my favorite scenes shows them trudging up a snowy hill outside the monastery, then sliding back down one by one, their long robes billowing, the sky echoing with their laughter.

But there is a seriousness too, derived in part from that long silence, in the young monk reading his daily portion of scripture; the aged tailor smoothing the white cloth as he cuts out a robe; the cobbler gluing a new sole onto a heavy work boot, and nailing it firmly down. For a moment, as they acknowledge the camera, it is as if the woman in a Vermeer painting had suddenly set down her jug, or folded up the letter she was reading, and turned to glance at you, the light still flickering on the wall behind.

I watched the film on a rainy Thursday afternoon, with an audience of perhaps thirty other people. Most of us came alone, and sat scattered in twos and threes along the empty rows, each preoccupied with our separate lives. But by the time the film ended, something had changed. We had become, however briefly, a community, united by the silence and the long hours of attentive looking, as if something of the monks' tranquility had entered us as well. The light trembled on the surface of the holy water stoop, and slowly returned to stillness. A bell rang out across the empty sky.

You seek me and you shall find me. Because you seek me with your heart, I will let myself be found.

SILENCE IS GOLDISH-BLUE

It is one thing to find tranquility in a snowy monastery high in the French Alps, and quite another to locate it in the modern world. As Picard says, bleakly, "The great cities are like enormous reservoirs of noise. Noise is manufactured in the city, just as goods are manufactured." Most of us have learned to live with the whirr and click of the refrigerator, the bleep of cell phones, the omnipresent hum of the computer. But that doesn't mean we actually *enjoy* those sounds. Alexander Graham Bell, who invented the telephone, was one of the first to suffer from its interruptions, even though he himself was partially deaf. His preference was to sleep till noon. But again and again, the phone would shrill him awake. A colleague remembers seeing the phone in his room stuffed with paper or wound about with towels.

"Little did I think," said Bell, "when I invented this thing, that it would rise up to mock and annoy me."

Despite the clarion call of his name, Bell clearly valued time for ruminative reflection. One feels he would have sympathized with the Carthusian monks, and with the writers and artists (and, of course, musicians), who have spoken out in defense of silence. "I think I am probably in love with silence, that other world," says poet Jorie Graham. "And that I write, in some way, to negotiate seriously with it." Jane Hirshfield agrees. "I've long believed that silence must be one of a poet's closest friends. If I were not able to enter the silence before words, how could I find any words I don't already know yet?"

Silence for them is resonant, inspiring, part of what makes possible the kind of "inner listening" that gives rise to poetry. This is something even children understand.

Several years ago, I was teaching poetry at a big school in the South Bronx. The desks were drawn together into groups of four, and the students were gathered round them, calm and concentrated. Gentle music was playing in the background. Slowly, the classroom teacher and I moved around the room, glancing over the children's shoulders, disentangling the sweet chicken-scratch of their poems. Suddenly one of the little girls looked up at me. "I *like* you," she said earnestly. "I like you too," I told her, smiling, startled at the unexpected compliment.

But when I thought about it later, I realized that it wasn't me she liked, as much as the atmosphere I'd helped to generate: something different from the usual noisy classroom, and (I imagined) from the ruckus of radio and television and frenetic family life that surrounded her at home. Children *enjoy* silence, I remind myself, looking at the words of nine-year-old Joseph, from a little school in upstate New York:

> *Silence is goldish blue.*
> *It is like seeing the moon in the rain.*
> *Silence is like standing by the window*

when all you can see is the sound of the wind blowing past
    you.
It is like standing in front of a gate in heaven.

All of us, child or adult, need time to find our way to that heavenly gate, time to sit back and listen to the sounds outside, and to our own, half-formed thoughts, to attend to the call of the birds and the roar of the air conditioner, and to our own interior voices as well: to let silence spiral deeper into silence. Mary Oliver writes about this beautifully in her book, *Winter Hours*.

> In the act of writing the poem, I am obedient, and submissive. Insofar as one can, I put aside ego and vanity, and even intention. I listen. What I hear is almost a voice, almost a language. It is a second ocean, rising, singing into one's ear, or deep inside the ears, whispering in the recesses where one is less oneself than a part of some single indivisible community. Blake spoke of taking dictation. I am no Blake, yet I know the nature of what he meant.

The speedy modern reader may not realize it, but poetry comes to us like the holy infant, wrapped in swaddling bands of silence. There is silence, often, in the place where it is made, or at most, a slow heart beat. There is silence in the thought that greets particular words and phrases, and in the care with which they're weighed and pondered, and again in their particular layout on the page. And finally there's the silence that surrounds the reading of the poem, and in the quiet intake of breath with which, so often, the poem is received.

For all the emphasis that is placed on words and imagery, poems need that silence, as a painting needs the naked canvas, or music needs the pause between the notes. Most poets know this, in however inchoate a way. They slow down, they listen, they learn to pay attention. They root themselves in what the Celtic bard Taliesen called "the cave of silence" from which all words are born.

THE SPACE BETWEEN

I have been writing about poets here, and poetry, because those are the subjects I know best. But all of us can benefit from some form of emptiness, of *ma*. When people are asked where they get their best ideas, again and again they answer, "In the bathroom," "On vacation," "Doing nothing." They begin, in other words, by "simply being." It makes sense that the two words should be anagrams, since any act of making does indeed *begin* with *being*. It is as if one had to shift one's center of attention down from the busy talking head into the slower, dumber, wiser, human body, and from there into the body of the project itself: the poem, the painting, the piece of music. "Listening," one says, because that is perhaps the best analogy for such expansive receptivity. But it is a "listening" that engages all one's breathing body, and one's spirit too. There is great tenderness and vulnerability in this. It is as if one were trying to marry (or at least make love to) the tiniest iota of the task at hand. When a caterpillar is closed inside the chrysalis, there is a point at which it totally dissolves: no longer caterpillar, nor yet butterfly: just a delicate fizz of possibility, a cusp of hope. Creation has this quality as well.

The British psychologist D. W. Winnicott used the term "play space" or "potential space" for this willingness to let things be, to "hold a frame around an experience" without labeling or judging it. Psychotherapist Eugene Gendlin thinks in similar terms, noting that his most successful clients are those who are able to stop talking from time to time, and simply sit, while they attend to some inarticulate internal process. *They are listening to something they have not yet found words for.* Gendlin calls the gradual clarity that emerges "the felt sense," and explains that it is not located in the head, but rather in the middle of the body, somewhere between the throat and the abdomen. The process he describes is akin to what the Japanese call *kufu*, which is to say, "asking the abdomen" or "thinking with the abdomen."

It sounds simple enough. But for the rational, practical part of ourselves, such "thinking with the abdomen" can seem terrifying. We are down in the mud, shoveling, uncertain. Our comfortable identities have been torn away. We are chipping blindly at the hard rock-face, reaching out to the unknown and the unborn. Allowing time *to listen, to slow down, to surrender*, can feel like a tremendous waste of time.

And yet, and yet . . .

Several years ago, the head of the Missouri Botanical Gardens wrote a letter to one of his graduate students. The student was studying the clematis, and had come up with a number of worthy proposals. His supervisor was sympathetic and appreciative. They were all good ideas, he said. But he had another, more important suggestion.

"Every time you get where there is one of these populations of plants, find a large flat rock, in the shade if necessary; sit down upon it for at least fifteen minutes by your wristwatch; and *do not try to think about your clematises*. Just think what a nice day it is, how pretty the flowers are, and the blue sky. Think how lucky you are to be doing this kind of work when the rest of the world is doing all the awful things they do not want to do. Just let your mind alone. Now I am not joking. Please do this, by the clock if necessary."

The student was dubious at first. But a few weeks later, he reported that he had indeed attempted the flat-rock approach. "Now it is probably just coincidence," he said, "but when I got up from the rock the first time and started down across the hillside, I noticed . . . "

"Chance favors the prepared mind," someone said. But more than mind is involved here, more indeed than chance. If we are flexible and patient, if we are able to persist, there comes a time when the work itself begins to respond, when a conversation starts to develop between one's project and oneself: each moment of clarity giving rise to the next. People talk about surprise and synchronicity, the influence of dreams. But to say that presumes that one remains a separate entity, "subject to influence." The truth is far more fluid and astonishing. It is as if one had indeed dissolved into the larger universe, and the universe itself were doing the making, as if, through the act of self-surrender, the writing had started to appear on the screen, the painting to paint itself, the music to play on its own.

LEARNING TO LISTEN

Joseph Campbell tells a story about a certain Zen master who was about to deliver a sermon to his students. Just as he opened his mouth, a little bird burst into song. The monk paused for a moment, and released his breath. "My friends," he said. "The sermon has been delivered."

Not all human beings speak in the same way, with fixed terms of identification and an orderly hierarchy of tenses. The Piraha, for example (pronounced *pee-da-HAN*), who live along the Maici and Marmelos rivers in northwestern Brazil, speak a language based on just eight consonants and three vowels, which seems not to be related to any other on the planet. They have no system of numbers, no fixed color terms, no words for "all," "each," "every," "most," or "few." Their talk sounds, says writer John Colapinto, "like a profusion of exotic songbirds, a melodic chattering scarcely discernible . . . as human speech."

Numerous scholars have tried (and failed) to master Piraha. Keren Everett, a missionary and longtime linguist, is someone who appears to have succeeded. For her, the key to the language is the tribe's singing, the way that they can sing, hum, and whistle conversations, dropping consonants and vowels entirely, and communicating only by variations in pitch, stress, and rhythm (what linguists call "prosody"). "It's not the kind of thing that you can write, and capture, and go back to," she says. "You have to watch, and you have to feel it. It's like someone singing a song. You want to watch and listen and try to sing along with them. . . . They give a lot of things using prosody that you never would have found [out] otherwise."

What does it mean to "listen deeply" in this way? Can westerners learn to hum or whistle conversations, or, at least, to follow along when others do? Years ago, when I was a student at Cambridge, one of the professors played us a tape of Italian poetry. Most of us did not speak or write Italian, or indeed any foreign language except French, something that troubled him not at all. He knew, of course, that we were not going to "understand" in any logical, straightforward way.

But he believed that some kind of recognition would percolate nonetheless. We would taste the flavor of the language, its rhythm and pace and emphasis, much as Keren Everett, with infinitely more time and persistence, finally learned the music of the Piraha.

"I want to speak to you without words," I said to my friend Maia once, after a lengthy long-distance conversation. I meant it partly as a joke; both of us were tired of shaping careful words into the plastic mouthpiece of the phone. But I also meant it seriously. I wondered whether it might be possible to communicate simply through the rise and fall of sound, as if our words were birdsong, or better still, to talk back and forth in silence: just the quiet intake of breath along the wire.

Max Picard would have understood what I meant. "When two people are conversing with one another," he wrote, "a third is always present: Silence is listening." For him, this is what gives depth and resonance to a conversation, when the words are not restricted to the narrow space between two speakers, but echo back from far away, from the attentive heart of silence.

Such speech is close to what the writer M. F. K. Fisher once called "the Green Talk," the ability to speak without sound—"a kind of transference of speech from one spirit to another"—an idea that had come to her in a dream. When people are especially skilled, she said, they can talk back and forth without smiling, or looking at each other, or making any physical contact at all. Long and witty conversations can go on between them. Fisher herself was not particularly adept. But she knew that it was possible to improve. Anyone could learn the Green Talk, provided there was some basis of love and sympathy. It was a rich, inaudible, deeply private colloquy, a genuinely magical exchange.

AS SLOW AS POSSIBLE

In May 2006, a chord change was played at St. Burchardi Church in Halberstadt, Germany, part of an organ composition by John Cage called "As Slow as Possible." The piece is to be played in tiny increments, once or twice a year, always on the fifth day of the month. The entire performance will last 639 years.

The concert started on September 5th, 2001, on what would have been Cage's eighty-ninth birthday. Because it opened with a rest, nothing was actually heard until February 5th, 2003, when the first chord was struck: two G sharps buttressing a single B. Such a tentative beginning is not unusual for John Cage, many of whose pieces open into silence. As he said himself, "[W]hen any composer in his right mind would be making things thicker. . . . I was getting thinner and thinner." Like the boy in the fairy tale who wanted to learn to shiver, he longed to immerse himself in total silence.

When Cage had the opportunity to sit in an anechoic chamber, he leapt at the chance: *at last*, he thought, *he would be able to hear nothing*. But far from being silent, the anechoic chamber throbbed with sounds: one thin and high and shrill, the other lower and more resonant. These were the sounds made by his own body: the high shrill workings of his nervous system, and the low throb of his circulating blood.

It was this experience, along with the white paintings of Robert Rauschenberg (whose apparently "empty" canvases act as a mirror, revealing ambient dust and shadows) that led Cage to compose 4'3", which is to say four minutes and thirty-three seconds of uninterrupted silence. This was first performed in the little town of Woodstock, New York, on August 29th, 1952. The pianist David Tudor set off a stopwatch, then sat down and closed the piano lid. Three times he moved his arms, indicating the three separate movements of the piece: thirty seconds; two minutes twenty-three seconds; one minute and forty seconds. Then he raised the piano lid and got to his feet. 4'33" of (adulterated) silence.

Early audiences were taken aback by such displays. And certainly it is easy to see such performances as sophisticated sleight of hand: the musical equivalent of the emperor's new clothes. But Cage himself was not trying to deceive anybody. On the contrary. For him, all audible phenomena could be understood as music, and silence (or what passed as such) was for him especially potent.

"I love sounds," he said. "And I actually like them more than what we've done to them." And again, "If you want to know the truth of the matter, the music I prefer, even to my own or anyone else's, is what we are hearing if we are just quiet."

AN INNER QUICKENING

Meredith Monk is a performance artist with an extraordinary singing voice, and the recipient of a MacArthur Genius Award. She is also a practicing Buddhist and a student of Pema Chödrön, with a strong appreciation for the art of listening. Over the past forty-five years, she has worked with voice, composition, dance, and film, sometimes alone, more often as part of an ensemble. She begins each day alone at the piano, singing and playing and trying out different musical ideas. Later, she brings those shards of material into rehearsal, and works them through with the ensemble. She enjoys the chance to share ideas and let go of a certain kind of control. But the time she spends alone is crucial too. "A sense of mystery has room to enter."

In the mid-1970s, Monk was staying at her sister's house in New Mexico. Each day, she would walk up into the hills, and just sit there in the blazing sun and wait. When an idea came to her, she would tape it or write it out. Later, after she had returned to New York, she developed those fragments into a series of pieces called "Songs from the Hill," all of them inspired by that particular landscape.

"Most of my work is very slow," she says. "It's not what people necessarily want in this world right now. They want to be titillated. They want entertainment. They want things to go by really fast." But she herself is drawn to something more profound: both medicine and antidote to our frantic jazzed-up world. "When things are very speedy, there may be a momentary pleasure, but usually when it's over, it's just over. There's no retention." What she calls "a poetry of the senses" works on a different level altogether. "The human voice is a language in itself. It can conjure up and delineate feelings and energies for which we don't have words."

Monk is the fourth-generation singer in her family. Her great-grandfather was a cantor in Russia, her grandfather sang in churches, temples, and concert halls here in the United States, and her mother too was a professional singer, "the original Chiquita Banana, Muriel Cigar, Schafer Beer, Blue Bonnet Margarine, and Royal Pudding Girl." Monk loved singing from very early on. Often, as a child, she would sing herself to sleep. But it was not so easy being a singer in a family of singers, and for a while she transferred her allegiance to movement and dance. She has always possessed a striking physical presence: a long, elegant, high cheek-boned face, set like a mask on top of a trim, androgynous body. But her true originality lay with her voice. Soon after she graduated from college, she went back to the piano and started vocalizing.

> One day I had a revelation that the voice could be an instrument like the body, that I could find a vocabulary built on my own vocal instrument and that my voice could move like a spine or a foot. I understood in a flash that within the voice are male and female, all ages, different characters, landscapes, colors, textures, and ways of using the breath, limitless possibilities of producing sound. . . . From that point on, I began a deep exploration of the voice as the first human instrument, an exploration that continues to this day.

Monk's work has met with much appreciation and professional success. But she admits that it isn't getting any easier. It takes time, she says, to sift through almost fifty years of work, "to drop the backpack." Nonetheless, she feels that her music has refined itself as she's grown older. The surface may seem simpler now, but the underlying elements are much more complex. After her partner, Mieke van Hoek, died, Monk wrote a piece in her honor, called "impermanence." It opened with a song made up only of broken phrases: "Last breath, last laugh, last rites, last word, last goodbye," sung by Monk in a haunting and hypnotic solo. In a later scene, the actors moved slowly about the stage in soft gray-blue costumes, while one man zipped in and out on roller-blades, here—*and gone!*— so suddenly, as death itself is sudden. Towards the end, the entire cast lay on the floor like human chrysalises, great soft empty shells, rolling, rolling, off the stage and away.

As a younger woman, Monk would not have dared to tackle a subject of such magnitude. She describes herself as an impatient person, "very speedy, you know, very impatient." But in the long deep river of herself, there's a part that is somehow not her personality, and that, she says, is where the work comes from. "That place is love. And I think that in that deep river, I'm very, very patient. So it's a patience practice. I'm trying to put myself into the material with every ounce of my being."

Van Hoek died from cancer of the heart. In the last month of her life, while she lay unconscious in the hospital, Monk sang to her all day long: folksongs, lullabies, songs she herself had written. Hearing is one of the last senses to depart the body, and she hoped that her voice would somehow carry through to Mieke, "like a little lantern in the darkness."

Monk still misses Mieke passionately. But in the years since, she has come to find some wisdom in that long enduring sorrow. "Billions of other people have lost their loved ones. . . . Billions of people are suffering. How should we be any different?" The Buddhist teacher Pema Chödrön writes about honoring one's wounded heart, one's gentle, tender heart. "But you can't feel that raw heart if you don't slow down," says Monk. "I'm not sure that you can have that raw heart and speed."

When Monk talks about her work, she describes "a slowing down and then a kind of quickening which is different from speeding. An inner quickening." Now in her sixties, she tries to pass on that gift to her younger colleagues, to share her strength with them, and her enthusiasm. She understands their struggles all too well. But at the same time, she tries to rouse them, "to go with their questions, their creativity," to listen to their dreams. As for herself, "When you do the same thing for your whole life, the things that are inessential start falling away. . . . You just go through life and try to be as kind as possible."

TEACH SLOW

The artist Paulus Berensohn was thought to be slow, even "retarded," as a boy, when in fact he was simply dyslexic. Now in his seventies, he has made his peace with slowness, which he sees as a necessary prerequisite for any art. The day we talked, he was wearing khaki jeans and a richly colored shirt in fiery reds and corals, over a black T-shirt reading OLD GROWTH. He looked lean and vigorous and tanned, his white hair pulled back into a ponytail, and his small eyes twinkling and alert.

"Creativity can be very fast and very spontaneous," he told me. But first there had to be time to dream and drift, to listen and attend. "Imagination comes into us before it comes out of us. It is a receptive, a feminine process . . . imagination for me requires slowness; *slow and savor.*"

Berensohn is a well-known potter, and a dancer too, who has published several books. He has worked with clay for more than forty years. Early on, he took up pinch-pot work, which he describes as "throwing in extreme slow motion." As he explains in one of his books, "The more I pinched, the slower I seemed to move; my breath deepened and my very posture . . . seemed to become less tense. . . . My pinch pots asked to be formed slowly, quietly, and with deep attention." Often he would close his eyes or lower his gaze in order to focus more completely on the feeling of the clay: how cold it was, how wet; how it felt, right at that moment. It was clear to him that both clay and potter needed time to ripen. Only then could he "breathe the spirit of his life" into the living clay.

Finding One's Way with Clay appeared in 1972, and became a surprise bestseller. For a while, Berensohn was full of ambition—he was going to write six other books, and give hundreds of workshops and teach—but then suddenly he became very sick, and couldn't work any more. He went to San Diego in search of alternative healing, arriving, by chance, on Christmas Eve. The next day almost everything was closed. But one movie theater was open, and it happened to be showing Bergman's *The Magic Flute.*

While the overture was being played, Ingmar Bergman flashes on one face after another, one face after another. But every ninth face is the face of a young girl, about nine years old. I knew immediately that it was his own daughter, and that he had made the movie as a teaching story for his child. It's all about the masculine finding its feminine. I came out of the theater saying to myself, *that's what will heal me.*

He started to drive back to his motel, across a long causeway.

In the middle of the causeway was this huge illuminated star, because it was Christmas. When I got back to the motel, I thought, well what am I going to do? I don't have any clay. But I opened a drawer and besides the Bible, there was a match-book with a needle in it, and three or four colors of yarn. This was a fantastic moment in my life. I had some cloth that I had wrapped around the chopsticks that I travel with. So I took that piece of cloth and I thought, "Oh, I'll stitch a star." I sat down in a chair and turned on the lamp above me, and threaded the needle and put the needle underneath the cloth, you know, and brought it up through the tissue of the cloth. As the point of the needle came through the cloth, the light of the lamp bounced off its tip and it became a star. I lifted up this needle, and it became a sword, a silver sword. And that was a gift of the feminine.

His friend the theologian Matthew Fox once described Berensohn as practicing "extrovert meditation." Berensohn himself prefers the word *active*. "Active meditation, you know, like active imagination." To this day, he still sews regularly. "I have seven art forms at least: reading, writing, clay-work, stitchery, bookmaking, dancing, doodling. And all of it is to slow me down." He is easily overwhelmed, he says, by the contemporary torrent of news and information and entertainment. "It can drive you crazy, especially if you're a hysteric. Or you can take it slow.

You can say, '*Take your time. Take your time to embody it.*'"

Not long ago, Berensohn woke from a dream of the Divine Mother. He knew it was she because she wore a broad ribbon tied diagonally across her chest, "like Miss America," emblazoned with the words, "Divine Mother." *I should ask her something*, he thought. *What should I ask?*

"Should I teach?" he asked tentatively. "What should I teach?"

"Teach me," said the Divine Mother. "Teach Slow."

Tactics

↵ From time to time, take three (or four, or five) slow luscious breaths. Remember too, the larger breathing body of the earth itself.

↵ Consider your own experience of silence. What does silence mean to you?

↵ *Consider the following quotations:*
"In my cabin I learnt the sheer luxury of daydreaming. It has been my making and my undoing too. How many days, weeks, months have I lost to it? But perhaps it isn't lost time at all, but the most valuable thing I could have done."

ROGER DEAKIN

"Wherever we are, what we hear is mostly noise. When we ignore it, it disturbs us. When we listen to it, we find it fascinating."

JOHN CAGE

CHAPTER NINE

Learning to Pause

The spirit, by its very nature, is Slow.
CARL HONORÉ

Drinking the Landscape

A s a child, I spent most of my time outside, climbing trees, or wandering in the woods and fields behind the house. I had a trail I liked to follow, with different sitting-places along the way: a crouched nest at the edge of a cornfield, another in the long grass between the hedge and the barbed wire, and two more under the spindle tree and by the barn. It was as if my trail made a kind of necklace, and these sitting-places were the beads along its string: mini-shrines or private altars, at which I alone paid homage.

If the simplest of walks is a stroll to the local park or round one's garden, the simplest of pauses is the glance out of the window or up at the sky: the glance *out* at something larger than oneself. Both walking and pausing allow in this larger world, making for a new and more generous sense of perspective. It was Charlotte Brontë who said, "I avoid looking forward or backward, and try to keep looking upward," but it might as well have been Mary Oliver or William Stafford, or the ornithologist Bill Eddie, who once described to me the sight of two hundred thousand pink-footed geese flying over Edinburgh, "And nobody—but nobody—looked up!"

Driving through Scotland in the 1950s, the poet Edwin Muir stopped his car one summer afternoon, and sat down to rest among the heather.

> The thin air was sweetened by a thousand scents rising into it from every tuft in these miles of moorland, mingling as they rose, so that one seemed to be breathing in the landscape itself, drinking it in with all one's senses except that of

hearing, which was magically stilled. . . . There was not one contour, one variation of colour which did not suggest peace and gladness; and the loneliness and silence surrounding the moor were like a double dream enclosing it and making it safe, one might have thought, for ever.

One is struck by the serenity of this place, and by Muir's grateful surrender to its beauty. Like the graduate student on his shady rock, or Meredith Monk "just waiting" for the next new song, Muir has no goal but receptivity. He describes himself as "breathing in the landscape itself, drinking it in with all [his] senses." Every slope of the moorland, every subtlety of color, delights him yet more deeply. Here, at its most gloriously manifest, is the power of the pause.

TIME & TIDE

The writer G. K. Chesterton once said that the truest form of leisure was the freedom to do absolutely nothing. In the United States today, it has also become one of the rarest. A recent survey by the U.S. National Recreation and Park Association found that 38 percent of Americans describe themselves as "always" feeling rushed. No other warm-blooded creature lives this way: ignoring seasonal patterns, ignoring rest. We alone keep working 24/7, under the false suns of our fluorescent lights. It is as if we hope to rid ourselves of the natural world entirely: discarding not just our own circadian rhythms, but also the larger cycles of the moon and stars, the tides, the solar year.

And yet, it is useful, surely, to have some grasp of what the experts call "chronobiology"—to recognize the ways in which our bodies are in fact entrained not to clocks or computers or our weekly schedules, but to the ancient, powerful rhythms of the larger universe. In the course of a day, our hearts will pound out a quiet drum of sixty to eighty beats per minute, speeding up as we race to catch a bus, slowing down when we take a nap. Our body temperatures will rise and fall by a degree or two, reaching peak efficiency late in the afternoon. Our cells will multiply and divide and replace themselves as necessary; hormones and enzymes will be produced. Women in their child-bearing years will move with greater or lesser ease through the different stages of their monthly cycles. Meanwhile, rain or shine, our attention will ebb and flow throughout the day: an hour and a half of concentrated attention, a short break; another hour and a half, another break.

The dominant culture pays minimal attention to such things, preferring to operate by a kind of cosmic "mono-time" (Jay Griffiths' word), in which one point on the clock is much like any other, whether it be twelve noon on a Sunday ("the unhappiest hour in America"), or 9 a.m. on a frantic Monday (the most common time for sudden heart attacks). Such brutal utilitarianism startles those who live with a subtler and more nuanced sense of daily rhythms. In one story, quoted by the writer Bruce Chatwin, a small army of porters is hired by a white explorer to transport some goods lickety-split across Africa. After several days of nonstop motion, the men insist on taking a break. Their boss tries to cajole them onwards, offering cash, and yet more cash, but the men play dumb, and will not be persuaded. They are waiting, they say, for their souls to catch up.

In the spring of 2006, the San Francisco art collective Rebar set up a park on the west side of Manhattan. Like most other visitors, they began by scouting out a parking spot. But instead of a car, they "parked a park" there for the day, complete with wooden bench and fresh green sod, as well as official-looking New York Parks Department signage.

"Well, I'm just going to go ahead and sit down," said Richard Johnson, who happened to be passing by. And sit he did, his back to the traffic, smiling cheerfully at the minuscule horizon of gleaming parking meters, while some photographer hurried up to snap a picture.

It comes as no surprise that those people who choose to pause at regular intervals report almost immediate effects in terms of personal well-being. William James is especially eloquent on this. "The transition from tenseness, self-responsibility, and worry, to equanimity, receptivity, and peace, is the most wonderful of all those shiftings of inner equilibrium . . . and the chief wonder of it is that it so often comes about, not by doing, but by simply relaxing and throwing the burden down." Rhythmic creatures that we are, it makes sense that we should choose to do this in a predictable way, whether in the form of feasts or holy festivals, or at regular secular intervals. The pause is delicious in and of itself. But repeated, rhythmic pauses, like our contemporary weekend, pauses that can be anticipated and relied upon, are ten thousand times more precious.

Rumi's translator Coleman Barks tells a story about a prisoner who is sent a little prayer rug by a friend. *A prayer rug!* He had been hoping for a file or even a crowbar, something to help him escape. But out of curiosity, or simply boredom, he begins to use the prayer rug, bowing towards Mecca five times a day: at dawn, at noon, midway through the afternoon, just after sunset, and before going to sleep. In the course of these prostrations, he notices a curious pattern on the rug, just at the *qibla*, the point where his head touches it. *What can it be?* He returns to the spot over and over, studying it carefully for several days. At last he understands what he is looking at. Woven into the rug is a special diagram: a guide to the lock in his cell door. Now at last he will be able to escape.

The point is clear: any repeated practice (tending a window box, sweeping the sidewalk in front of the house) can be a source of spiritual nourishment, of liberation.

A PALACE IN TIME

For most of us, even those raised in secular households, the Sabbath is the "pause" that we know best. The Bible tells us, "In six days God made heaven and earth, and on the seventh day he rested and was refreshed." The Hebrew word "refreshed" (*vaiynafesh*) has also been translated "exhaled" or "infused with soul"—a tender poetic usage implying that soul itself only comes into being when the body has a chance to relax. The scholar Abraham Heschel elaborates on this in his little book, *The Sabbath*. "The seventh day is a *palace in time*," he writes. "It is made of soul, of joy and reticence."

And again, "What was created on the seventh day? *Tranquility, serenity, peace, and repose.*"

There have been many forms of Sabbath over the course of human history, many forms of holiday and holy day. The Christian Sabbath has been in existence since 321 AD, when Sunday was ordained a day of rest throughout the Roman Empire. Muslims celebrate their Sabbath on a Friday; Jews, of course, on Saturday. The Babylonians celebrated a lunar Sabbath, as do many contemporary Buddhists. In every case, the intention is the same: to set aside a time outside of time: one day a week in which to relax, to pray, to come home to our family and ourselves.

My friend Arthur Strimling is a wise, kind-hearted man, with a head of close-cropped curly hair and beautiful fluid hands. He directs an intergenerational theater group in New York City; he is also the resident storyteller at a Brooklyn synagogue. Raised in a secular Jewish household, he has returned, in the last few decades, to the spiritual traditions of his ancestors. Observing the Sabbath has now become very real for him, he says, and has brought with it a slowly evolving relationship to prayer. Many of those prayers are in Hebrew, which he doesn't understand. But he has memorized the translations. And he finds great satisfaction in the chanting itself, and in the support of the community. "That sense of welcome and of being held is very powerful."

As a boy, Strimling was seen as "incredibly headlong"; he was always being told to slow down, something he did not find easy. The phrase "Slow down!" still carries a certain sting. He played football and other sports, and was known as a jock. But he was a daydreamer too, and a dedicated reader, already able to value "time out of time, time that was inward, time that was very pleasurable and still."

Years later, as an actor, he began to practice yoga every day. He took up aikido too, "fast motion, but from a very still center." These days, he also practices tai chi. And surprisingly to me, he loves the subway. "I can read a book on the subway almost like I can't do anywhere else. There's no phone, there's no refrigerator, there's no other books around, there's no jobs I ought to do. There's nothing. There's just the subway. So that's a slowing down place for me."

We talked together about the Sabbath, and taking time to pause, quoting Heschel to each other, and the Buddhist teachers Chögyam Trungpa and Suzuki Roshi. "It's not just the pause itself," I said. "It's the repetition of that pause, week after week, year after year." Strimling agreed. "There's a genius in repetition. We do an immense amount of repetition in our culture, but we don't honor it. We don't make it sacred."

As a storyteller, he used to feel jealous of singers, because audiences would be willing to hear the same song over and over again, whereas with a story they always wanted something new. He has tried to teach his congregation to listen more deeply. "I know you've heard this before," he tells them. "I know you think you know how it comes out. But listen again. A story's like a song, you know. It's really worth the being in it again."

Every year at Rosh Hashanah, the Jewish New Year, Striming has the chance to tell the story of Abraham and Isaac. "You can say, 'Oh I've heard that story. I've seen that movie. I've heard that joke.' Or you can do what children do automatically, which is to want every telling to be the same." From Strimling's perspective, the children are the ones who've got it right. "As a culture, we're conditioned to want newness. If you can persuade people to want something new, then they have to spend the money to get it. But by always looking for the new we rob ourselves of a deepening relationship to the old. The pleasure keeps on growing. It begins to have a history."

The same, for him, is true of the Sabbath day itself. "You've experienced it a lot of times before. But also it is always the first time."

FERTILE SADNESS

One September, a friend asked me to join her at a rented house on Cape Cod. The sun shone; the days were calm and uncluttered, mine to inhabit as I wished. I could get up early and wander through the woods to the broad white beach; I could read or swim or hang out in the kitchen; I could stay up to watch the full moon shimmering on the lake behind the house. And yet that handful of peerless days was actually very challenging for me. I felt restless and obsessed, guilty that I wasn't "doing more." It was hard to know what best to focus on: tiny private sculptures made of driftwood, the fat paperback book I wanted to finish. *Should I draw? Should I write in my journal? Read far into the night and sleep in late?*

I am not the only one who finds it difficult to pause. Music teachers report that their otherwise talented students have a hard time playing rests. Technicians excise the modest stretches of "dead air" from poetry and concert recordings. Friends yearn for precious time alone, and then squander it in unimportant chores. No less a figure than Oscar Wilde wrote that "to do nothing at all is the most difficult thing in the world, the most difficult and the most intellectual. . . . [The] contemplative life, the life that has for its aim not *doing* but *being,* and not *being* merely, but *becoming*—this is what the critical spirit can give us. The gods live thus."

Perhaps because so many of us are so obsessed with *doing, being* tends to feel awkward and uncomfortable at first, let alone *becoming.* Slowing down enough to relax and enjoy one's private Sabbath can open up a Pandora's box of complicated feelings, all of them clamoring for our attention. Faced with that internal ruckus, it can seem easier to abandon any pretense of rest, and retreat to our familiar patterns of busyness and addiction, including so-called "therapeutic" shopping. It is poignant, in this context, that "buys" should be an anagram of "busy."

Such a response is common even when the "pause" is imposed from the outside. Rosie and I lived together for almost six years. We had a beautiful old house, a luscious garden. When she broke up with me the misery and grief seemed unrelenting. This was *pause* carried to the nth degree: pause become *chasm,* become *chaos,* a fury of loss and discombobulation. In the midst of that tumult, I was given some unsolicited advice. "Keep occupied," one neighbor advised me seriously. "Eat ice cream," said another, and proceeded to give me directions to her favorite store. "You know where Herrells is? Right in downtown Northampton?" No matter that it was January, the bitter core of the New England winter, or that I don't much care for ice cream at the best of times. The point was to indulge myself, fast-forward past the pain, suture the wound over the still-beating heart, and do whatever I could manage to *keep busy*.

Luckily for me, I disobeyed.

I can't take any credit for this; I could barely think. It was as much as I could do to drive to class and mark my student papers. I was ashamed of that slow, unwieldy, lumbering part of me. I wanted to get well *soon*. But at the same time, I did somehow know that as other, wiser friends reminded me, "It takes as long as it takes," and "The only way out is through." Clichés, yes, but accurate. I needed the time to let things fall apart, to sob and scream and write in my journal, to let myself be utterly bereft.

Six months after the breakup, I was walking down Main Street when I caught sight of a snail on the path ahead. It was an ordinary brown snail about as big as my thumb, with a yellowish-brown body and thin translucent horns. I watched as it moved with infinite slowness over the hot asphalt (already grayed with its own trail), its high humped shadow tilted alongside. At last it reached the edge of the sidewalk, then, little by little, oozed itself over the 90 degree angle, and down into a cool and hidden place among the stones.

Like me, I thought to myself. *Like me.*

For most of the following decade, I lived alone in southern Vermont. I went to sangha regularly, and took time each day to pray and meditate. I taught here and there, enough to pay my bills. I traveled back and forth to Scotland. But mostly I just read. I read poetry and Buddhism and psychology and art. I read letters and biography and memoir. I read philosophy and sociology. I read literary criticism. I read early in the morning before breakfast, and late into the night, the books stacked up beside me on the bed. It was as if I were enrolled in an intensive private program all my own.

At the time, I had no idea why I was doing this. "It interests me," I would have said, if you had asked. "It costs nothing. It's a sort of company." But when I look back, I see that, like the prayer rug in Coleman Barks's story, the books were what allowed me to break free. They talked to me, they talked to each other, they showed me how to think.

Fall if you must fall, said a slogan that I clung to at the time. *The one you will become will catch you.* The books I read are in the endnotes at the back. The person I became is writing this.

I did not become "well" again, in the way I once expected to be well. But I'm well enough. As Thoreau once wrote, in relation to his own difficult feelings, "There is a certain fertile sadness which I would not avoid, but rather earnestly seek. . . . My life flows with a deeper current, no longer in a shallow and brawling stream."

That fertile sadness shows itself most easily when I am outside, swimming idly in a summer lake, or tramping along the edges of a field. Sometimes, more rarely, it appears in meditation, as if a door has clicked shut on the usual verbal racket, and I am left standing alone under the stars. At times too, it comes in company, and for a brief moment I am able to slow down, to honor *ma*, and to listen for the silence between words. I go on missing Rosie, her good quicksilver brain and tender heart, and realize I most likely always will. Some *koans* are intractable, some mysteries not intended to be solved. But the emptiness inside is also full.

TWO ORDINARY HOURS

As a child in Scotland, I was taken every week to Sunday Mass. I remember trying to like it, trying to immerse myself in some imagined form of sanctity. I said my prayers, I sang along with the hymns. When the time came for communion, I made my hands into a little gnarly cave, pretending myself back in the Roman catacombs, and received the host with reverence, its dry wafer dissolving against the ridged roof of my mouth. But even then I knew that I was bored.

Apart from the sermons (which were variable) and the brisk narratives of gospel and epistle, Sunday Mass was the same drama playing again and again in the same stale theater: the same flat gestures, the same half-comprehended words. There was no time at all for silent contemplation, no time, indeed, for prayer. *Where was the consolation people found in church?* I had no idea.

Sangha was different. You sat there on a cushion or a little stool, counted breaths or practiced *metta* meditation, sending good wishes out and out in ever-widening circles. It was uncomfortable at first, *just sitting*. But there was pleasure in that enveloping silence. Forty minutes of sitting meditation, ten minutes of walking meditation, a short reading, a *dharma* discussion, another ten minutes of meditation: two hours total, twice a month, less than fifty hours in the entire year. It was nothing; it was everything I needed.

When Rosie and I lived together, we had a tiny gesture before meals: a moment where we shut our eyes, held hands, and simply breathed. It was not a moment of grace so much as gratitude, of re-alignment. It allowed us time to catch our breath, to be present for each other, to enjoy the food we were about to eat.

Buddhist practice is filled with such moments. There is the *gasho*, the little bow of greeting, hands held upright, palm to palm. You *gasho* to your prayer bench as you take your seat, to the other members of the sangha, to the image of the Buddha. And you *gasho* too during dharma discussion: acknowledging each person before they start to speak, and again when they are finished. Such formalities create a pause, a modest threshold. Like a Quaker meeting whose silence tingles with the possibility of revelation, the talk is energized by the surrounding quiet. Out of that quiet, deep and surprising things are sometimes said. Like talking with beloved trusted friends: you discover things you scarcely knew you knew.

The word "threshold" is drawn from the Middle English *threschen*: the act of threshing or beating grain; it is what separates the wheat from the chaff. To make time to attend sangha is to create just such a threshold in one's own life, separating the inside from the outside, the past from the future, the sacred from the profane. It is to open a little gate between time and eternity, in which, despite the rush of daily life, two ordinary unprepossessing hours have the chance to flourish.

A HOME ALTAR

My local sangha met only twice a month, and though its influence was immense, I needed other practices as well. Spirituality was not a luxury to me then. It was necessary bread: the hard and gritty sustenance of every day. Luckily there are many tactics one can practice on one's own, from simply taking the time to pause and breathe (before leaving the house, for example, or picking up the phone) to tiny one-word prayers of praise or gratitude. Some people recite mantras every morning; others prefer to focus on more elaborate seasonal rituals. The practice varies in a thousand different ways. What matters is the attitude with which it's carried out: the playful/prayerful heart of the intent.

One thing I enjoyed was keeping a home altar: a box or chest of drawers spread with a piece of colored cloth, and decorated in whatever way seemed right. I was embarrassed at first to have created such a thing, as if my very soul were on display. But in later years, working on a project that for me was radioactive in its difficulty, I began to use the altar more consistently. It became a place to pause between meditation and the desk, a place to pray for friends and family, and also for myself.

> *May I be brave & steady, clear of mind & heart.*
> *May I be free of fear & anger & self-pity.*
> *May I be generous & loving & compassionate.*
> *May I not forget to laugh.*

My current altar includes a little tag-sale Buddha, a photograph of the Buddhist teacher Thich Nhat Hanh, and a scattering of pretty stones and shells. I play with it as if I were a child. Last fall I added a string of scarlet beads, the ashy makings of a wasp's nest, three small mementoes from a market in Tibet. When I was searching for a place to finish writing this, I laid down a tiny house-shaped dish, a miniature book. Each day I pause and light an incense stick before I set to work.

Some mornings I will also light a candle, draw a soul card or two, or consult with the *I Ching*. The Benedictine monk Brother David Steindl-Rast believes that lighting a candle can itself be seen as prayer. "There is the sound of striking the match, the whiff of smoke after blowing it out, the way the flame flares up and then sinks, almost goes out." From his point of view, "all this and the darkness beyond my small circle of light is prayer." I am less sure of this than he. But I like the velvety smell of melting wax, the gentle, tender flickering of the flame, and once again, I like the chance to pray.

> *May I remember how lucky I am to be alive.*
> *May I be free of misery & resentment.*
> *May I remember to breathe & laugh & love my friends.*

Remembering those far-off Scottish Sundays, dulled with repetitions of the "Our Father" and the "Hail Mary," I have a sweet feeling of independence in reciting my own prayers. Staring at the delicate limbs of the maple tree outside my window, I think of those I love, too early dead, and I do indeed recognize how fortunate I am. The ordinary, the habitual, shifts for a moment, and I look up, restored, able to meet and greet whatever comes.

THE HOLY MAN & THE PARTRIDGE

My mother tells a story about St. John the Evangelist, the disciple Jesus loved. One day he was sitting with a hen partridge on his wrist, gently caressing her feathers, when a hunter happened to pass by.

"How can it be," he asked, "that a holy man like you should choose to waste his time in such a way?"

The saint smiled, and answered with another question. "And you, as a hunter, why don't you always keep your bow tight strung and at the ready?"

"If I did that," said the hunter, "my bow would lose its strength and flexibility. It wouldn't serve me when the moment came to shoot."

"Just so," replied the saint. "And in the same way, I take the chance to relax, so as to give myself more fully to my prayers. It's a mistake to be so committed to one's practice that one never allows any time for recreation."

THE GREAT SONG

Brother Steindl-Rast understands that it is not possible to say prayers all the time, but he believes, nonetheless, that we should "pray unceasingly." When a party of soldiers was marooned on a Greenland icecap during the Second World War, they knelt together in the winter sunshine, repeating the "Our Father" over and over again. It was the only prayer they knew, and they chanted it incessantly, as children chant a lesson they have learned by heart. *Our Father, who art in heaven, hallowed be thy name.* It was as if all hope of rescue lay in maintaining that unbroken stream of words.

Sent to boarding school at the age of eight, I invented a primitive mantra, which I used to repeat to myself after lights out, in an effort to go to sleep. *Fairies dancing, fairies dancing,* I would say under my breath, trying to visualize a fairy ring, each sprite dressed in the white seed-heads of a blown dandelion. While less effective than the "Our Father," this little phrase was not entirely useless. It did not dispel my homesickness, but it did at least distract me, helped keep some of the terror and the loneliness at bay.

If the experts are right, and 80 to 90 percent of all human thought comes under the heading of "negative rumination" (which is to say that it's repetitive and dysfunctional, if not thoroughly dispiriting), then it makes sense that prayer should be used as an antidote, insistent and inspiring. Some people prefer one all-purpose prayer for all occasions. (My favorite is a brisk two-liner, attributed to an Irish nun: "For what is past, *thanks;* for what is to come, *welcome.*") Others feel each task, each passing moment, should be honored in its specificities.

The *Carmina Gadelica* is a stout compendium of hymns and incantations, collected by Alexander Carmichael in the Highlands and Islands of Scotland towards the end of the nineteenth century. It contains more than five hundred different prayers. There are prayers for the seasons and for different times of day, prayers for various forms of manual labor (milking cows, setting up a loom, going fishing), as well as for the small domestic tasks: for kindling the fire and smooring it (banking it up at night), for consecrating seed. Here, for example, is part of a traveler's prayer, a so-called "Journey Blessing":

> *Bless to me, O God,*
> *The earth beneath my foot,*
> *Bless to me, O God,*
> *The path whereon I go;*
> *Bless to me, O God,*
> *The thing of my desire;*
> *Thou Evermore of evermore,*
> *Bless Thou to me my rest.*

One tends to think of a prayer as an *asking*, a request. The word itself derives from the Old French, *preier: to ask, to demand, to question, to inquire*. But not all prayers take the form of an appeal. Prayer can also be a dialogue, a mutual listening. Mother Teresa said that she did not pray to God so much as listen. When she was asked what she heard, she replied that God was listening too. In other words, the channel between them was open. One is reminded of the lines by the medieval mystic Meister Eckhart, "The eye through which I see God is the same eye through which God sees me."

It is difficult to write about such things, since they are, by their very nature, outside the realm of words. But if we hope to keep that channel open, it behooves us all to listen very carefully. Steindl-Rast points out that the word "obedience" derives from *ob-audiens*, which is to say, "thoroughly listening." "We get no letters from the world of emptiness," said the Zen master Shunryu Suzuki, "but when you see the plant flower, where you hear the sound of bamboo hit by the small stone, that is a letter from the world of emptiness."

The ancient Celts believed that the world was sustained by a great song or *oran mor*, a tremendous resonating melody which ran beneath all things. "Listening" in Mother Teresa's terms might ripple out from the creator God to all the ways in which creation itself is manifest: the crash of waves on a rocky shore, the cry of the seagulls circling overhead. It is easy to imagine this merging, almost imperceptibly, with song. Carmichael notes that the elders he interviewed would at times intone their hymns and prayers, their "low tremulous unmeasured cadences" not so different from the wind or from the sea itself. Often they withdrew to some sheltered place, so that nobody could see or hear them. At eighty years old, even at ninety or a hundred, they would make their way down to the shore, "to join their voices with the voicing of the waves and their praises with the praises of the ceaseless sea."

There is a great reciprocity being practiced here: a profound understanding of the unity between the human and the natural worlds. It is interesting to compare the words of a modern mystic like Thomas Merton, "Let me seek then, the gift of silence, and poverty and solitude, where everything I touch is turned into prayer, where the sky is my prayer, the birds are my prayer, the wind in the trees is my prayer, for God is all in all."

DRINK YOUR TEA

Twenty-six hundred years ago, a little Indian boy lay resting in the shade under a rose-apple tree. It was the time of the spring plowing, and he watched the men and oxen as they worked their way up and down the lengthy furrows. In the newly turned soil, he could see the frantic insects struggling to escape, and the torn shoots of grass where they had laid their eggs. He felt strangely sorry for them, as if they were members of his own family. But at the same time, he was thoroughly awake to the beauty of the day: the birds singing in the clear sky, the sweet scent of the apple-blossom. *Both/ and*, he felt: both sorrow and joy were possible, and an all-encompassing peace.

That child was of course Siddhartha Gautama, who would grow up to be the Buddha. Years later, battling to reach enlightenment, he would remember how he had lain there, in the cool shade under the rose-apple tree. Perhaps, after all, one didn't have to strive for liberation. Perhaps openness and acceptance were enough. "Can one reach God by toil?" asks Yeats in his autobiography—and immediately answers his own question. "He gives himself to the pure in heart. He asks nothing but attention."

Such attention is at the core of spiritual practice. The Buddhist teacher Thich Nhat Hanh, or "Thây," undertakes every task in the spirit of mindfulness, from tracing the word "BREATHE" in his warm, robust calligraphy to mulching the monastery garden. During the week I spent at Plum Village, his retreat center in the south of France, I was given a taste of what it might mean to live in such a way.

Plum Village is set in the rolling countryside of the Dordogne, surrounded by vineyards and orchards and rustling willow trees. Most of the monks and nuns are Vietnamese, like Thich Nhat Hanh himself, but visitors arrive from all over the world. Each day follows the same simple pattern, interweaving prayers and meditation with meals, community work, and private recreation. Time feels both intricately patterned and miraculously spacious. For me, this was especially true of walking meditation.

At Plum Village, walking meditation takes place early in the morning. My first day, I set off slowly into the darkness, trying to match each footstep to my breath. After the crowded Buddha Hall, the time alone seemed especially precious. I could see the crescent moon overhead, and one brilliant planet on the far horizon.

> *I have arrived*
> *I am home*
> *in the here*
> *in the now.*
>
> *I am solid*
> *I am free*
> *in the ultimate*
> *I dwell.*

Gradually the sky began to brighten. Prayers formed themselves unbidden, for one friend who was sick, and another who was dying, yet another on the brink of a divorce. I caught the rank scent of a fox from a nearby hedge. *One step, two steps, breathing in, breathing out.* Another visitor passed me on the road, her long white trousers gleaming in the dawn.

Back at the Buddha Hall, the nuns sat motionless in their long rows, their robes the color of bitter chocolate, of dark turned earth, gold cloth splashed like daffodils across their shoulders. I noticed the gritty gray of their shaved heads, and the Matisse-like poise of one of the young acolytes, with her calm attentive face and graceful hands. What joy it was, this chance to meet each other without words!

The clock chimed for breakfast at eight o'clock: a choice of bread and cereal and different kinds of fruit, including fresh green figs. The nuns stood in line, courteous and unhurried. No one spoke a word. "Bois ton thé," read the poster on the wall. "Drink your tea." At eight-fifteen, when the clock chimed the quarter hour, everyone sat still and simply breathed. We did the same at fifteen-minute intervals throughout the day. Because talk was only allowed at certain times, our mouths and busy brains were forced to take a rest, making space for a more widely focused attention in which each moment shone from within: the small frogs crouched on their lilypads at Lotus Pond, the roo-coo of the doves, the young nun in her gray habit, playing soccer all by herself one quiet afternoon.

Over the course of my stay there were two days of retreat, each of which included a lengthy walking meditation, led by Thich Nhat Hanh himself. The Japanese word for Buddhist practice is in fact the same as "walk," and the practitioner (*gyoja*) is also "the walker." Because Buddhism is understood to be a path, the "one-who-walks" is following in many holy footsteps. During the retreat, Thây's monks and nuns were joined by many local friends and followers, as well as by visitors like myself: a total of more than two hundred people. We surged up the hill behind the Buddha Hall, walking slowly through the orchard that gives the monastery its name. It was hot and humid, and the air was filled with the scent of plums and the buzzing of intoxicated bees. I picked up a fallen plum and pressed it to my mouth, sucking at the fermented golden flesh.

"Please enjoy your spiritual childhood here and now," Thich Nhat

Hanh had told us. "Make it a cozy time you can come back to in the future. We grow older, and one day we will die. Take care of the joyful present so that it can be the joyful past."

When we reached the summit, he lay down to rest, crumpling like a folding doll onto a plastic mat, his wrinkled brown head resting on someone else's blanket. One of the nuns poured him a drink from a miniature teapot. I watched him as he drank, gazing out beyond him at the distant fields, and then down at the familiar European flowers: the clover and silverweed, eyebright and scarlet pimpernel. People tend to think of Buddhism as grounded in an acknowledgment of *dukkha* (suffering), but Thây was right, it is also a celebration of the here and now. Those silvery leaves, those tiny blossoms: everything in its place.

In his books, Thich Nhat Hanh advises people "to water the seeds of happiness" in one another, and during that week, I often saw him as a gardener, all of us raising our faces to his great watering can. "The robe is my home now," said one of his disciples, an ex-prisoner. "Thây taught me how to breathe, how to be a human being, how to walk." In comparison to the western ethos of speed and accomplishment, such mindfulness can seem almost intolerably slow. It is not so easy to relinquish one's commonplace ego and become *unsui*, "clouds and water," like a wandering monk, to abandon one's cell phone and laptop and fax machine. But at Plum Village, one does come to feel it might be possible.

SCOTTISH EQUINOX

The poet Alastair Reid grew up in Galloway, in rural Scotland, not far from the place where Edwin Muir sat down to rest among the heather. His father was a country minister, his mother a doctor, and he remembers his childhood as kindly and gentle, "for we were bound by the rhythms of the soil, always outdoors, helping at neighboring farms, haunting small harbors, looking after animals, or romping in the oat and barley fields that lay between our house and the sea."

When his father read from the pulpit of "a land overflowing with milk and honey," Reid was overcome by the beauty of the image, never doubting that it was drawn directly from their own home ground, for one of his chores was to fetch from the local creamery a jug of milk still warm from the evening milking. It was a rich life, and one he remembers vividly to this day. "When we eventually left Galloway for the flintier east, a glass closed over that time, that landscape. We had left the garden behind, and how it glowed, over our shoulders, how it shines!"

I myself grew up in the "flintier east" of Scotland, but I have lived in New England for more than a decade now, celebrating spring with homemade maple syrup, summer with baskets of fresh strawberries, fall with the brazen glory of the leaves. Even winter has its seasonal crescendos: the dark-green scent of Christmas, the chance to tramp across the shadowy blue fields on a pair of beautiful old-fashioned snowshoes.

It is written in Ecclesiastes that "To everything there is a season, and a time for every purpose under heaven," but in our new world of instant gratification this is increasingly untrue. When goods and services are available 24/7, there is no Advent calendar with its miniature numbered doors, no Lenten fast, none of the taut exhilaration that comes from having something to look forward to. "Longing, we say, because desire is full / of endless distances," writes the poet Robert Hass. But the distances are being erased now, and the longing too, as all seasons merge into one long triumph of consumption.

The solar calendar divides the year into four quarters, marked by the winter and summer solstices, and the spring and autumn equinoxes. For more than twenty years, my friend Maia and I have found a way to honor these quarter-days, *choosing* to celebrate them, to make a ritual together, even though I live in Massachusetts now, and she is far away in California. We pray, we meditate, we write, we draw; sometimes we sing or chant, sometimes we simply listen, each in our separate lives; braiding together our own quirky ceremonies with a handful of practices borrowed from Celtic, Buddhist, and Native American traditions.

Because I teach for a living, and am often on the road, I have carried out these rituals in dozens of unlikely places: on a tiny knoll on the island of Iona, in the blazing red-rock canyons of Nevada, on a rainy rooftop in New York City, even on a moving bus. The process is both grave and deeply playful. Over the years, I have learned to trust myself to its authority, to surrender to a different, sacred time.

Planning starts about three weeks ahead of the festivities, as Maia and I struggle to clarify our thoughts with a long transcontinental phone call. *Where are we in our lives right now? What are we trying to accomplish as friends, as writers, as human beings? What colors are we drawn to? What attitudes of mind? Is there a special theme we'd like to focus on?*

In September 2003, I celebrated the fall equinox in the southwest of Scotland, close to Alastair Reid's sturdy childhood manse. That year, Maia and I had decided to set ourselves a private task, tackling something we had never done before, something that had the quality of risk or daring. We also pledged to look at whatever seemed "off" or out of kilter in our lives, and to do what we could to restore the balance. Imagining a gray-white Scottish sky with seagulls wheeling, I decided to wear an especially brilliant red.

I woke the morning of the equinox to heavy drenching rain, and spent three hours at my desk, bent over a demanding piece of writing. Prospects for the ritual seemed grim. But then a long letter arrived from my friend Barbara, all the way from Portland, Oregon, and towards noon, the sky began to clear. By one o'clock I was ready to eat lunch, and then stop by to visit Alastair Reid, who was staying at a house just down the road. We talked and drank coffee together, and soon I was on my way to the little town of Wigtown, jolting along at thirty mph in a borrowed van.

I did not feel especially comfortable behind the wheel, but there were errands to run, groceries to buy, books to track down. I spent an hour on the library computer, answering messages from France and Spain and western Massachusetts. By the time I emerged, the rain had stopped, and the light was brilliant and exhilarating. In fact, it was such a gorgeous afternoon that I decided to throw caution to the winds, and drive down to the Isle of Whithorn, the very tip of the peninsula, to conduct my ritual.

The sun was dappling the fields as I passed through Sorbie, and glinting on the gray stone walls. The Isle of Whithorn was almost deserted, and I wandered about like a tourist, reading up on local history. The remains of an Iron Age fort have been found there, but it is best known for St. Ninian, who brought Christianity to Scotland in 397 AD, and whose stone chapel, Candida Casa, still stands near the harbor. A little whitewashed marker has been built to honor him, set on the hill above the bay.

Slowly I climbed the hill, pausing from time to time to look around. I was struck by the beauty of the landscape at that hour: the fields so bright as almost to seem lime green, the sea dark blue as watered silk, with little dashes of white foam. At its zenith, the sky was pure cerulean blue. You could see the Isle of Man on the far horizon, gray-blue and steeple-y, and when I turned to the left, looking up the body of the peninsula, there was a rainbow arching across the fields, gleaming over the pale blue sky and grayish clouds, as if pointing with one delicate finger: *here, you belong here.* A notice board informed me that one could see five kingdoms from that little peak: England, Scotland, Ireland, the Isle of Man, and—heaven itself. "Look, see, eternity is all around!"

I walked downhill into the fresh wind, the whole body of the earth shivering and glittering around me, and stood alone in the chapel, praying in turn to each of the seven directions: to the north and south and east and west, to the sky above and the ground below, to the place within. I prayed for my immediate family, for Maia, and for Rosie too. "Help me to let go of her," I prayed. "Help me to find peace."

The municipal notice board confirmed that I was only one of many such pilgrims, each with her own urgency and pain.

> *Celebrating St. Ninian 397-1997*
> *Inaugurated 11th May 1997.*
> *Dear Visitor-Pilgrim,*
> *You are invited to add your own stone*
> *to this cairn as a symbol of an act of*
> *witness which you have completed*
> *or which you now pledge.*

Obediently, I went searching for some stones. I found a heart-shaped one for myself; a small, milk-splashed one for my sister, Isabella; a stone shaped like a bird's head for Maia; and a flat gray stone for Rosie, ringed with two white lines. Gently I placed them on the cairn beside the gate, pledging to bravery and balance and the habit of joy. And then drove home, via a little restaurant called the Steam Packet, where I ate a bowl of chicken soup, rumbling home just as the dusk came on, learning to work the headlights in the old white van.

Much later, I thought back over that day and realized how precisely balanced it had been, how entirely equinoctial. There had been the rain in the morning, and the bright sun in the afternoon; the privacy and diligence of my little house, and the beauty and expansion of the Isle of Whithorn. I had worked on my own writing, and received a letter from a friend; I'd sent emails out across the globe. I'd been quietly responsible in a daily way, and I'd also been attentive to the needs of the spirit and the passing of the seasons. And in doing so, I had arrived, as so often, at a place of peace. Why has this come to seem so difficult? After all, as William Stafford writes in one of his poems,

> *If you let the silence of*
> *afternoon pool around you, that serenity*
> *may last a long time . . .*
> *This whole world is yours, you know. You can*
> *breathe it and think about it and dream it after this*
> *wherever you go. It's all right. Nobody cares.*

Tactics

↝ Create a home altar for yourself, and incorporate its presence in your prayers.

↝ Native Americans lived in accordance with a changing cycle of moons; for the Ojibwa, March was *the moon on the crust of the snow*, June *the moon of the strawberries*, and October *the moon of the falling of the leaves*. How might you describe the seasons and cycles of your own home territory?

↝ *Consider the following quotations:*
"Sunday deserves to be, not a No-day, but a Yes-day."

ALASTAIR REID

"What is Above is Within, for everything in Eternity is translucent. The Circumference is Within."

WILLIAM BLAKE

CHAPTER TEN

Across the Bridge of Dreams

*What if you slept? And what if, in your sleep, you dreamed?
And what if, in your dream, you went to heaven and plucked a
strange and beautiful flower? And what if, when you awoke,
you had the flower in your hand? Ah, what then?*
COLERIDGE

Love Soup

I WAS STANDING IN THE MIDDLE OF MY aunt's enormous apartment: room after room leading out of one another, ever more spacious and surprising. She had gone out, and I was alone in the kitchen. A pan of milk seethed and hissed in front of me, and a chicken leg lay (oddly) on the windowsill. I was about to make what I thought of as Love Soup, a strange, magical brew with the power to relieve all the miseries of loss and self-obsession. *But where should I begin?* I asked myself. Perhaps I should coat the chicken leg with oil and garlic, and stew it in the milk. Then I could add some couscous and some carrots. But that chicken leg looked awfully red and raw. Would it be safe to eat?

Just then, I heard my aunt's voice in the corridor, "Darling, I am home!"

I told this dream to my dream group that same evening. My culinary anxieties amused them. They pointed out that I'd had everything I might need to make the soup. "You could add an onion," someone said. "Some salt and seasoning. A little celery."

I drove to town next day and bought two chicken legs. My friends were right: I already had most of the other ingredients. There was a can of coconut milk in the cupboard, and a packet of spicy Thai seasoning. I could start at once. By then it was snowing outside, the land muffled and bright under a cobalt sky, the air splintered, charged with ice crystals. Small blizzards bellied out across the fields, as if some invisible giantess were emptying her flour sack in the woods.

Meanwhile, I was making my first pot of Love Soup.

I took onions and garlic, chopped them up fine, and sautéed them

237

in olive oil. I added celery and carrots, a carton of organic chicken broth, and plenty of fresh water. When this had come to a boil, I stirred in the Thai seasoning and the pieces of hacked up chicken leg, and left it all to simmer for what seemed a long, long time. Last of all, I added the coconut milk and a sprinkling of cilantro. The soup was fierce and nourishing. I ate it for lunch and supper that same day, and for several meals thereafter.

And that would be the end of the story, except for this. Despite a broken night, cranky and insomniac, I was at my desk by ten-thirty the next morning, and *wrote beautifully that whole weekend.* I had been working on this book, the "talking" section, and I wrote nine or ten pages the first day, and another eight or nine the second: joyful, confident, and unafraid. "It's only a dream," people say. But the Love Soup—the healing power—was real.

HUNGRY FOR SLEEP

Just as we pause during the day to pray or catch our breath, so we descend into unconsciousness each night, grateful for the "sabbath" imposed by our biology. Every human being has the power to dream (as in fact do all mammals, with the curious exception of the spiny anteater and the duck-billed platypus), and for thousands of years we have been fed by gifts and insight from that other world. We return from sleep with healing remedies for ourselves and others, with songs and stories, poems and prayers; with the image for a painting, the steps to a new dance, the answer to some private koan or scientific question.

But in contemporary America, such opportunities are under siege. The average citizen sleeps between sixty and ninety minutes less a night than he or she did a century ago, which in turn means less time to dream, to lie in bed and brood, or to ponder missives from our sleeping selves. We are suffering, in fact, from a chronic national sleep deficit. A recent ad by Carpenter Co. Labs filled a full page in *USA Today.* Offering readers the chance to get their sleep questions answered—and at the same time, promoting its own remedies for insomnia — it showed an unshaven man in striped pajamas, caught in the middle of a jaw-breaking yawn. "America, you're not sleeping well," it read. "You know it . . . we know it."

About seventy million Americans have trouble sleeping, according to a recent survey by the non-profit National Sleep Foundation. As many as three in ten have become very sleepy, or even fallen asleep at work over the course of the past month. There are numerous reasons for this, ranging from the growth of the global economy to shift-work, long working hours, and a sharply accelerating pace of life. Business-people rise at dawn to field calls from Tokyo and London. Parents stay up too late in search of child-free, adult time. Sociologist Arlie Hochschild describes the hard-pressed working mothers, who long, to the point of desperation, for more sleep. They "talked about how much they could 'get by on' . . . six and a half, seven and a half, less, more. . . . These women talked about sleep the way a hungry person talks about food."

It bears remembering just how recent all this is. Before the invention of the electric light bulb in the late nineteenth century, most people did actually sleep nine-and-a-half hours every night: an amount that now seems almost impossibly luxurious. Until that time, fire was the only source of light, in the form of candles and rush lights, gas lamps or kerosene. Working people rose and slept according to the sun. These days, by comparison, we live in a perpetually illuminated world. The defense establishment, the financial markets, television, radio, and computers are now operative 24/7, along with many businesses, supermarkets, movies, night and evening classes. *What are the consequences of this, for ourselves, our dreams, our creativity?*

One third of our life is spent asleep, and about a fifth of that spent dreaming; which is to say that we dream for about an hour and a half each night, or between four and five years over the course of a lifetime. Dreams are signaled by REM sleep (short for "Rapid Eye Movements") when our eyeballs shift about under their closed lids. Throughout the night, REM sleep alternates with non-REM sleep, in spells ranging in length from ten minutes to an hour, growing longer and longer towards morning. Such sleep is critical to human well-being.

When volunteers in a lab experiment are deprived of the chance to dream, they experience what is called "REM rebound"; that is, they "dream overtime" as soon as the opportunity arises. In the meantime, their performance suffers. Denying people REM sleep impairs their ability to solve problems and to think creatively. Their readiness to laugh and take a joke is also compromised. In addition, scientific studies have shown that challenging work may itself require more dreaming. Top-notch students at an intensive language course found they needed more REM sleep than usual if they were to succeed in their work. Less successful students (who presumably did not work so hard) showed no such increase in REM sleep.

Despite the glaring obviousness of this research—which shows beyond doubt that we are all "more productive, good-humored and satisfied with life" if we get our full complement of rest—the average American continues to skimp on sleep. (More than half the population admits to trading sleep for television.) This has widespread consequences, not just for personal happiness and achievement, but in terms of the larger world and the quirky revelations dreams can bring. The writer Laurens van der Post records an occasion on which Jung addressed a friend (perhaps van der Post himself) "You tell me you have had many dreams lately, but have been too busy with your writing to pay attention to them. You have got it the wrong way round. Your writing can wait, but your dreams cannot, because they come unsolicited from within and point urgently to the way [that] you must go."

THE BLUE STAIRCASE

People who study dreams are known as oneirologists (from the ancient Greek *oneiros* meaning "a dream"). Theirs is an enormous subject, reaching back far into the past, from the songs and stories of the native Australians to the esoteric traditions of India and Tibet and the visionary Sufism of Islam. There is, in fact, a vast treasure house of thought having to do with dreams, some of it focusing on their mystical and creative aspects, some on the more practical and analytical. What interests me here is *what can be brought back—something of beauty, something of use*—and how that may be shared with the waking world.

In Ancient Babylon, and later, in Greece and Rome, dreams were seen primarily as a source of healing, granted by Asclepius, the god of medicine. Pilgrims would gather at one of his many temples, where they would fast and purify themselves, making offerings of incense, oil, and wheat cakes, and sacrificing sheep or oxen. At night, they would lie down to sleep on the newly flayed skins, surrounded by the small yellow snakes of the region, praying for a revelatory dream: a process known as incubation. Originally, the god himself appeared to them; later, the dream became the means (like my Love Soup recipe) of receiving medical advice from the divine. Aristides, author of the *Sacred Orations* (150 AD), struggled to describe his own experience:

> One listened and heard things, sometimes in a dream, sometimes in waking life. One's hair stood on end; one cried and felt happy, one's heart swelled out but not with vain-glory. What human being could put this experience into words?

Aristides, at any rate, emerged from the temple with some clear instructions: he was required to use emetics, to go barefoot in winter, and even to cut off one of his fingers. Extreme advice, perhaps. But for him it was entirely worth it. He had been suffering from a long illness, and now, finally, he was cured.

The Native American vision quest was also meant to result in potent dreams, in their case induced by prayer and drugs and fasting. For the Iroquois, especially, dreaming was seen as the language of the soul, "more real than reality." The Jesuit missionary, Father Fremin, who spent time with the tribe in the late seventeenth century, wrote that "The Iroquois have, properly speaking, only a single divinity—the dream. To it they render their submission, and follow all its orders with the utmost exactness." In *Shaking the Pumpkin,* the poet Jerome Rothenberg records two such "Dream Events" taken from the Iroquois tradition:

After having a dream, let someone else guess what it was. Then have everyone act it out together.

Have participants run around the center of a village, acting out their dreams & demanding that others guess & satisfy them.

Father Fremin confirms this behavior in his text. Someone who had dreamed of bathing would run from cabin to cabin, in each of which he'd have a kettleful of water thrown over him, no matter what the weather. Similarly, among the Huron, a warrior who dreamed that he was bitten by a snake, would go in search of an antidote as soon as he woke up. Some dreams were clearly personal, whereas others were seen as gifts to the entire tribe. Rothenberg tells of a Papago shaman who used to name the village children for the images he encountered in his dreams:

Among such names [were] Circling Light, Rushing Light Beams, Daylight Comes, Wind Rainbow, Wind Leaves, Rainbow Shaman, Feather Leaves, A-Rainbow-as-a-Bow, Shining Beetle, Singing Dawn, Hawk-Flying-over-Water-Holes, Flowers Trembling, Chief-of-Jackrabbits, Water-Drops-on-Leaves, Short Wings, Leaf Blossoms, Foamy Water.

Other shamans might return with the words to a new song, the design for a sand painting, or instructions for choosing a totem animal or a healing herb. If their words were occasionally cryptic or abrupt, that was hardly surprising. As one Papago woman explained, "The song is very short because we know so much." Like Mary Oliver's journal entries, which were intended to return her to the "felt experience," the dreamer's words acted as a verbal trail by which he or she could reenter the dream. Here, for example, is the "Song of an Initiate" from the Huichol people, a piece that is both lyrical and evocative, and at the same time, utterly mysterious:

climbed the blue staircase up to sky
climbed where the roses were opening
      where roses were speaking

heard nothing   nothing to hear
      heard silence

i climbed where the roses were singing
      where the gods were waiting
      blue staircase up in the sky

but heard nothing   nothing to hear

      heard silence   silence

THE CELTIC BARDS

The poet Taliesin, who lived in Wales during the second half of the sixth century, described himself as a "diviner and a leading bard," one who knew "every passage of the cave of silence." In the following poem, he invokes his own skills and multiplicity:

I am Taliesin
I sing perfect meter which will last till the world's end
I know why an echo answers again
why liver is bloody, why breath is black and why silver shines
   . . .
I have been a blue salmon
a dog, a stag, a roebuck on the mountain
   . . .
upon a hill I was grown as grain
reaped and in the oven thrown
   . . .
I have been dead, I have been alive, I am Taliesin.

243

Like the Huichol initiate, the Celtic bards were healers and vision-aries, what Jerome Rothenberg calls "technicians of the sacred." Their training was a formidable one. Over the course of twelve years, they were expected to learn at least a hundred and fifty oghams (or alpha-bets) by heart, as well as almost six hundred tales, and two hundred and fifty poems in various forms and meters. They were also taught prophetic invocation and shamanic healing. They were helped, in other words, to dream good dreams, and to use them as a bridge between the worlds.

No one knows just how this was accomplished, but it is clear that it involved at least one night alone on the mountains or in an isolated cave, perhaps enhanced by some initiatory potion. The experience could be terrifying. Taliesin writes that "whoever spends the night alone on the top of Cader Idris or under the Rock of Arddu on the Llanberis side of Snowdon will be found in the morning dead, mad, or a poet."

As they lay in the darkness, the young bards would increase their receptivity by placing their hands crosswise over their face, a palm over each eye. On some occasions they would gorge themselves on raw meat (beef, pork, even cat) hoping to receive an augury from the totem animal. In time, they learned to befriend their dreams, drawing from them that occult knowledge known as *fios* or *imbas*: simultaneous ac-cess to both inner and outer worlds. In confirmation of their achieve-ment, they would be entitled to wear a special shamanic cloak or bird-mantle, made of swan and mallard feathers, and to carry a branch of gold or silver or bronze, hung with tinkling bells, symbolic of the ever-fertile, otherworldly tree, which is the tree of poetry.

It is not known how long the bardic schools were in existence, for they had their origins in prehistoric times. But in Ireland they lasted well into the seventeenth century. An account by the Marquis of Clanricarde, dated 1722, describes a typical "poetical seminary." Students were housed in a low, snug hut, out of reach of any noise. This held little but beds, a table, and some seats, as well as pegs on which to hang one's clothes. There were no windows, and the doors were kept tight shut. The teacher would assign a particular poem, determining both subject and rhyme scheme, and the students would work on it through the night, and on into the following day, composing on their finger ends, or reciting incantations into their hands, each one lying in the dark on his own bed.

On the second night, candles would be brought in, and the poems could finally be written down. The students would get up and dress, presenting their work to the teacher, one by one. Those whose poems were approved would be given a fresh theme for the following day.

"The reason of laying the Study aforesaid in the Dark was doubtless to avoid the Distraction which Light and the variety of Objects represented thereby commonly occasioned," explained the Marquis. "This being prevented, the Faculties of the Soul occupied themselves solely upon the Subject in hand, and the Theme given; so that it was soon brought to some Perfection according to the Notions or Capacities of the Students."

In a poem written in Irish around the same time, a graduate of one of the schools criticizes an acquaintance for "making art on horseback." He himself, he says, much prefers the traditional method:

> *Myself now, when I make a poem,*
> *I prefer, guarding me from error,*
> *A screen against the sun; to be under a roof,*
> *A dark bed to protect me.*

Without that, he feels, he would not be able to compose:

> *If I did not close my eyelids*
> *Against the brilliant rays,*
> *Like a veil between me and my lay,*
> *I would loose all my skill.*

WRITERS DREAMING

"All good writing is a guided dream," said the Argentinean writer Jorge Luis Borges. It is an attitude with which the nineteenth-century

Romantics—Coleridge especially—would have profoundly agreed. Several of his contemporaries courted both dreams and nightmares, deliberately exacerbating them by the use of opium, laudanum, or laughing gas. But Coleridge had no need of such encouragements. Since childhood, he had been subject to terrifying nightmares that made him "dread to go to bed or fall asleep," and that often woke him screaming.

> [October 1803] A sad night—went to bed after Tea—& in about 2 hours absolutely summoned the whole Household to me by my Screams—from all the chambers—& I continued screaming even after Mrs. Coleridge was sitting and speaking to me! O me! O me!

Not surprisingly, Coleridge took opium to help him quell his nightmares, rather than to elicit more. Nonetheless, he continued to study and record his dreams, often commenting on them in considerable detail. He wrote, for example, about "hypnagogic hallucinations"—"those Whispers just as you have fallen asleep or are falling asleep—what are they and whence?" and puzzled over the vocabulary involved, "to *fall* asleep—is not a *real* event in the body well represented by this phrase?" His visionary night self with its rich language of "Images and Sensations" both baffled and intrigued him. "I must devote some one or more Days exclusively to the Meditation on *Dream*," he wrote in his notebook. "Days? Say rather Weeks!"

Several of Coleridge's best known poems, among them "Kubla Khan" and "Frost at Midnight," draw on the imagery of night and dreams. "Kubla Khan" came to him, in fact, within a dream. In the summer of 1797, he was living in an isolated farmhouse on the edge of Exmoor, in southwest England. He had not been well for some time, and the medicine he was taking caused him to fall asleep, just as he was reading the following sentence: "Here the Khan Kubla commanded a palace to be built, and stately garden thereunto. And thus ten miles of fertile ground were inclosed with a wall."

For the next three hours, Coleridge went on sleeping, even while he was simultaneously engaged in a lengthy act of composition. "Kubla Khan" emerged with the utmost fluency, words and images rising up before him, "without any sensation or consciousness of effort." In its original form, it was some two or three hundred lines long.

The idea of poetic creation *as a gift* goes back to ancient times, but Coleridge was one of the first modern writers to submit to it so consciously, seeing the imagination as a living force that "dissolves, diffuses, dissipates, in order to re-create," and allowing it to infuse both the modest details of his daily life and the starry constellations of his dreams. In "Frost at Midnight," written in February 1798, he sits awake far into the night, with his son, a sleeping infant, by his side. The poem is brooding and contemplative, its details crisp and freshly observed, creating a portrait of affectionate fatherhood that still feels remarkably contemporary.

Coleridge died in 1834; Robert Louis Stevenson, born only sixteen years later, in 1850, would have sympathized with his interest in dreams, and with his terrifying nightmares too. At six years old, he had been kept awake by "the noise of pens writing" (a charming premonition of his future career), and for most of his childhood he was "an ardent and uncomfortable dreamer," as he explained in his autobiographical essay, "A Chapter on Dreams." His room, at night, would seem to swell and shrink, and his clothes, hanging on a nail, first loomed up to the size of a church, and then "drew away into a horror of infinite distance and infinite littleness." This signaled for him the beginning of a nightmare. He fought hard against it, but, like Coleridge, his struggles were in vain, "sooner or later the night-hag would have him by the throat, and pluck him, strangling and screaming, from his sleep."

Stevenson's dreams varied enormously; sometimes he would be haunted by nothing more than a certain shade of brown, which did not bother him at all during the day; at other times, the demands of school and the Final Judgment would compound themselves into an appalling nightmare, in which he seemed to stand before a Great White Throne, required to make some vital recitation. "[H]is tongue stuck, his memory was blank, hell gaped for him," and he awoke in terror, "clinging to the curtain-rod with his knees to his chin." The extreme sensibility persisted, but over time the nightmares lessened, and the boy started to take "long uneventful journeys" and to see "strange towns and beautiful places" as he lay in bed. He also began to read inside his dreams, such marvelously enthralling tales as to make him impatient with real books ever after.

Later in life, plagued by insomnia, Stevenson told himself stories as a way of going to sleep. At first these were casual productions. But after he started to write professionally, he began to rely on his dreams as a source of inspiration. He gave credit for these to his "Brownies" or "Little People," who, like the elves in the fairy story, worked away all night while he was fast asleep. It was they who provided the plot for his bestselling novel, *The Strange Case of Dr. Jekyll and Mr. Hyde,* which sold forty thousand copies in Britain in the first six months, then swept stupendously across the States. Stevenson had thought up the original subject of the book, as well as the characters and setting, but it was the Brownies who gave him the core idea of a willed, then unwilling, transformation, as well as three crucial scenes.

Many contemporary authors have testified in similar fashion to the shaping power of dreams, among them William Styron and Isabel Allende, interviewed by Naomi Epel for her anthology, *Writers Dreaming.* Back in 1974, Styron was struggling with an intractable manuscript, when he dreamed of a woman with her arms full of books, a blue number tattooed just beneath her sleeve. Clearly she was a Holocaust survivor. Styron went straight to his desk, and wrote the opening paragraphs of what later became *Sophie's Choice.*

Isabel Allende had a similar struggle with her first novel, *The House of the Spirits.* She wrote and rewrote the final pages, trying to get them right. Then, at three o'clock one morning, she woke from a dream in which she'd seen her grandfather, lying in black on his black bed. She herself was sitting on a black chair, also dressed in black, talking to him about her book. When she woke, she realized that the book had been meant for him from the beginning, which meant that it would necessarily end with his death. "So the epilogue has the tone of a person sitting beside her grandfather, who is dead . . . telling the story very simply. The dream gave me that."

Some writers do not keep a record of their dreams, preferring to let them "work underground." But Allende keeps a little notebook by her bed. If she wakes with a dream, she goes through to the bathroom, in order not to wake her husband, and quietly writes it down. Later she copies it into her computer. She describes her dreams as like a storage room that can't be entered during daylight hours. "Sometimes I reach back into that storage room and bring out some information, write about it, and then it becomes true." At times, it's like a kind of premonition. But she feels, too, as if the information were always there, somewhere in the collective memory, and she simply had to tune in.

It is easy to disparage that ordinary self, the one who listens, the one who pays attention, when so much is given by the dream. Still, as Stevenson pointed out, that humdrum self is an excellent editor and amanuensis, and a more-than-competent secretary. Such skills are crucial too. "I pull back and I cut down; and I dress the whole in the best words and sentences that I can find and make; I hold the pen too . . . and when all is done, I make up the manuscript and pay for the registration; so that, on the whole, I have some claim to a share . . . in the profits of our common enterprise."

HARVEST OF DREAMS

Years ago, Emerson described how tantalizing dreams could be, seeming to suggest "an abundance and fluency of thought not familiar to the waking experience," and at the same time, piquing us with their independence. Nonetheless, he felt that there was much to be gained from them. "We know ourselves in this mad crowd, and owe to dreams a kind of divination and wisdom."

The question of how best to harvest that "divination and wisdom" was a growing concern throughout the nineteenth century. Some dream retrievals were extremely practical. The zoologist Louis Agassiz struggled for weeks to identify a certain fossil fish, until finally he gave up in despair. But then for three nights in succession the fish appeared in his dreams, all its features perfectly restored. On the third night, still groggy with sleep, Agassiz sat up in bed and began to sketch. Next morning he hurried back to the fossil, and started to chisel away at the surrounding stone, using his drawing as guide. To his amazement, the fish exactly matched his dream, and he was able to identify it with ease.

A similar tale is told of a certain Dr. Hilprecht, professor of Assyrian at the University of Pennsylvania. Hilprecht had been given a drawing of two pieces of agate taken from an ancient Babylonian temple, and asked if he could identify them. He thought perhaps they might be finger rings. But then one night, a priest came to him in a dream, and led him into the temple treasure house, explaining that the fragments were, in fact, parts of an inscribed votive cylinder. When he looked again at the drawing, Hilprecht realized that this was indeed entirely possible. Later that year, he was able to visit the museum in Istanbul where the fragments were kept. He took them up and fitted them together, and immediately the inscription was complete.

There are many such stories, some more fully documented than others. The abolitionist Harriet Tubman dreamed precise escape routes for the underground railroad which carried so many slaves north into freedom. Elias Howe dreamed the eye in the needle that led him to invent the lock-stitch sewing machine. The German chemist August Kekule von Stradonitz dreamed of a snake swallowing its own tail—and so discovered the ring shape of the benzene molecule.

Not all dreams and visitations are of such high caliber. "We work in the dark—we do what we can—we give what we have," wrote the novelist Henry James. On one occasion, his brother William, the philosopher, dreamed that he'd discovered the secret of the universe. He struggled awake just long enough to scribble a few words in his notebook, and woke the next morning to discover these immortal lines:

> *Higamus, hogamus,*
> *Women are monogamous;*
> *Hogamus, higamous,*
> *Men are Polygamous!*

But despite such moments of bathos, poets and writers, artists and inventors continued to record their dreams, and to turn to them in search of inspiration. "I can never decide whether my dreams are the result of my thoughts, or my thoughts the result of my dreams," wrote D. H. Lawrence to a friend. "My dreams make conclusions for me. They decide things finally. I dream a decision."

IMAGINARY BEINGS

When Frida Kahlo was a little girl, she had an imaginary friendship with another child. She would breathe on one of the windowpanes in her room until a mist formed, white and cloudy, and then she would draw a "door" with her finger.

> *Through that "door"*
> *I would come out, in my imagination,*
> *and hurriedly, with immense happiness, I would*
> *cross all the field I*
> *could see until I reached*
> *a dairy store*
> *called PINZON. . . . Through*
> *the "O" in PINZON I en-*
> *tered and descended impetuously*
> *to the entrails*
> *of the earth, where*
> *"my imaginary friend"*
> *always waited for me.*

Thirty-four years later, Kahlo could barely recollect what her friend looked like. But she did remember her joyfulness, the way she laughed a lot, "soundlessly," and danced "as if she were weight-less." The child Frida would copy her friend's every move, and as they danced together, would confide her secret problems. "Which / ones? I can't remember." Later, she would return home through the same imaginary door. *How long had they been together?* Frida had no idea.

But in any case, it didn't matter. She would erase the "door" with her hand, and run with her secret to the farthest corner of the patio. There, alone under a cedron tree, she would laugh and shout aloud, astonished and delighted by her happiness.

As Westerners, we tend to make hard and fast distinctions between reality and imagination, between the waking world and the world of dreams. But not all people operate like this. The Sufi mystical tradition includes a kind of halfway house known as *alam al-mithral,* where imaginary beings have a real existence of their own. It is always difficult to translate across cultures, but Kahlo's imaginary friend would seem to belong to such an intermediate realm. Like the *fios* or *imbas* of the Celtic bards, it is one with which many writers and artists are familiar. Flaubert, for example, though he worked hard, diligently researching the background of his books, often wrote from what he himself called "visions." It would be easy to confuse this "inward vision" with classic hallucinations. But that would be a mistake.

> During what is properly called hallucination, terror is always present; you feel your personality escaping, you think yourself about to die. With the poetic vision, on the contrary, *something enters into you . . .*

Sometimes the vision would take form slowly, "piece by piece, as the parts of a scene slide on to the stage," and sometimes it would pass by, swift and fleeting. But in either case, there was a certain urgency involved. "Something passes before your eyes; then you must throw yourself eagerly upon it."

Without the necessary time and space, it would be almost impossible to entertain such visions. Lin Yutang praises the simple act of lying down, free to dream or cogitate or muse. He points out that many harried businessmen would make twice as much as they do if they would only permit themselves an hour's solitude awake in bed. There, comfortably stretched out in their pajamas, free of their stiff collars and heavy shoes, they would finally be free to think at their leisure, "for it is only when one's toes are free that one's head is free, and only when one's head is free is real thinking possible."

Among such productive idlers were Walt Whitman, Edith Wharton, and G. K. Chesterton, each of whom liked to lie in bed comfortably late in the morning, propped up against their respective pillows, busy with writing board and pen. Like the eighteenth-century Irish bard who preferred to close his eyes against the brilliant sun, they felt that without "a dark bed" to protect them, they would lose all their skill.

BEFRIENDING THE DREAM

Freud claimed, famously, that dreaming was "the royal road to the unconscious," and there is no question that his *Interpretation of Dreams* (published in 1899, but dated 1900 to coincide with the new century) ushered in a new era of theory and research that held sway until his death. Nonetheless, for many of his readers, the symbols came to seem too literal, the interpretation a touch too heavy-handed. In the course of Freud's analysis, the mystery and poetry of the dreams—their sheer surprising *gift*—was almost entirely destroyed.

Jung's attitude was very different. For him, there was little difference between dreams and poetry: both worked through imagery and symbol, and it was the task of the analyst to recognize this, without forcing a translation into acceptable social terms. He felt it was his task to help the dreamer "to honor the forgotten language of himself," asking of any particular dream, "What does it want? For what conscious attitude does it compensate?" This was not the same, he emphasized, as asking, *What does it mean?*

The contemporary Jungian James Hillman writes in similar terms: "To ask of a dream, what does it mean, is as misguided as to ask the same question of a person or a poem, or of a sunset." Instead, he says, one should attempt to *befriend the dream*. "Befriending the dream begins with a plain attempt to listen . . . to set down on paper or in a dream diary . . . just what it says."

Jung himself provides an impressive role model for this approach.

From childhood on, he had a tremendously rich and complicated dream life, much of which he recorded in a series of dream journals, among them the famous *Red Book*. He filled this heavy parchment volume with elaborate hand-painted dreams: a portrait of his shadow, cowering in ulster and top hat; a fiery cross, blazing above a contemporary urban landscape. Later, he transferred some of these dream images to the walls of his house in Bollingen. His friend Laurens van der Post found those murals "so decisive and electric" that he could barely sleep in the same room with them. One image was especially haunting. This was the old man Philemon, with his handful of keys, his bull-like horns, and his dazzling bright blue wings. Jung held hundreds of conversations with this being, using what he called "active imagination," a willed state somewhere between dream and waking life. Philemon was for him a sage, a wise and brilliant spirit, the loving father he had never had. "He said things I had not consciously thought," reported Jung.

Any of us can take the time to draw our dreams, or to converse with the images that recur. In her essay "Dream as Story," Jungian analyst Edith Sullwold encourages people to use clay and paint, movement and music to explore their experience more fully. It also helps to share our dreams with friends and family, whether casually, or in a formal dream group. When dreams are made welcome in this way, they can become a powerful source of healing, providing courage for the road ahead, and helping to integrate what has been forgotten or denied.

For many years, the conductor David Blum kept a record of his dreams, illustrating each one in great detail. After he was diagnosed with cancer, the images in his dreams became his guides. "The dreams are larger than I am," he said. "They explain me more than I can explain them."

DANDELION CLOCKS

Among our multitude of dreams, there are some that seem astonishing even to ourselves, which, in Emily Bronte's words, go through one's life "like wine through water." Such dreams seem larger and wiser than ourselves, as if they had reached us from a place outside of time. Henry Vaughan's poem "The World" has this quality of mystery and revelation:

> *I saw Eternity the other night*
> *Like a great Ring of pure and endless light,*
> > *All calm as it was bright;*
> *And round beneath it, Time, in hours, days, years,*
> > *Driven by the spheres,*
> *Like a vast shadow moved, in which the world*
> > *And all her train were hurled.*

Some years ago, I too had such a vision. This was long before the breakup, when I was still living happily with Rosie. In the dream, I was standing with a dandelion in either hand, each stalk bearing a full head of white seeds, round and luminous and about twice their normal size. These seed heads were, I knew, my soul and hers. They were fragile, obviously, but also radiant, and I understood that although they were "clocks" they would not be blown until we died, when their seeds would scatter into eternity. It made me glad to think of death as a sower, not a reaper. I realized too that although the two flowers were the same (indeed, identical, to all appearances) and would vanish in the same way at the end, they were also, for the moment, individual, bounded orbs.

I gazed at those dandelions for a long time: the delicacy of each lifted seed, the air between, the sense of that shriveled core at the heart of it all that was so utterly unimportant. *This is your soul* was the message, and when you looked more closely, you could see that of course the soul was perfect: not worn by human age or strain. It had a gorgeous radiant aura all its own. It was strangely comforting to have this revealed in such simplicity and truthfulness. It is an image I've returned to many times.

Many years later, in researching the material for this book, I came upon a reference to the way psychics understand the manifestation of human consciousness. Apparently, every human being, when viewed as an energy field, seems to be made up of a dazzling, egg-like shape, from which issues threads or filaments of light. This image is confirmed in greater detail by the Irish seer George Russell, here describing a particular vision:

> There was a dazzle of light, and then I saw that this came from the heart of a tall figure with a body apparently shaped out of half-transparent or opalescent air. . . . [T]hroughout the body ran a radiant, electrical fire, to which the heart seemed the center. Around the head of this being and through its waving luminous hair . . . there appeared flaming wing-like auras. From the being itself light seemed to stream out in every direction; and the effect left on me after the vision was one of extraordinary lightness, joyousness, or ecstasy.

It is perhaps not accidental that the word "dream" is itself linked to this ecstasy, drawn as it is from the Old English *dream* meaning "joy" and "music" as well as the Old Frisian *dram* meaning both "dream" and "(shout of) joy." Lucid dreamers— those people who can "wake up" inside a dream, realize that they are dreaming, and at the same time recall their daily lives—often describe their inner universe as one of light. The medieval mystic Hildegard von Bingen illustrated her visions, as did the poet William Blake. In both cases, these appeared when they were sleeping, and in modern parlance, would be understood as lucid dreams.

Not surprisingly, there are links between lucid dreaming and meditation (the regular practice of meditation has been found to increase the frequency of lucid dreams), as well as between dreams and prayer. Brother David Steindl-Rast claims that we pray unconsciously, dream after dream, and that such open-hearted, open-ended prayers are among the most effective. There is a special word in Arabic, *i-stingara*, for a "request for spiritual or practical assistance in the form of a dream." But at times, it seems, the very urgency of our need may be enough.

After she had published *The Color Purple*, Alice Walker was faced with a barrage of contradictory responses: on the one hand, the book was being attacked; on the other, it was being praised and winning prizes. During that time, she had several "dream-visits" from people she had known before they died, and from her immediate ancestors as well.

> But then, at my most troubled, I started to dream of people I'd never heard of and never knew anything about, except, perhaps, in a general way. . . . Once a dark, heavy-set woman who worked in the fields and had somehow lost the two middle fingers of her right hand took hold of my hand lovingly, called me "daughter," and commented approvingly on my work. . . . I remembered her distinctly next morning because I could still feel her plump hand with its missing fingers gently and firmly holding my own.

Tibetan Buddhists pray for lucid dreams, hoping to teach themselves that both dreams and waking existence can be seen as equally dreamlike. They believe that if we can learn to live consciously inside our dreams, we will be able to practice that same skill in waking life, and so pass through the doors of death with some measure of clarity and grace. Seen in these terms, writing is just another form of preparation, a quiet rehearsal for our own mortality.

Meanwhile, there is much to be learned on both side of the threshold. Or, as Rumi wrote some eight hundred years ago:

> *The breeze at dawn has secrets to tell you.*
> *Don't go back to sleep.*
> *You must ask for what you really want.*
> *Don't go back to sleep.*
> *People are going back and forth across the doorsill*
> *where the two worlds touch.*
> *The door is round and open.*
> *Don't go back to sleep.*

Tactics

↶ Allow plenty of time to sleep, and if possible, to wake up slowly.

↶ Keep a dream journal, and write down your dreams. Make time to talk them over with your friends.

↶ *Consider the following quotations:*
"I've dreamt in my life dreams that have stayed with me ever after, and changed my ideas; they've gone through and through me, like wine through water, and altered the colour of my mind."

EMILY BRONTË

"I have learned that dreams are more accurately set down in drawings (with color pens if dreaming in color) than in words. I divide the page into three sections because dreams are often in three acts, and do have beginning-middle-end."

MAXINE HONG KINGSTON

CHAPTER ELEVEN

A Universe of Stories

The world is a better place for having its stories told.
GRACE PALEY

Family Stories

I HAD ARRIVED IN GALLOWAY IN THE MIDDLE of September, a week or two before the equinox. An old man met me at the station, and helped me lug my heavy suitcase to the car. He was in his seventies, tall and rangy, an exact contemporary of my friend Alastair Reid. They had known one another as boys.

"And you are?"

"Christian," I told him. "Christian McEwen."

"McEwen," he repeated thoughtfully. "McEwen. You're not related to *Finn* McEwen, I suppose."

"Not Finn," I said. "But Finnie. Robert Finnie McEwen. He was my great-grandfather."

"Finnie! Yes!" The old man was exultant. "That's it. He rented the big house back in the early 1900s. Galloway House. So that was your grandfather."

"Great-grandfather," I corrected.

"That was your great-grandfather."

The old man had never met my great-grandfather. But he knew the stories. He had lived all his life in that little corner of southwest Scotland, and for him every rock and tree and rounded tussock had a tale to tell. Naturally he would have heard of the legal man, the stranger, who had come down from Edinburgh in 1905 and moved into Galloway House with his wife and children. And naturally too, as a man of almost eighty, with the well-stocked mind of the dedicated oral historian, he would have a sense of the larger extended clan.

"Are you any relation to *Hugo* McEwen?"

This was like the card game Happy Families.

"He's my first cousin—"

"Ah—"

Hugo, it turned out, was a contemporary of his own son, Finn, from whom I was renting High Lodge. And the Lodge (a quirky little rock and sandstone house, with two pointed gables and a wide view over the bay) had been built to mark one of the entrances to Galloway House. Almost a hundred years after my great-grandparents and their four children had left the area, I, however temporarily, was moving in.

Barring the absence of bloodshed and betrayal, this seems to me a quintessentially Scottish story, a story of land and memory, people and place, stretching with casual efficiency across time. I was delighted by our conversation, as if a shimmering tartan shawl had been magically unfurled from inside a hazelnut, a fairy shawl woven of mist and thistledown, with the colors of the heather running through it, and the sharp green of infant beech leaves. The old man's questions drew me back into the embrace of such a shawl, and I luxuriated in it. I was part of the family again, part of the clan.

At the same time, of course, I wanted to break free. That shawl meant the past, meant class and history and tradition, which I had spent much of my life trying to escape.

For us as children, growing up at Marchmont, it was hard not to believe that everything interesting had happened long before we were born. The past colored everything we knew, from the blue-gray Cheviots on the far horizon to the songs we sang and the stories we were told. The pale faces of our ancestors stared down from the high walls of the dining room. We ate at tables they had eaten at, used the knives and forks that they had used. Every day we walked as they had, following the nannies down the long front drive. Our present was no more than a thin white scrim, a narrow margin, dwarfed by the busy, word-producing racket of the past.

At twenty-one, I left the British Isles, and took off—in triumph— for the United States. My first week in New York, friends took me to dinner at a vast apartment somewhere on the Upper East Side.

"How long have you lived here?" I asked my host, gazing out at the glittering lights across the river.

"Oh, a long time now," he said. "Two years at least."

"*Two years?*" I echoed. Marchmont had been built in the 1750s. My family had moved there before the First World War, and were still seen locally as newcomers. Two years meant nothing, even to me: a couple of Christmases, two or three inches of growth. What could he possibly mean by "a long time"?

It is the sort of question Howard Mansfield tries to answer.

AMERICAN AMNESIA

Howard Mansfield is a lively energetic man, a writer and historian, with several projects always on the go. His quirky wit is immediately apparent, as is his head of dark and curly hair, each tendril of which seems to have a mind of its own. He describes his corner of New Hampshire as "kind of a poky place. Not hip. Not cool. There's something kind of frumpy about it, you know." But that is exactly what he likes about it. The "pokiness" allows him space and solitude, time to read and relax and find his way.

Mansfield grew up on Long Island, at a time when it was still rural enough for human history to leave its mark. He remembers a certain corner where a young couple crashed their car just days before their wedding, and how his father would be reminded of the tragedy each time they passed the spot. Today that area is heavily congested and built up. "The death of a young couple would still upset," he writes. "But probably only for a day or two." After that, "the sheer push of a million daily routines" would erase all memory.

Mansfield's grandparents were Jewish immigrants, who refused, for obvious reasons, to talk about the past, or what they always called "the Old Country." Mansfield understands that attitude all too well. "The message is, 'Cling to the past, and you'll be wiped away.'" But as a historian, the specificities of time and place are crucial to his understanding. Until standard time zones were introduced, every city, town, and hamlet had a rhythm of its own. In a recent book, *Turn &*

Jump, Mansfield examines diaries, journals, and daily newspapers, in an effort to isolate that vanished time, and somehow find a way to make it visible. *What was considered rapid?* he asks himself. *How long did it take to get a letter? How long did people dwell on something? How long did memory survive?*

In most cases, it was not for very long. As Americans, amnesia has become part of our identity. "We're an immigrant culture," he tells me. "A frontier culture. There's always a third, fourth, fifth act. There's a sense you can improve your lot at any time. Try your luck somewhere else."

Such an attitude can look supremely optimistic. But it has a sad and vicious undertow as well. As Mansfield explains, "In every building leveled and every building cleared, we say, 'We just don't want to hear about it any more.' We have made our bargain. We have speed and power, but no place. Travel, but no destination. Convenience, but no ease." It is as if we had traded memory for momentum, fidelity and rootedness for the flash of an anonymous plastic card. Milan Kundera says it best, perhaps, in his novel *Slowness.*

> Our period is obsessed with the desire to forget, and it is to fulfill that desire that it gives over to the demon of speed; it picks up the pace to show us that it no longer wishes to be remembered, that it is tired of itself; that it wants to blow out the tiny troubling flame of memory.

OTHER PEOPLE'S STORIES

Across the length and breadth of human history, such insistent amnesia would have been seen as very odd indeed. Every culture on the earth tells stories. The human brain is specifically wired to create coherent narrative. And for the past fifty thousand years, such storytelling has been among the unquestioned pleasures of each ordinary day. Jubal Merton, who grew up in the English village of Akenfield in the early 1900s, remembered twenty or more people gathering together each evening just to talk.

They sat on the verge if it was fine and on the benches inside the shop if it was wet. . . . It was the good time of day and we all looked forward to it. We told each other about the things that happened to us, only a long time ago. People didn't usually tell each other things that were happening to them at that moment! But if it had happened years ago—no matter how awful it was—you could tell it.

They sang songs too, and practiced step dancing. But by 1969, when Merton was interviewed, nobody did that any more. As he explained, "All that is finished now. People are locked in their houses with the television and haven't any more time for talk and the like."

In the States, television has been widely available since the late 1950s, and despite competition from more recent media, it is still the focus of most contemporary homes. Human beings have been using fire for at least half a million years (some say as long as 790,000 years) so our desire to gather together round a shimmering light source is one that is deeply familiar. (The word *focus*, in fact, is drawn from the Latin for "hearth.") But where a fire shifts and crackles, requiring to be fed, a television asks nothing but one's slumped attention. The average person may look away from the screen as many as 150 times an hour, but he or she will also be drawn back. If a glance lasts longer than fifteen seconds, it is likely to stretch out into at least ten minutes.

Community is one of the first casualties of that seductive presence, and with it the shared history of that community, its local tales and habits and traditions. Such loss extends from the outer perimeter of friends and neighbors to the heart of the nuclear family. Whereas a fire allows for silence, storytelling, laughter, above all, perhaps, the act of reverie, television has a flattening, deadening effect. The child will play with his toys only half as often when the television is turned on; his parents will respond to him at least a fifth less often than usual, and his grandmother's concentration will be broken. Many families now spend more time watching TV than they do actually talking together; some, indeed, scarcely seem to talk at all, and prefer to communicate by reading one another's blogs. It is as if ordinary, unprocessed human storytelling had somehow grown too slow, too unpredictable, too *dull.*

The writer Sam Keen believes that we have become saturated with those media-generated stories; that we are, as he says, "written on from the outside." Other people's lives invade our dreams and nightmares, the quiet reaches of our private thoughts. Medieval towns were built around churches, their steeples pointing towards heaven. Present day suburbia is twisted inward towards the ubiquitous glowing screen. But there is, in his terms, no organizing principle, no shaman or storyteller to act as guide. Few of us have time to process the stories that we hear, to link them up with other stories, to construct a plot, a pathway through.

One could argue that the popularity of memoir and "reality TV" is in fact some kind of antidote to this: an effort to regain centrality in our own lives, in the face of the media juggernaut of loss and grief we can do so little to assuage. It is possible to see the flood of victim and survival narratives (the explosion, for example, of recovered memory stories in the early nineties) as an attempt to right the balance in human terms, to reclaim our stories for ourselves. But such tales of escalating horror lead, all too soon, to numbness and withdrawal, and perhaps to a distrust for more subtle, gentler memories. What we really hunger for is something else: the luxury of time to mull things over, to lay out thoughts and memories as a child might play with seashells on the beach, *to see how things fit together, where they best belong,* to build a shelter with a trusted friend, and then to set up house in it, and call it ours.

THE STORYTELLER

Walter Benjamin's essay "The Storyteller" was first published in 1955, some fifteen years after his death. More than half a century later, it is still very much worth reading. Benjamin presents it as a consideration of the work of the nineteenth-century Russian novelist Nikolai Leskov, but the area he covers is in fact far broader and more generous.

Like Howard Mansfield, like Jubal Merton, Benjamin believed

that the art of storytelling was coming to an end. For him, this was precipitated by the devastation of the First World War. "A generation that had gone to school on a horse-drawn street-car now stood under the open sky in a countryside in which nothing remained unchanged but the clouds." Those soldiers who did return unhurt came home silent, unable to communicate what they had seen. Meanwhile, via radio and newspapers (if not yet television), the air was charged with information, the news of the world unspooling fresh each morning, factual, accurate, unremitting, and, in Benjamin's words, "shot through with explanation."

Benjamin himself was not especially impressed by information or analysis. From his point of view, much of the art of storytelling was to keep a story free of exegesis. He would have agreed with the poet Valéry, who wanted "to give the feeling without the boredom of its conveyance." Leskov was a master of this, as was Chekhov. Where journalism was dependant on facts, on the diligent accumulation of data, Benjamin saw storytelling as deeper, richer, altogether more mysterious. He believed that stories should contain *something useful:* a moral, a proverb, a piece of practical advice: something durable and concentrated. For him, good stories were like seeds that had been locked up, deep inside the storage chambers of the pyramids. Millennia might pass. But still they would retain their germinating power.

Whether the storyteller had come from far away, or, like Alastair Reid's old friend, had somehow been able to stay put, rooted in a familiar childhood landscape, the implication was that he had had time to brood over his tales, to come to a sense of their weight and heft and potency. A storyteller had to *earn* the right to a particular story, and this was true of the audience as well. Without "enough time," enough leisure and patience, the story might be heard, but it would not be remembered or passed on. Once again, a pause, a gap, was necessary, if the gift were to be successfully communicated. Only then could the listener read the expression on the storyteller's face, catch her gestures, or learn to mimic the movements of her entire body. In Benjamin's words, "Boredom is the dream bird that hatches the egg of experience."

The philosopher Martin Buber liked to repeat a certain story, told him by a Hassidic rabbi. This man's grandfather had been lame for many years. But when he was asked about the Baal Shem Tov, whose disciple he had been, he at once began to evoke his master in great detail, describing how he used to dance each time he prayed. In the course of telling this, he naturally began to act it out, and before he knew it, found himself caught up in an ecstatic swirling dance. At that moment, his lameness fell away, and he was healed.

"And that," explained the rabbi, "is the way one is supposed to tell a story."

Stories are miraculous and life-changing, not just because of the nugget of truth at their core, but because they are *whole body events* communicated through every fiber of one's being. In a world of information overload, made up of thin, single-stranded surf-by interactions, such thorough nourishment is undeniable. My friend Terry Iacuzzo, a professional psychic, says she can always tell when someone is describing a real-life relationship, as opposed to one that is occurring only in cyber-space. People who have spent actual time together will be alert and energized from top to toe; soul and spirit, body and intellect, are all involved. A cyber-space romance is far more verbal and jazzy and narcissistic. Its sphere of influence is restricted, like a plastic bubble round a person's head.

Stories unfold across years and decades; they need time to ripen, time to be listened to and understood. The stories that were told at the evening gatherings in Akenfield were not the little happenings of the present day. They were drawn from events that had occurred years earlier, whose shape and meaning had only gradually become apparent. And they were told by older people, while the younger ones just listened. The elders might be ignorant of all the latest gadgets, but they had lived long enough to know what was worth telling: they could see the larger picture; the seeds they carried still had strength to flower.

THE LISTENING AUDIENCE

By the early 1990s, I had a job as writer-in-residence with the intergenerational theater group Roots & Branches, which was directed by my good friend Arthur Strimling. Once a week, elders from a Jewish senior center would meet up with a small group of acting students from Tisch School of the Arts, itself part of New York University. Strimling would pick a theme, and everyone would tell stories together and come up with scenes and improvisations, which were gradually reshaped into a full-length play.

One of the seniors was a man called Samuel Isaacs. Sam was in his seventies, square and stooped, with a shining bald head and a stomach that pushed out under his shirt. His hip hurt, and he found it hard to walk. He hated our weekly warm-ups, and much preferred to huddle in the corner over that morning's bagel and cream cheese and a steaming cup of coffee from the deli. I think he felt that warm-ups were unnecessary, at least for him. The rest of us could do them if we wanted to. He was different, still the curly headed cherub of his early years, the pampered child, his mother's little darling.

"I was the kind of boy women adored," he told us once. "I had the curse of beauty. It's hard to believe that now. But when I was a boy, I was very nice looking."

No one finds it easy to leave the bosom of a loving family for the harsh reality of a working life. But for Sam this was perhaps especially so. And though he was employed for many years as a social worker, and then as a tax auditor for the IRS (a job he loathed), there was a sense in which he never did grow up. The world frightened him, or so he told us, and he spent as much time as he could going to concerts and plays and to the movies. He loved books, and had a tremendous library.

"That was your real life, wasn't it?" I asked him once. "In the evenings, and at weekends?" "No," he said. "I didn't have a real life." And then he corrected himself. "*This* is my real life."

When Sam first joined Roots & Branches, he was extremely suspicious. He didn't trust the other members of the group, and he had a hard time taking directions. The improvisations troubled and upset him. But by the time I joined the company in 1991, that dubious, belligerent Sam had almost disappeared. Each week he opened up more and more. He was *telling himself to us*, risking his truth: his anger and sadness and frustration, his moments of yearning and hopefulness and joy. He was like someone with a gold mine in his back yard, who has suddenly realized just how valuable it is. The stones were flying, the dirt was all over the place, the glittering depths were gradually being revealed. For him, there was the profound pleasure of self-recognition and discovery; for the rest of us, the excitement of generating live and original material. It was clear to everyone that this was an experience that could not have occurred in private. The listening (and eliciting) audience was essential.

When the tsunami reared itself out of the Indian Ocean in December 2004, leaving death and destruction in its wake, playwright Eve Ensler flew to Sri Lanka, and spoke to the survivors there. At every refugee site she visited, people would line up, "as if waiting for food," in order to tell their stories. As each one came forward, the others would gather round to listen, all of them at different stages of grieving. Telling such stories, particularly to an outsider, was, Ensler wrote, a "crucial ritual." No technical skills were required. All that mattered was that she had time to listen.

Such "listening" derives from over eighty years of American documentary work, starting in the 1930s with folk-life archivist Alan Lomax, and culminating in the work of the extraordinary Studs Terkel, who blazed the way across the last half century with his award-winning radio and oral history projects. Warren Lehrer and Judith Sloan (whose work I quoted in "The Great Good Place") are part of that same tradition. Their book, *Crossing the Boulevard*, grew out of a three-year interviewing project based in Astoria, Queens, the most ethnically diverse community in the United States.

In recent years, the torch has been picked up by radio documentary maker Dave Isay. Isay (and what genial ancestor blessed him with that name?) is the founder of StoryCorps, now the largest oral history project in U.S. history, and the author of several books, including the aptly titled *Listening is an Act of Love*. The StoryCorps Project opened in New York City in 2003, and has since spread across the entire United States. Any member of the public may check into a booth for forty minutes, to trade "wisdom stories" with a friend or family member. At the end, participants are given a professional-quality CD with a recording of their interview. If they agree, a second copy is placed in the Library of Congress, and excerpts may be used on the radio, or as part of local community displays. But Isay's chief concern is to create an enjoyable experience for the storytellers themselves; it is for him, "A project that tells people that they matter."

It is, as he says, a remarkably simple idea. But in a media dominated by bad news, with a persistent focus on rich people and celebrities, it is also truly original and democratic. Isay hopes that, over time, it will teach us all to be better listeners, nourishing intergenerational connections, and encouraging everyone to elicit more stories of their own. "With a little luck," he says, "StoryCorps will one day grow into an oral history of our nation."

JUST IN CASE

Years ago, long before I met Arthur Strimling, he had a dear friend called Barbara Meyerhoff. The story that follows is itself about storytelling: a story that Strimling learned from Meyerhoff, and that I have borrowed (with gratitude) from him.

Back in the 1970s, Barbara Meyerhoff was teaching urban anthropology at the University of Southern California, and asked her students to conduct an oral history interview of their own. This was not to be with a friend or family member, but instead with someone "on the periphery of their vision," someone they might see every day, but whom, until then, they'd never really noticed. One of her students, a hunky physical education major by the name of Seth, decided to interview his family's live-in housekeeper. This was the person who had picked up his socks and cleaned his room for his whole life, the one who'd ironed his shirts and made his bed. He knew her first name, Carmen, but that was all. And so he went with his tape recorder to her little room behind the kitchen, the little room with its single bed and its single chair, and he asked her to tell him the story of her life.

It turned out she'd been born in Mexico in poverty. That as a child she'd almost starved to death. That she had smuggled herself across the border at night, and made her way to Los Angeles, where, for a while, she found work as a prostitute. There'd been a stint in jail, a series of turbulent relationships, and then a stretch where she'd worked three jobs simultaneously, putting her brother through school. And finally, there she was, under Seth's own roof, taking care of someone else's children six days of the week so that, once a week, on Sunday, she could finally spend some free time with her own.

This is not an unusual story. But for Seth it was a revelation. He was blown away.

"So, did listening to Carmen's story change you in any way?" Meyerhoff asked him later.

"Yeah," said Seth uncomfortably. "Yeah. Now when my brother starts to tease her, I go, 'No, don't do that. . . .'" He didn't have the words. But there was no doubt that the experience had changed him. In Strimling's terms, Seth had begun to grow a soul.

Then Barbara Meyerhoff gave her students one more task. They were to go back to the person they had interviewed, and they were to thank that person, to give them some kind of gift: a transcript of the interview, a bunch of flowers, a poem. So Seth went back to the little room behind the kitchen. He sat down on that one chair, and he thanked Carmen for everything she'd given him.

"But no, *niño*," she said. "It is I who must thank you."

"Why?" he asked, bewildered.

"Because every night I come up to my room and I lie on my little bed, and I tell myself the story of my life—just in case someone should ever ask."

TOLD POETRY

The poet Verandah Porche grew up in Teaneck, New Jersey. Her mother liked to talk, whereas her father was, she says, "a particularly silent person." The children used to refer to her father as "The Word," and to her mother as "The Word Revealed." Her family, like Howard Mansfield's, were Jewish immigrants, with some fiercely painful, and fiercely hidden, stories.

Both my parents believed that pain should be hidden. And of course I was born right on the heels of the Holocaust. I can understand, looking back, why there was so much too horrible to tell.

Porche learned those "core stories of real terrible pain" only very late, in her teens and early twenties. She finds it ironic that she, who as a girl was thought to be so heedless, should have developed such a passion for listening. But that is in fact what she has done, listening to people's stories, writing them down, and in the process inventing a life and livelihood in what she calls "told poetry."

Porche moved to Vermont in the late 1960s, as part of the "back to the land movement," and published her first book of poems not long after, which meant that she was eligible to work as a writer-in-the-schools for the Vermont Arts Council. This in turn opened the door to a series of residencies in local nursing homes, working mostly with older rural women. To begin with, each participant would be given pencil and paper and an individual TV tray, so they could write their poems and stories for themselves. But it soon became apparent that they didn't really want to write; they wanted to *have their stories told.* It was clear too, that their writing voices were rather different from what Porche calls "their recollective voices," and that their "recollective voices" were, in fact, considerably more interesting. "I became fascinated with the idea of poems that fell out of the air—'found poems, told poems'—poems that grew out of conversation." She would lose track of the information she was being given, because she was so struck by the language people used. "The way that they spoke, their think patterns and speech patterns, just stopped my mind. And I wanted to hold onto those things. They fascinated me."

Early on, she used one of her childhood memories as a prompt, describing the smell of gefilte fish in her grandmother's kitchen. A woman called Hazel Amidon pulled herself up from her reclining chair, and began to talk about her own grandmother, and how she had scrubbed the floor with lye. *"She didn't have much to do with, but she did with what she had,"* she told Porche. Thirty years later, Porche can repeat the sentence perfectly, delighting in its precision, "just the single syllable staccato punches of that line." She marvels at the potency that lay compacted there. "There was a whole belief system mixed in with the sensation of the kitchen floor and the lye and the brush and all. It just seemed like pay dirt."

An elegant woman, stylish and original with enormous hooded eyes, Porche had no professional models for what she was doing. "I was just making a living," she says now. But little by little, she began to develop her role as literary amanuensis. At first she worked with a pencil and chart paper, simply taking dictation. Then she bought a laptop computer, and shifted from group work to what she calls "one-on-one transmission." Someone would start to talk, and she would listen. Sometimes she would introduce the task more formally, explaining that they were creating "a piece of personal literature . . . a shape to hold a memory or an imagining or a reflection." But mostly, she would just start typing in a wild shorthand. "And when people reached a part that really fascinated me we would slow down and try to focus on that."

She realizes now how much her questions and curiosity helped to shape the finished product. The work was a kind of triad, braiding together her voice and theirs and then the third voice that was the artistic one. Not everybody understood what was involved. But they were usually more than pleased by the results. "Oh, you make me sound so much more interesting than I am!" they'd tell her, or, "Nobody ever asked me *that* before!"

"It's as though specific asking creates the pathways for the specific telling," Porche says. Most people, she feels, don't think to ask sufficiently interesting questions, or pause to savor the answers. Her own mind is naturally "very hectic, *hither and yon, hither and yon.*" But the work has given her the opportunity to slow down. It has also resulted in numerous publications over the years: chapbooks, poetry pamphlets, magazines, and other memorabilia, as well as paying the mortgage on her beautiful dilapidated farmhouse. From Porche's point of view, the talk is what makes it all worthwhile. That access to "repetition and variation . . . intimate cheek by jowl, lip to ear work," has given her life a richness and adventure she still relishes, the sudden pleasure of "the chance revelation," and "the slowness of the courtship" leading up to it.

GRACE NOTES

Telling stories can be a pleasure in and of itself; it can culminate in a performance, like our Roots & Branches work; in a legacy project, like StoryCorps; or in some version of "told poetry." It can also lead, very directly, to the writing of short stories. After all, as Grace Paley used to say, "When a story is told for the second time, it's fiction, no matter what."

Grace Paley published three collections of short stories over the course of her long life, as well as a book of essays and articles, and two volumes of poetry. But she herself wrote only poems till she was almost thirty. "I really was not all that interested in stories when I was a kid writing. I just went on writing poems all the time." At seventeen, she studied briefly with the English poet W. H. Auden. He took her out to lunch to discuss her work. "You really use words like this?" he asked her. "And this, and this, and this? *Subaltern?*" There she was in the South Bronx, writing poems with a cut-glass British accent. "So I got from him that I'd better learn my own language."

Paley had grown up with at least three languages: the Russian, Yiddish, and English spoken at home under her own immigrant roof, and the wider life of the immediate neighborhood. Children in those days (the 1920s and early 1930s) lived and played on the street, and their parents too would sit out on boxes and chairs and talk by the hour. For someone like Paley, it was all "terribly interesting. . . . they would be talking about in-laws, children, husbands, wives, what it was all about."

Storytelling, as she came to understand it, was not really possible without story-listening, and that, for her, meant listening with both ears: the greedy, ardent ear of childhood, and the traditionally educated literary ear. For years, teaching at Sarah Lawrence, she would begin each class by reading aloud a poem or two, or a few pages of prose. "I wanted them to listen to stories, to listen to people talk, *to listen.*"

She knew, of course, that writing stories was not a simple matter of transcription. There is a difference between the well-honed anecdote—the story that has been told a thousand times over, and that is both dulled and polished in the telling—and the story that appears as revelation, in response to the right interlocutor, the quirky unexpected question. If you tell a story too often, she said, there's no point in writing it. "There has to be some of the joy of mystery. . . . You write what you don't know about what you know." Crucial to her own work was a certain kind of idleness and receptivity.

> I have a basic indolence about me which is essential to writing. It really is. Kids now call it space around you. It's thinking time, it's hanging-out time, it's daydreaming time. You know it's lie-around-the-bed time, it's sitting-like-a-dope-in-your-chair time. And that seems to me essential to my work.

That indolence gave Paley the time she needed to brood over her stories, both the real and the invented. Most people write from just one voice inside themselves: the scholar, the aesthete, the fierce, unhappy child. But in Paley's case, all the selves are there at once: a giddy, talky chorus around her busy kitchen table. And there are other people's voices too, other sounds and rhythms, other lives. "If you speak for others . . . you'll really begin to be able to tell your own story better," she told her students. She advised them to read their work aloud to each other, to slow down and pay attention. "Because the eye is such a speedy thing. The eye goes *zzt, zzt, zzt,* you know? The ear says, 'Wait.' "

Or, as she put it in "A Poem about Storytelling," describing the artist-writer, *aka* Grace Paley, her own indolent, hard-working self:

> *She will listen*
> *It's her work   She will be the listener*
> *in the story of the stories*

SUNKEN MEADOW HEIGHTS

I have been teaching poetry for more than a dozen years, flying in for intensive weekend workshops all over the United States. Often, as the plane swoops in over the asphalt runway, I wonder about the original inhabitants of the land. *Who made love under that stunted bush? Who did their washing by that sparkling waterfall?* The street signs bear names like miniature elegies: "Lakeview Drive," "Plumtree Lane," "Orchard Street," "Singing Brook." It is hard not to lament the ugliness and monotony that have overtaken so many specific, storied places.

Close to where I lived as a child, there was a farm that went by the name of "Sorrowlessfield." The name dates back to the battle of Flodden in 1513, the worst defeat ever inflicted on a Scots army. Five thousand men were killed, many from the surrounding Border country. But the son of the house returned home unscathed, and all his men with him. Hence, the rejoicing; hence, half a millennium later, the triumphant name. Or that, at least, is what I was always told. When I asked my brother John for confirmation, he told me that in fact the name is considerably older. It originates not with Flodden, but four centuries earlier, with King David I, who granted the land to his friend, the Baron de Sorules. So much for its dazzling antecedents!

Tim Robinson, writer and cartographer extraordinaire, lived for twelve years on the Aran Islands, off the west coast of Ireland. The largest of these is only nine miles long by two and a half miles wide, but every windy slope and rocky inlet is dense with brilliant, contradictory Gaelic names. Scholars talk in disparaging terms of the "corruption" of certain names; they forget that corruption is by its nature fertile. Most place names, says Robinson, are perpetually gathering and shedding different meanings. The mythical "Lake Isle of Innisfree" probably derives from the Gaelic *Inis Fraoigh*, which is to say, "the island of the heather." But the attraction of Yeats's poem lies in that one anglicized syllable, "free." As Robinson says, "One doesn't dream-visit his isle for its heather, but for its freedom from the cares of the city."

Here in the States, we have become inured to fake names, many of them concocted (by the real estate agents? by the city fathers?) with no regard at all for either history or topography. Instead of Station Road or Plastics Avenue, we are greeted with such absurdly oxymoronic monikers as "Ridge Dale" and "Sunken Meadow Heights" or, for that matter, the New York City suburb of "Forest Hills," itself built on a low-lying tract of treeless ground.

But for those who know and love their home territory, naming names can be a pleasure, in and of itself. The Indian national anthem is nothing but a litany of beloved names. David Abram tells a lovely story about the anthropologist Keith Basso, who worked for many years with the Western Apache in the Cibecue Valley of Arizona.

> While stringing a fence with two Apache cowboys, Basso noticed one of them talking quietly to himself. When he listened more closely, Basso discovered that the man was reciting a long series of place-names—"punctuated only by spurts of tobacco juice"—that went on for almost ten minutes. Later, when Basso asked what he'd been doing, the man replied that he often "talked names" to himself. "I like to," he told the anthropologist. "I ride that way in my mind."

Basso himself mapped 104 square kilometers in and around Cibecue, and identified almost three hundred place names, most of which took the form of complete sentences: for example, "big cottonwood trees stand spreading here and there," "coarse textured rocks lie above in a compact cluster," or "water flows down on top of a regular succession of flat rocks." The details are as compact as a haiku, as bright and precise as a picture postcard. It is easy to imagine the cowboy playing them over in his mind while his hands went on tinkering with the fence.

Language, said French phenomenologist Merleau-Ponty, is how the world speaks through us. "Language is the very voice of the trees, the waves, and the forests." To destroy that landscape (or to betray it by one's speed or inattention) is also to destroy those stories, for the land itself is a mnemonic, primed to remind us of all that has happened there.

For Australian aboriginals, each craggy rock, each softly mounded sand dune, has been called into being by the Ancient Ones, their ancestors, leaving behind a trail of words and music. Succeeding generations inherit those "Songlines" and the responsibility to preserve them, singing over the same ancestral songs, and following the same slow tracks. As writer Bruce Chatwin explains, "By spending his whole life walking and singing his Ancestor's Songline, a man eventually [becomes] the track, the Ancestor and the Song."

It is one thing to accomplish this at an ordinary walking pace; quite another when a Land Cruiser is involved.

Some time in the early 1980s, Chatwin was traveling though the Australian outback, along with a couple of friends, when a native man called Limpy asked to join them. He wanted to visit the Cycad Valley, a place of great importance to his own Songline, which had to do with the Tjilpa, or Native Cat. Chatwin made him welcome, and for seven hours, they just kept driving. Then, about ten miles from the Valley, their vehicle crossed a certain little creek, and Limpy sprang up like a jack-in-a-box, and began to mutter fiercely under his breath. Some time later, they crossed that same creek again, and Limpy bounced back into action, shoving his head through both windows of the Land Cruiser, and rolling his eyes wildly over the surrounding countryside. Once again, he began to mutter under his breath, a swift, persistent hiss, like the sound of wind through branches.

Chatwin himself might not have understood, but his driver, Arkady, knew exactly what was happening. Limpy had learned his Native Cat couplets for walking pace, which is to say, at about four miles an hour, and they were traveling at twenty-five. Quickly, Arkady shifted down into a lower gear, and the Land Cruiser slowed to the pace of a walking man. At once, "Limpy matched his tempo to the new speed. He was smiling. His head swayed to and fro. The sound became a lovely melodious swishing; and you knew that, as far as he was concerned, he *was* the Native Cat."

Limpy was fortunate. His ancestral territory had remained unspoiled, and he himself was well-prepared: he still knew all the stanzas of his song. With a little help from Arkady, land and words could be brought back into harmonious alignment. Not everyone is so lucky. Language, as well as land, is under siege, and to lose one's language is to lose access to the world that it describes. There are some sixty-five hundred languages in the world today, of which two die off every month. Each one contains colors and clarities known only to itself. In his poem, "Losing A Language," W. S. Merwin outlines the immensity of that loss:

> *many of the things the words were about*
> *no longer exist*
>
> *the noun for standing in mist by a haunted tree*
> *the verb for I*
>
> *the children will not repeat*
> *the phrases their parents speak*
>
> *somebody has persuaded them*
> *that it is better to say everything differently*
>
> . . .
>
> *nobody has seen it happening*
> *nobody remembers*
> *this is what the words were made*
> *to prophesy*
>
> *here are the extinct feathers*
> *here is the rain I saw*

A UNIVERSE OF STORIES

As human beings, we have all grown up listening to stories, even if they were the ersatz stories of the public media. We have all grown up on this rubbly round planet, even if our own home ground kept shifting, because our parents' work required them (and us) to move. As adults, we may not choose to honor place or story, or to remember either one with much precision. But they remain inside us nonetheless, returning in our dreams, our private imagery: the times we paddled in the city fountain, the tall and gnarly tree we liked to climb.

We may live "story-less" for decades at a time, barreling forwards into a world of sleek efficiency, where only factual information seems to count. But story will catch up with us in the end. According to the Cree people of Manitoba, stories are "round," and so too is the act of storytelling. When they're not being told, stories live off by themselves in their own villages. They gather at night, and talk to one another. But from time to time, a story will leave its village, and seek out a human being to inhabit. That person will become, as we say, "possessed" by the story, and will be impelled to carry it out into the world, "singing it back into active circulation."

Barbara McClintock won a Nobel Prize for the discovery of gene transposition in corn, a feat she accomplished, she said, by *listening to the corn*, "learning the story" of each individual plant. "I was part of the system," she explained. "I was right down there with them." Being possessed in this way (as I have found myself possessed by slowness in this book) is both a privilege and a challenge. Inhabited by story, one is also an inhabitant *of* story, held, once again, in the larger cycles of the cosmos. In Celtic mythology, the storyteller was Cernunnos, lord of the animals, a wise, majestic, antlered god. On the Gundesrup Cauldron, he sits cross-legged on the ground next to a great stag, holding a torc in one hand, and a ram-horned snake in the other. Fluently he moves between the worlds, part deer, part man; seer and visionary and healer.

"A tale is better than food," said the Celtic scholar Robin Flower.

Or perhaps it is more accurate to say that a tale itself *is* food. The right story at the right time can be a powerful kind of nourishment, lifting one out of confusion and bewilderment into a place of enchantment, a little pool of eternity. The child lying back drowsily on her pillow, while her father repeats her favorite story for the twenty-seventh time, is experiencing that enchantment. She knows, as the frazzled adult may not, that stories are concentrated medicine, concentrated forms of knowing. Beyond the beauty of the words and phrasing, the satisfaction of structure, lies something else: a thousand lifetimes of compacted human wisdom.

But as we have seen, it takes a certain patience to be available to this: a certain openness, a receptivity. The dominant culture does not especially value storytelling. Imagination is allowed to flaunt its wings, like a dragonfly glancing down across the surface of the water. But such casual visitations are not enough. We need to prepare a place for it, to make it welcome. As the artist Paulus Berensohn said in a recent interview, "Imagination, inspiration and intuition are all arts of the ear." In other words, they all require *deep listening*.

To find the nourishment that resides in stories, we have to allow ourselves to listen. The world is full of joyous messages. The surrounding landscape is radiantly alive. Just as Agassiz used to ask his students to draw and redraw the same dried fish, and the monks practiced *lectio divina,* reading and rereading the same short piece of scripture, so we too can learn to push past boredom and familiarity to a brand-new place of freshness and discovery.

The Russians have a term, *ostranyenie*, which may be useful here. Often translated as "defamiliarization" or "estrangement," this word, invented by the critic Viktor Shklovsky, means, literally, "to look at the familiar and have it become strange again." That "becoming strange" is what we need to learn, both in terms of listening, and of telling stories.

Any little tale can act as impetus, knitting us back into the fabric of the universe, and at the same time, reminding us of the marvel that it is to be alive. One of my favorites has to do with Theodore Roosevelt, who, as well as being president of the United States and the winner of the Nobel Peace Prize, could apparently hold his own with any naturalist or scientist of his day. It is recounted by his old friend William Beebe. After an evening of convivial talk, the two of them would saunter out onto the lawn, where they would search the sky for the shimmering patch of lights at the far left-hand corner of the Great Square of Pegasus. When they had found it, with or without glasses, one of them would recite:

> *This is the Spiral Galaxy in Andromeda.*
> *It is as large as our Milky Way.*
> *It is one of a hundred million galaxies.*
> *It is 750,000 miles away.*
> *It consists of one hundred billion suns,*
> *each larger than our sun.*

They would pause to imbibe the immensity of all this, and then Roosevelt would turn to Beebe and grin.

"Now I think we are small enough! Let's go to bed!"

A darkened lawn, a shimmering patch of sky; a universe of stories, the story of the universe.

Tactics

ᴥ Interview the oldest members of your family. Ask them to tell you a story they learned from someone who was very old when they themselves were young.

ᴥ Make a list of the stories you think of over and over again. Choose your favorite, and tell it from a different point of view, first to a trusted friend, and then in written form.

ᴥ *Consider the following quotations:*
"I have liked remembering almost as much as I've liked living."

WILLIAM MAXWELL

"Remember only this one thing," said Badger. "The stories people tell have a way of taking care of them. If stories come to you, care for them. And learn to give them away where they are needed. Sometimes a person needs a story more than food to stay alive."

BARRY LOPEZ

CHAPTER TWELVE

A Day So Happy

Take someone who doesn't keep score,
who's not looking to be richer, or afraid of losing,
who has not the slightest interest even
in his own personality: He's free.
RUMI

"I want! I want!"

IN MAY 1793, WILLIAM BLAKE PUBLISHED A strange little etching. It shows a naked sprite poised at the foot of a long ladder that leads up and up into the sky, grazing the slim crescent of the moon. The sprite's voice is visible in the caption underneath. "I want! I want!" it says.

American astronauts landed on the moon in 1969. But here on earth, the sprite's thin voice still whines across our airwaves: confirmation of our "hungry ghost" economy. In the Buddhist tradition, the hungry ghost has a huge belly and a tiny throat, but however much it eats, it's never satisfied. In the same way, we in the United States live with continually exacerbated "wanting mechanisms," always hurried, harried, obsessive, greedy, yearning. Such greed and neediness shows up even in our children, as Naomi Shihab Nye writes in one of her poems:

> Since when do children sketch dreams with price
> tags attached?
> Don't tell me they were born this way.
> We were all born like empty fields.
> What we are now shows what has been planted.

What has been planted is the *I want! I want!* of advertising, which thrives on envy and dissatisfaction. Advertising tells us that happiness can be bought if we will only put our minds to it, that we need only acquire the right house, the right appliances, the right car and TV and personal computer, and perpetual satisfaction will be ours.

In the last sixty years, we have listened attentively to such messages, and done our best to put them into practice. We consume twice as much now as we did in 1945. Our houses are three times as big as they were then. We are forever stockpiling more possessions. But happiness has continued to elude us.

According to a recent health survey, Americans are, in fact, the unhappiest people on the planet. 9.6 percent of us suffer from depression or bipolar illness—the highest rate of all the nations surveyed. Even the very richest among us claim an average happiness of 5.8 (on a scale of 0 to 7), the equivalent of the Inuit people of Greenland, and the cattle-herding Masai of Kenya. Meanwhile, the South Pacific island of Vanuatu, whose people live in mud huts with no electricity or running water, and whose only currency is pigs, has been rated as the happiest place on earth.

I wrote the bulk of this chapter in October 2008, when the seven hundred billion dollar bailout package had just been signed into law. The aging colossus of American capitalism had already begun to falter. It was clear, even then, that our easy assumptions of privilege, our many years of greed and peace and prosperity, were finally drawing to a close. Not even the richest and most well-ensconced could be certain of what lay ahead. At such times, the capacity for happiness is far from trivial. It is, instead, one of the few crucial strengths we have available: potent antidote to self-absorption and despair, welcome guide to grace and gratitude and praise.

THE ART OF HAPPINESS

The Buddhist teacher Thich Nhat Hanh says that the most precious gift a parent can provide is the gift of his or her own happiness. Happy parents give rise to happy children who themselves grow into happy adults. But what exactly constitutes that happiness? It's not something that our culture knows very much about.

The *DSM IV* (the *Diagnostic and Statistical Manual of Mental Disorders*) is the ur-text of the American Psychiatric Association, found on the shelves of every psychiatrist, psychologist, and psychotherapist in the nation. It lists each flickering ailment in the human psyche, from autism to pyromania. But there's no matching catalogue of mental well-being, distinguishing joy and pleasure, gladness and delight; no carefully alphabetized definitions of glee and gusto, felicity and bliss, rapture, jubilation and enchantment. Even now, professional books and articles having to do with anger, anxiety, and depression outnumber those dealing with joy and happiness by some fourteen to one.

Only in the last couple of decades has this begun to change, with the publication of Martin Seligman's *Authentic Happiness*, and the now classic opus, *Flow*, by his friend and colleague Mihalyi Csikszentmihalyi (pronounced "cheeks-sent-me-high," Seligman informs us, helpfully). Both have been instrumental in shifting focus from pathology and mental illness to what they call "positive psychology," or, in layperson's terms, *the art and analysis of human happiness*. According to Seligman's modest formula, happiness is determined by someone's personal "set-point" (which may well be genetic), plus the current conditions of their life and whatever voluntary activities they choose to undertake. As he explains it:

$$H = S + C + V$$

where S (the set-point) equals 50 percent; C (circumstances) equal 10 percent; and V (voluntary activities) account for the remaining 40 percent. What is striking here is how little satisfaction is contributed by such longed-for attributes as fame and fortune, good looks, education, social status, even health. Nor do more intractable facts such as age, sex, ethnicity, or local climate appear to make much difference to the equation. According to Seligman, all these things are subsumed under "circumstances," and account for no more than 10 to 15 percent of our total well-being.

Seligman does admit that some circumstances are more favorable than others. Climate may have little bearing on one's happiness, but the larger social structure matters a great deal. A wealthy, peaceful democracy is much preferable to an impoverished dictatorship. It also helps to have a job, or creative work, that one enjoys, and to be gregarious and outgoing: to make time for church or volunteer work, a sustaining social network. Marriage, in particular, is what is called a "robust" indicator of happiness. But none of these categories is ultimately definitive. Seligman's V (voluntary activities) still account for some 40 percent of the total. In other words, there are choices that will enhance it, both internal and external, choices that engage what Seligman calls one's "signature strengths," and that in turn open into joyful self-forgetfulness or "flow."

"How do you manage to be so happy all the time?" her friend Linsey Abrams asked short-story writer Grace Paley. "Even when things really aren't going very well?"

"I just decided," Paley told her. "At one point in my life, I just decided to be happy."

From Seligman's point of view, Paley *decided* to look with curiosity and gratitude at the past, and with hope and optimism at the years to come. She *decided* to savor the momentary pleasures that came her way (the smell of woodsmoke drifting across the yard, "the sun caught / in white and black winter / birches") and to give herself over to the practice of her own inimitable skills, in her case, a deliciously original literary voice. She also recognized how much happiness could be enhanced by indulging her own "basic indolence"—sitting late over breakfast with family or beloved friends; allowing time for reading, resting, gardening, dreaming.

BUDDHISM AND THE BRAIN

Most of us need to spiral inwards into calm and silence, to root ourselves in strength and steadiness, before we send out new tendrils of interest and activity. The fifteenth-century Tibetan scholar Tsongkhapa recognized the importance of this, using the analogy of a tapestry hung in a dingy, unlit room. If you have a "radiant, steady lamp," it will be easy for you to examine the tapestry, and to study its various images. But if your light is too dim, or the wind causes it to flicker, you won't be able to see the hanging properly. To do this, you need heart-felt commitment and sustained, focused attention: skills that Buddhist training can provide.

Buddhism has been concerned with the nature of the mind—and what one might call its "deepest flourishing"—for more than twenty-five hundred years. The Buddha's most senior disciple, Shariputra, was an expert meditator, able to track not just every individual movement of his mind, but *seventeen separate parts* of each movement. The Buddha himself was impressed by this achievement.

"It is as if you had taken a cup of water and described where each of the molecules originated. It is well done, Shariputra."

For many years, Western scientists refused to believe such skills were even possible. But recently, they have begun to recognize that our brains (even adult ones) do possess "neuroplasticity" after all, which is to say that they're adaptable, constantly evolving in response to new experience. Just as it takes some ten thousand hours to become an expert at chess, or to play the violin professionally, so too, it takes a lengthy apprenticeship to rewire the inner workings of one's mind. But with patience and persistence, it can be done. The tale of Matthieu Ricard is a case in point.

Ricard was born in France in 1946. His mother was a painter, his father a renowned philosopher. As a child at his parents' dinner table, he met people like André Breton and Igor Stravinsky: poets and musicians, artists and academics, the cream of French bohemian and intellectual life. He enjoyed their company, and had considerable respect for their achievements. But in themselves, they did not seem especially wise or perspicacious. That, as he saw it, was one of the failings of modern philosophy: that its ideas could be run "in neutral gear," and have almost no effect on its practitioners.

Then, in the mid-1960s, he saw some films about a group of lamas who had fled Tibet after the Chinese invasion, and was struck by what he called their "moral excellence." When a friend returned from Darjeeling having actually met these men, Ricard decided to set out on a similar pilgrimage. His first teacher was an elderly Tibetan lama called Kangyur Rinpoche. At that point, Ricard spoke very little English, while the Rinpoche spoke none at all. But in his presence,

Ricard experienced something that made words entirely irrelevant: the opportunity to "mix his own mind" with that of his teacher. Day after day, they sat in meditation together, and Ricard found himself moved to the core by the older man's serenity and strength. Years later, he remembered him "radiating goodness and compassion, sitting with his back to the window that looked out over a sea of clouds."

"You can't go and meet Socrates, listen to Plato debating, or sit at St. Francis' feet," he told his father. "Yet suddenly, here were beings who seemed to be living examples of wisdom."

It was the fall of 1966, and Ricard was twenty years old. He returned to France, and completed a PhD in cell genetics, spending the school year in Paris at the Pasteur Institute, and the summer months in Darjeeling. He made a number of original discoveries, and was seen as a promising young scientist. His superiors wanted to send him to the States, to continue his research. But in 1972, when his training was complete, Ricard went back to India, to study with Kangyur Rinpoche.

Ricard remained with Kangyur Rinpoche until the lama's death in 1975, and with his second teacher, Khyentse Rinpoche, for a further twelve. In 1979, he was ordained as a Buddhist monk. For the last thirty years, he has lived at the Shechen Monastery in Nepal, helping to publish many of the sacred texts of Tibetan Buddhism, and to translate them into English and French. He has also published several books under his own name, including a manual entitled *Happiness: A Guide to Developing Life's Most Important Skill.* In the meantime, he has acquired a different kind of fame, as a key subject in some crucial research having to do with the effects of meditation on the brain. His work with Richard Davidson, at the Laboratory of Affective Neuroscience in Madison, Wisconsin, is perhaps the best known.

As one of twelve experienced meditators, each with more than ten thousand hours of meditative training, Ricard was placed in an fMRI (a functional magnetic resonance imager), and required to meditate in turn on altruistic love and compassion; on attention *per se*; on so-called open presence; and on the visualization of mental images; in each case alternating thirty seconds of "down time" with ninety seconds of Buddhist practice.

While he was doing this, the fMRI measured the blood flow in different parts of his brain, mapping its workings in exquisite detail. The watching scientists were able to see a significant increase in what is called the left middle frontal gyrus, the area of the brain that is linked with joy and enthusiasm. It was clear that Ricard was a master of what Buddhists call *sukha*: a state of flourishing that arises from balanced composure and true insight. Not even the loudest "startle" experiment (115 decibels of white noise, equivalent to a gunshot going off beside the ear) was able to faze him. As scientist Paul Eckman explains, "When an emotion arises, Matthieu recognizes it simply as a cloud which passes by."

It would be easy to believe Ricard had always been this way. But when Eckman asked his mother about what he was like as a teenager, her response was: "very difficult." "I was quite a typical Parisian student," adds Ricard. "The word *happiness* did not mean much to me." He had some sense of his own potential for development, but no idea of what that might involve. Looking back, he pays tribute to his own truly remarkable teachers, and to the opportunity he has had to put their teachings into practice.

But as he says, "It's a matter of really transforming yourself, not just dreaming or twiddling your thumbs." The contemplative life asks considerable commitment. But that doesn't mean that it's impossible. Few of us could ever hope to be Olympic javelin throwers. "But all of us, if we practice, can learn to throw the javelin further."

CRISIS & OPPORTUNITY

Often, as I stand in yet another line waiting to show my driver's license and my boarding pass, waiting to set my coat and shoes in yet another plastic trug, I wonder how it would be if my flying mates and I were a little less preoccupied and self-absorbed, a little less comfortably naïve. What if we were refugees waiting for food or water to be distributed? What if we had lost our cars, our homes, our bank accounts? What if, like a fifth of all the people in Iraq today, we had been internally displaced? Would we still be tapping away at our BlackBerries, turning the tired pages of our magazines, grumbling at all the time we had to wait?

When I began teaching in the 1980s, my older students were in their mid-sixties and early seventies, which meant they had been young adults during World War Two. They remembered London during the Blitz: the blacked-out windows, the broken buildings, the empty craters where someone's house once stood. But they remembered the kindness, too, the generosity. Like the fireweed and brambles that colonized the torn-up bomb sites, human virtue flourished in the chaos.

In a recent essay, Rebecca Solnit describes the warmth and neighborliness in the days after the 1989 Loma Prieta earthquake. Sixty-three people in the Bay area died in the quake, and its blackouts and freeway collapses caused chaos for millions more. But as she writes, it also "shook us out of our everyday grudges and created a rare sense of fellowship." Crisis created camaraderie. It was no longer possible to be punctual or efficient in the usual ways, nor to maintain the greedy *want-want-want* perspective. Instead, there was the gift of present time, in which "nobody went to work and everybody talked to strangers."

If William James is right, and most of our usual misfortunes stem from loneliness, then crisis heals at least one chronic ailment, plus granting the rare chance to be heroic. After the planes crashed into the World Trade Center towers, hundreds of thousands of people were evacuated from Lower Manhattan—not by the police or the Coast Guard or the fire department, but, as Solnit points out—by a private armada of sailboats and barges and ferries, manned by ordinary untrained citizens. Simple self-interest would have sent them straight back home. Instead, crisis blossomed into opportunity.

Sometimes the journey is a shared and public one; sometimes it is considerably more private.

When my brother James killed himself in the summer of 1983, I was staying with friends at a farm outside Poughkeepsie. Stunned,

I sat for hours at an upstairs window, looking down at the swaying purple blossoms of the loosestrife, the small birds flirting and playing in the willow trees. My brother had died on June 18th, but by the time I learned the news it was late on 21st, and my friends had already planned a Solstice celebration. Each of us was to fix a candle to a cedar shingle, and set it floating across the dark waters of the pond: carrying a wish, a hope, a silent prayer.

After supper, a group of us gathered together at the water's edge. One by one, we lit a candle, and sent our rafts spinning out across the pond. I had prepared two shingles, one for James and one for me. Carefully, I placed them in the water. Other people began to talk and move away. But I stood watching for a long time, the small flames glinting like fireflies in the darkness. I had no words just then, but the image alone was sustaining: *light on water, light on water, light.*

Next morning, when I went back to the pond, James's raft and mine were side by side, bobbing together in the dark green reeds. Even in the midst of misery, I felt strangely grateful.

TURNING INWARDS

For Solnit, such crises work like a "crash course in consciousness," forcing us to be aware of our own mortality, and deepening our awareness of the present moment. When my friend Maia fell sick with an especially virulent strain of chronic fatigue, she was thirty years old: a single mother with two young children, going to school and working, and trying to maintain some sort of creative life. She was an all-A student, and had published several of her poems. But she was getting almost no sleep. In retrospect, she says, "It was ridiculous, what I was trying to do."

Maia and I talk on the phone at least twice a month, but I haven't seen her face-to-face for almost twenty years. I stare at her photograph: the rippling blonde hair, the wide-set blue eyes, trying to conjure her up, this dear friend, now in her sixties. It is hard to admit, but Maia has been sick for more than half her life. Clearly there have been losses at the very deepest level. She can hardly imagine how it might feel to be healthy again. Most of all, she says, she misses energy and spontaneity: those times when one has an idea, and is free to act on it immediately and with abandon. "You feel the joy of exuberance and stamina and all of that," she tells me. "Being sick means that you don't have that any more—that's broken."

But the opportunities are real and potent, too, not least in the surrender to a deepened receptivity, a strangely clarified and focused mode of looking. As she explains,

"Turning inward is so much more continuous. You discover not just the outside of things, but the inside, too. It's as if you are studying color and light for days and days; as if you're slowing down so much that you could slip between the molecules. You can watch clouds being born, really see them in the act, not as something accomplished, but gathering together and then withering away and disappearing and being utterly gone. You watch the whole entire cycle that you never usually see because it takes such time and stillness.

"And in the same way you can accumulate knowledge of people's feelings, you can watch them accumulate and reinforce each other, and you realize they belong to the same family of disappearing forms. People talk of the 10,000 things, but instead of the 10,000 things, there are really only a few moments and gestures. So it's a great compensation. It's astonishing really, how intricate it is."

In recent years, Maia has volunteered as a phone mentor, teaching Buddhist meditation to beginning students. Often, she is exhausted by the daily challenges of her life. But then again she finds her way. "The best part of the day is when the students call. I forget everything, just to be with them." Her gift to them becomes a source of energy: in helping them, she also recovers clarity and inspiration for herself.

In 2005, Maia's stamina was tested to the utmost, when her beloved partner died suddenly in his sleep. I thought she would implode from grief. Instead, it was as if she were beatified. "Charlie's death stunned me into this immense gratitude, *gratitude inside of sorrow*, a kind of magnification of vision and meaning."

When she found him, he had already been dead for several hours. She knew that one was supposed to call the coroner straight away.

But she wanted to spend that last piece of time alone with Charlie. And she did. She spent the whole night singing and talking to him, weeping and praying. Everything she did was infused with gratitude.

"Gratitude for our twenty-four years together. For death coming like that, in his sleep. For his kindness and wisdom."

That time, for her, was deeply necessary. "There's a certain ceremonial quality that can only be done slowly. Hurrying and rushing is ground in which gratitude can't grow. There's a whole universe in every act, if you are only slow enough, present enough, to perceive it."

GRATITUDE & GENEROSITY

Meister Eckhart told us centuries ago that if our only prayer were *thank you,* that would be enough. But for many of us, gratitude comes grudgingly and awkwardly, if it comes at all. How, then, might we best teach ourselves a deeper courtesy, not with a brow-beaten guilty "should," but from the heart?

The Japanese have a practice called *naikan* (pronounced "nyecon") specifically designed to nurture gratitude. It was developed in the 1940s by a Buddhist businessman called Ishin Yoshimoto, and is currently used in marriage counseling and addiction centers, as well as in schools and business settings. The word *naikan* means "looking inside" or "seeing oneself with the mind's eye," and that spacious, open-hearted self-reflection is exactly what *naikan* practice is all about. Those who want to try it set aside a week of uninterrupted time, during which they think back over the story of their lives, focusing in turn on their mother and father, friends, teachers, siblings, colleagues, partners, and children, and asking of each the same three questions:

> *What have I received from this person?*
> *What have I given to him or her?*
> *What troubles or difficulties have I caused?*

Little by little, they allow the answers to surface, first covering the period from birth to nine years old, and then from nine to twelve, and so in three-year increments up to the present time. They do this with the greatest specificity they can muster. Not, "My parents always celebrated my birthday," but rather, "On my sixth birthday my parents gave me a red wicker sewing box. On my seventh birthday, they gave me a watch with a pale blue leather strap. On my eighth birthday, they bought me a bright blue bicycle, which I loved."

In working through these questions one by one, and in facing what is called "the missing fourth question" (*What troubles or difficulties has so-and-so caused me?*), participants come to recognize just how much they have received over the course of their lives, and how deeply their own story is entwined with everyone else's. Rilke said once that reaching out with joy "alters the past within us, and dissolves the foreign body of pain," and this certainly seems to be the message of *naikan*. Too often, we believe that our past is set in stone. *Naikan* teaches us to question this, emphasizing that our lives are based, at least in part, on what we choose to notice, and that this is something we have power to alter.

Such radical rewriting does not come easy. *If I am not the tale of my miserable traumatic childhood, then who am I?* But it can also be immensely liberating. We live in an era of tremendous uncertainty, where there is much to fear and lament. Nonetheless, like the English poet Helen Dunmore, we can find ways to be "glad of these times":

> *Driving along the motorway*
> *swerving the packed lanes*
> *I am glad of these times.*

> *Because I did not die in childbirth*
> *because my children will survive me*
> *I am glad of these times.*
>   . . .

> *glad of central heating and cable TV*
> *glad of email and keyhole surgery*
> *glad of power showers and washing machines,*

A Day So Happy

glad of polio inoculations
glad of three weeks paid holiday
glad of smart cards and cash-back
. . .

I do not breathe pure air or walk green lanes
see darkness, hear silence,
make music, tell stories

tend the dead in their dying,
tend the newborn in their birthing,
tend the fire in its breathing,

but I am glad of my times

The practice of *naikan* tends to jumpstart that sense of gratitude, transforming chronic low-grade guilt into the "happy problem" of reparation. One can also start from gift-giving in the first place. My friend Kathy O'Rourke says that her grandfather always advised her to be generous, especially if things were going badly. "If you're feeling poor or miserable, give something away—time or money or material goods—and immediately you'll feel better."

It is easy to dismiss this as naive and unrealistic. But I will never forget a scene I witnessed on a subway train in New York City, when a young Hispanic mother and her two small children tried to give some money to a homeless man. The children were dressed in their best clothes, a stiff suit, a little dress, as if they were on their way to church or Sunday school. They approached the man shyly, each holding out a dime. At first he frowned and shook his head and refused to take the money. But their mother was urging them from behind, and the children persisted.

Finally the man allowed them to drop their coins into his cup. But then something completely unexpected happened. He put one hand on the top of the cup, shook it up and down with an elaborate flourish, and, with a smile, extracted two shining quarters, presenting one to each astonished child. They had given him twenty cents and he had multiplied it two and a half times. He was not a homeless man that day, he was a magician and a millionaire. He had all the money he could ever need.

The dancer and choreographer Twyla Tharp would have loved this moment. In her book on creativity, she urges her readers to be generous. "If you are generous to someone, you are in effect making him [or her] lucky. That is important. It is like inviting yourself into a community of good fortune." In other words, *generosity is generative* (they come, in fact, from the same root, the Latin *genere:* "to engender, or be born"). Kindness is itself a creative act.

In his memoirs, Pablo Neruda tells a story from his very early childhood. He was outside playing, exploring the back garden, when he came upon a hole in the wooden fence. As he watched, a child's hand appeared, and almost immediately vanished, leaving behind a magnificent toy sheep. The sheep's wool was torn and faded, and its wheels were missing. But for Neruda, it was a miracle. He ran home and returned with one of his own treasures, a ripe pinecone, smelling deliciously of resin, and set it down in the place of the sheep. He never saw the other child again. But that small, mysterious exchange remained with him for the rest of his life, "deep and indestructible, giving [his] poetry light."

ENOUGH ALREADY

An act of spontaneous generosity (like Neruda's; like the one I witnessed on the train) has the power to color the whole day. It is infinitely more powerful, in terms of lasting happiness, than an act of spontaneous self-indulgence. For all the blandishments of the advertising industry, it is entirely possible that we need not more but less than we imagine. "I make myself rich by making my wants few," said Thoreau, famously. There is a similar story about Socrates, who turned to one of his disciples as great quantities of gold and jewels were being carried through the streets of Athens. "Look how many things there are which I don't want!" he cried, exultantly.

As psychologists have repeatedly pointed out, money does not buy happiness. The "happy poor" are often more serene and satisfied than the stressed-out rich. Most Americans would agree with this, having ourselves come to believe that there is a "negative correlation" between happiness and progress. Some 5 to 10 percent of the U.S. workforce now define themselves as "downshifters," eager to trade an eighty hour work week for a slower, saner, less materialistic life. The current recession, deepening into depression, may force almost all of us to think in just such terms. Meanwhile, we need not wait for some grand Utopian future. As Howard Zinn says, "To live now as we think human beings should live, in defiance of all the bad around us, is itself a marvelous victory."

Not long ago, I spoke with the Scottish writer Fiona Houston, who had decided to spend a year "living in the eighteenth century." She posed for me at the door of her house, dressed in a coarse gray dress with a striped apron, a dark plaid shawl crossed over her breast, and a frilled mob cap pulled down over her hair, as if she had just stepped out of an eighteenth-century painting. Barring extraordinary emergencies, her clothes and food and daily life would mimic those of a self-sufficient country woman of that era.

Houston was in a good position to conduct such a prolonged experiment. She lives in the Scottish Borders, not far from Edinburgh, in a fine old house with a few acres of garden. Because of this, she knew she would be able to grow most of her own food. She also has a croft on her property: a small stone outbuilding dating from the 1790s. Friends helped to build a cabinet bed and wooden shelves, and a new floor was installed, along with an old-fashioned stove. On the first day of the New Year, she moved in.

The croft could get extremely cold at times, she told me, and the work itself was hard: chopping wood, preparing the appropriate food. Sewing by hand could be demanding, too. She missed certain contemporary amenities: radio programs, music on CD, the taste of ripe bananas. But for the most part, she was happy to be inhabiting another century. Time, in particular, moved very differently there. "I'm not wasting time in motor cars. And I'm able to say no to all sorts of extra things that people might ask me to do. It's a more economical use of time."

Her daily walks gave her great pleasure, too. She had seen a kingfisher hunting down along the river, and the white flowers known as ladies' smocks growing there. "I saw the first geese flying north, and heard the first curlew and saw March hares. All in the same walk. Fantastic."

Some of her greatest joys were ordinary domestic ones, like waking to see her pewter plates and handmade crockery lined up on their shelf. "And sometimes in the evening, at twilight, we've got light coming through the west now. I'll be sitting here writing letters. And I just stop and stare, you know. I just enjoy it, savor it."

Meanwhile, she was "using the wild much more." She had discovered a recipe for Derbyshire oatcakes, half oatmeal and half whole wheat, which she ate with pesto ground from hazelnuts and wild garlic, and served with a fresh salad. It was clear, listening to her, that much of her pleasure lay in her own resourcefulness. "The human impulse to make and mend and improvise is very strong. And modern life completely denies it. So when I made my plate-drainer, *yeah!* I'm always making bits and pieces for the garden. And instead of thinking what can I buy, it's *what can I make it out of? How can I do it?* Which is a great feeling."

Few of us have the resolve (or indeed the resources) to suspend our lives for a year, while we experiment with living in another era. But we too can learn to savor what we have, rejoicing in our hard work and our inventiveness, as Fiona Houston did. "Is this really necessary?" we can ask of each new choice. "Will this *truly* make me happier?"

"Renounce and enjoy," said Gandhi. And for him, the secret of life lay in those three small words.

SLOW IS BEAUTIFUL

"Stay here forever," said the little girl in the Brooklyn Botanic Gardens. We were in the Japanese Pavilion, leaning over the rail to watch the fish. Cherry blossoms swirled like confetti in the dark water.

"No," said her father. "Gonna see more fish—" and he dragged her away from the ones she was already looking at: their shadowy bodies, their smiling mouths, their multicolored scales. Black and gold and pure albino white; cadmium yellow/charcoal; silver-blue-green-gray. The little girl protested, but her father didn't listen. "More fish," he said, as if more and different were always, unquestionably better. *More fish. Again more fish.*

Oryoki, the Japanese word for a begging bowl, means "just enough." The Irish word *go leor* (anglicized as "galore") also meant "sufficiency," at least at first, sufficiency being a synonym for plenty. But over time, "plenty" has metastasized into "more than enough," and finally into "too much." There is nothing wrong with having "too much of a good thing" on a feast day, or for a celebration. But when one comes to take that "more" for granted, requiring excess on every ordinary day, then its celebratory aspect is destroyed.

"Stay here forever," said the little girl. All she wanted was to watch the fish: to dissolve into that moment of enchantment. It was as if she already understood its precious rarity. "Slow down a little," we remind each other. "You've got to take the time to smell the roses." Beauty is transient; here, and swiftly gone. We need to be alert, if we are not to risk missing it altogether. "I don't know anything about consciousness," said the Zen teacher Shunryu Suzuki. "I just try to teach my students to hear the birds sing."

As we've seen, however, this is more easily said than done.

For years, Rosie and I used to share such moments, staying up late to watch the eclipse, racing out of the house to view a magnificent double rainbow. She was my soul mate, my co-perceptionist, her joy and exultation amplifying mine. After she left, the world seemed much diminished. I wanted to reach for her arm, to point out the groundhog sunning himself on the rock outside the window, or the fox mooching through the long grass, to delight in the instant when my year-old cat sprang like a lion under the hoofs of a browsing deer, and sent it bolting up the hillside. I still saw these things, it's true, but not so fully, so whole-heartedly. It was a long time before I was able to achieve such charged ecstatic looking on my own.

In ancient Greece, the *beautiful* and the *good* were seen as almost indistinguishable: ethics and aesthetics not contradictory, but matching values. For me too, faced with very practical decisions: *what to do next, where best to live,* beauty became a reliable and trusted guide. *Choose beauty,* I told myself repeatedly. *Pay attention.* I was living in a friend's house at the time, looking south from Vermont towards the Massachusetts hills. The cloudscapes were tremendous, sunsets especially. Again and again they caught me by surprise: pale turquoise washed with green, scored with coral and soft gold, a spill of egg-yellow against steely gray. They came to me *gratis,* free—a grace, a daily blessing—and I felt for them enormous gratitude.

All three words in fact derive from the same root, the Latin *gratia,* meaning "thanks," itself akin to the Sanskrit *gurtas,* and its derivative, *gir,* "a song of praise." This etymological trail, in which grace opens into gratitude, and gratitude flowers into praise, is a humanly accurate one, perhaps especially for artists, for it is precisely this readiness to be moved, this interest and curiosity, that draws us towards *making* of whatever kind: poetry or songwriting, dance or music, photography or art.

But for this to happen, there must be a second pause, a second stretch of quiet concentration: the moment in which the work itself is born. After long days of pilgrimage, the poet Basho used to light his lamp and take up pen and ink, closing his eyes, bringing to mind the sights he'd seen and the poems he'd composed along the way. Only thus could he retain—and ultimately share—something of his original experience. A life like his is indeed chequered with solitude. Daytime is nourished by the dreamy power of night, clock time by the wisdom of eternity. If *slow is beautiful,* in terms of the initial inspiration, *beautiful is also slow,* in terms of making art. In the words of the Beat poet Gary Snyder, such work helps return us to the natural dignity of life "at its normal, natural, ancient, slower pace."

One of my favorite accounts of this is given by Confucius's grandson Tsesse, praising what he called "the doctrine of the half-and-half," or what we ourselves might call "the golden mean." Tsesse had no conception of an independent woman artist, but his pronouns can be changed easily enough. In all other ways, his vision is exceptionally benign. He imagines someone whose life is neither celebrated nor obscure, neither indolent nor hectically active. This person reads, but not too much, is informed and capable, but neither a scholar nor a specialist. Each night, he sleeps long and well, and wakes up rested, blessed with a revivifying dream. Slowly, he makes his way towards his study, settling himself down before a bright window and a clean desk. At that moment, he finds himself inspired, free as all of us would like to be, to write good essays, good poems and good letters, free to paint good paintings, and to write good inscriptions on them. The world opens itself to him, in all its myriad beauties, and he responds with a full heart.

SEIZE THE DAY

In almost every Indo-European language, the word for happiness is linked with the word for luck or fate or fortune. It derives from *happe*, the Middle English word for chance, hence "happenstance," and "hapless" and "perhaps." In other words, it contains a strong element of uncertainty. Efforts to annihilate that uncertainty lead, not surprisingly, to "unhappiness" or what Buddhists would call "suffering." For almost all of us, happiness depends enormously on *letting go*, dropping our own willed insistent management, and opening into a more flexible and spacious, and above all, *playful* relationship with time.

The writer Susan Griffin tells a story about the French poet Robert Desnos. He had been captured by the Nazis, and sent to a concentration camp. On this particular day, he was being driven to the gas chambers, along with many others. The mood was somber; no one felt able to speak. But when the truck reached its destination, Desnos leapt down, and grabbed the hand of one of the other prisoners. Unlikely as it sounds, he began to read the man's palm.

"Ah," he said. "I see you have a very long lifeline. You will marry and have three children. You will be very happy." His exuberance was startling. It was also contagious. As he proceeded down the line, one prisoner after another held out an eager palm. And the predictions were always the same: riches, longevity, children, abundant joy.

The minutes passed, and Desnos continued to read palms. Who knows why the camp guards did not stop him? Perhaps they were intrigued by him: his courage, his sheer audacity. It was as if, in some curious way, his imaginative authority overpowered their uniforms, their guns. In any case, the events of that day, which had seemed so painfully predictable, spiraled round and took another turn. All the prisoners, Desnos among them, were ordered back onto the truck, and returned to camp.

"Art," said the novelist Saul Bellow, "has something to do with the achievement of stillness in the midst of chaos . . . an arrest of attention in the midst of distraction." There is an art to living as well as an art to writing, and at that moment, Desnos personified both. When he leapt down from the truck and began telling fortunes, his playfulness seemed almost instantaneous. But such quicksilver wit is grounded in a time outside of time, a trust in fortune and in happenstance. It is the gift of Kairos, the trickster god, the god of lucky coincidence. "You must take Kairos by the hair, or he escapes—"

The writer E. B. White said that habitually creative people were "prepared to be happy," and for the most part, I'd agree with him. I think of Virginia Woolf, alert to the most modest daily pleasures: a new nib to her pen, a passing omnibus. I think of the painter Claude Monet, brush always at the ready. When he painted clouds, he had to act with some dispatch, because on an average day, a given effect lasted barely thirty minutes. In that brief half hour, he had to catch all the changing colors of the sky, the shifting clouds, the sudden bursts of light. Like Desnos, he had to "seize the day," surrendering to that magic state called "flow"—a transcendent, concentrated swathe of time, in which the self dissolves into its present task, and all ordinary self-consciousness falls away.

When we look back across the small track of our achievements, we tend to set most store by the skills we've had to work for: the A+ for math, or the painfully acquired ability to play the piano. But twined in and out of our more dogged accomplishments, there's almost always something that comes easy, something we do happily and skillfully and without too much effort. Such a gift is our true north in terms of finding our way, lighting up the path as it appears under our feet. No less a person than Descartes believed that what he called "interior joy" had the power to "make luck more favorable."

> I have often noticed that the things I have done with a happy heart, and with no inner repugnance, have a habit of succeeding happily, even during games of chance, where only fortune rules.

A DAY SO HAPPY

"Refuse and choose," I said at the beginning of this book. Refuse the rush and skim and misery of distraction; insist, wherever possible, on taking time. I think here of the many poems that have been written encouraging us *simply to pay attention*, from Whitman's long, resounding inventories to Adam Zagajewski's "Try to Praise the Mutilated World," published in the *New Yorker* the week after 9/11. And I think too, of the artist Georgia O'Keeffe, and the words she wrote in a long ago letter to a friend: "[N]obody sees a flower really—it is so small—we haven't time—and to see takes time, like to have a friend takes time."

Taking time to look, to look again, is itself a joy, reminding us of those moments when the veil of the ordinary is drawn aside, and what is seen is (scintillatingly) revealed as miracle. Czeslaw Milosz's poem, "Gift," describes just such an epiphany.

> *A day so happy.*
> *Fog lifted early, I worked in the garden.*
> *Hummingbirds were stopping over honeysuckle flowers.*
> *There was no thing on earth I wanted to possess.*
> *I knew no one worth my envying him.*
> *Whatever evil I had suffered, I forgot.*

To think that once I was the same man did not embarrass me.
In my body I felt no pain.
When straightening up, I saw the blue sea and sails.

My friend Maia says that if you have an open heart, you are fed by everything: "Everything becomes the breast." The more one can disengage from one's own self-centered myopia, the more the world, in all its glory, rushes in to fill the gap. Gratitude creates a space in which *nothing is not welcome*: the fog, the hummingbirds, the blue sea and the sails. And when this is true for the writer or the artist him- or herself, it can also become true for those who read or see or otherwise appreciate their work.

The painter Jon Schueler was an American Abstract Expressionist, who settled for a while on the west coast of Scotland, near the little fishing town of Mallaig. He filled his canvases with rich and swirling marks, which at the same time mirrored the surrounding seascape, and the islands of Eigg and Rum and Skye. Perhaps because he had served in the Air Force during the Second World War (and therefore knew the sky in three dimensions) he was particularly fond of painting clouds.

Early in 1971, Schueler had a show at the Mallaig Village Hall. Tea and biscuits were served, and a sizable crowd turned up, among them a man called Robert Poole, his wife, and their two sons. The family stayed on for much of the afternoon. In fact, they seemed so interested that Schueler asked them back to his studio to look at his other work. Some time afterwards, he ran into Bob Poole in the street, and was invited to his office for a cup of tea.

"I wanted to explain," said Poole, "why your paintings meant so much to me."

His wife was a sensitive woman, he said, who loved poetry. But she'd had a serious nervous breakdown a few years back, and after that she'd lost her sense of color. "Everything turned to gray. Nature was gray, she lived in a world of gray." The poor woman was in despair. She began to believe she would never see color again. But then, Schueler's show opened at the Village Hall, and she went with her family to look at it. And while they were looking at the paintings, Mrs. Poole regained her sense of color.

"That's why we stayed the rest of the afternoon," her husband said. "The color was there for her, even in the grays. And that night in our house, she could still see color, and the next morning when she woke up. She took a long walk along the shore of Loch Morar, and the color never left her, nor has it to this day."

I love this story, the shy way Schueler tells it in his autobiography, Poole's careful thanks, the unassuming, life-transforming miracle. *Art, attention, gratitude and grace. A quiet healing, ordinary joy.* I know these things in my own body. For several years now, my head has felt loose on my shoulders, and I too have felt oddly permeable, no longer so tightly wound. Little shards of self fly off into the wind, and frankly, I am glad to see them go.

In the same way as one pulls the petals from a daisy, *she loves me, she loves me not,* so too one can pluck one letter at a time from familiar words, revealing the core beneath. Verandah Porche (who invented the term "pluck words") is especially fond of examples like "slaughter" and "laughter" where the missing letter not only transforms the meaning of the word, but alters its sound as well. My own favorites center on a little cluster of words that seem, like *koans*, to conceal a deeper meaning. It is as if one bit into a juicy peach to find its wizened stone, or broke apart an egg to show its golden yolk. For example, when *where* is plucked, it reveals the answer *here; less* is the hidden wisdom crouching inside *bless; your* gives way to the more generous-hearted *our;* and the small domestic *hearth* expands into the cosmic *earth.* Most miraculous of all, perhaps, *eyes* open into an all-confirming *yes.*

In the *I Ching,* when a line of the oracle reaches its most extreme, expansive state, it swings back, like a pendulum, into its own opposite. The technical term for this is *enantiodromia.*

It seems possible to me that our culture of speed and confusion, busyness and overwhelm, has reached just such a state, and that the time has come for the quick double-flip of transformation, from greed to gratitude, from isolation and depression to community and calm. "Let your last thinks all be thanks," said W. H. Auden, and certainly there is much to be thankful for.

Or, as Wu-Men put it long ago,

> *Ten thousand flowers in spring, the moon in autumn,*
> *a cool breeze in summer, snow in winter.*
> *If your mind isn't clouded by unnecessary things,*
> *this is the best season of your life.*

Tactics

✦ In *The Prelude,* Wordsworth wrote of what he called the "curious props" that sustain our daily lives.

> *the curious props*
> *By which the perishable hours of life*
> *Rest on each other, and the world of thought*
> *Exists and is sustained.*

What are your own curious props?

✦ There is a *New Yorker* cartoon where a monk is shown opening an empty box. "Nothing!" he exclaims. "Just what I always wanted." What kinds of "nothing" make you happiest? See if you can manage to give yourself such presents, and encourage your friends to do the same.

✦ *Consider the following quotations:*

"I think and think and think, I've thought myself out of happiness one million times, but never once into it."

JONATHAN SAFRAN FOER

"The present is the important thing. That's why it's the same word as gift."   JOHN MCEWEN

Afterword

I lost my beloved, I looked for him everywhere.
I looked for him in the hills, I looked for him by the sea.
I found him at last
in a corner of my own house.

(From ANDREW HARVEY in *A Journey to Ladakh*)

COMING TO OUR SENSES

As a child, I wanted to live on an island, in a little stone house look-ing out over the sea, with the white gulls circling overhead. For the past few years, I've been living by myself on an island known as *Slow*, exploring the ways in which ordinary joy might flourish in a culture addicted to speed and over-work. The philosopher William James believed that every life had the same potential for depth and richness and integrity. "But that potential is lost when your days are spread so thin that busyness is your true occupation."

The struggle to find time is so pervasive that it is easy to feel daunted, as if only the rarest and most costly equipment could track down those precious particles of freedom, that sack packed tight with childhood's golden hours. But this is just not true. As should by now be apparent, *all the time in the world* can be as close as our own breath, our own modest unremarkable daily choices. "A little can be a lot if it's enough," as my friend Mariel's grandmother liked to say.

The solution has less to do with "fighting back" against a culture of hyper speed and its attendant screens, than with turning the other cheek: choosing again and again "to take the slow way home." Not long ago, I had an early appointment at a big hospital in Boston. It would have been possible to join the frantic freeway at the height of the morning rush hour. Instead, my friend chose to drive me there by a series of small back roads, winding in and out among the woods and farms and sleepy, half-awakened houses. As a result, we arrived at the hospital more than forty minutes early, grateful and refreshed.

Every chapter of this book is a source of similar anecdotes. Because so few of us have time to read, I have filled it to the brim with stories and quotations, suggestions and ideas, made of it a compendium to which readers can turn again and again in search of nourishment. Cultural commentators like Maggie Jackson and William Powers have written of the "deep thinking" that can be accomplished in the course of reading—the insights and epiphanies, the unexpected joys. The poet William Matthews, obliged to leave his home in Troy, Ohio, remembered later how much courage came to him through books. "Leaning against the base of that tree, and in that high window, the work of the rupture was slowly and stubbornly performed in the silent thrall of reading."

In the course of writing this book, I have amassed a small library of philosophy and psychology, sociology and Buddhism, as well as revisiting many familiar works of poetry and literature. It has been a delight to have had an excuse to reread the Romantics and the Transcendentalists, to follow in the tracks of William and Henry James, of Robert Louis Stevenson and Virginia Woolf, and on into the present day. At times, I felt as if I were entertaining these people in my own front parlor, offering them tea and toast and slices of dark rich fruitcake, making sure to pass the milk. More often, I've been curled up in a corner by the fireside, while the grown up talk continues overhead. I've listened to the different writers as they've listened to each other, trailing them through the pages of their letters and biographies, noting the many convivial friendships, and the ways too, in which literary influence can arc across time, so that Wordsworth was read by Thoreau who was read by John Muir who in turn was read by Theodore Roosevelt, leading him to write the bills that inaugurated the

National Park system—a proof that poetry (and poetic prose) can, at least occasionally, make "something happen."

As Emerson said, "There is then creative reading as well as creative writing."

But for all their compacted clarities and inspiration, books alone are not enough. We can read the label on the bottle a hundred thousand times, we can devour it with our eyes, quote its instructions to our friends—but in the end, we have to take the medicine. Others can model wise practice and good sense but *finding time* is something each of us must accomplish for ourselves. If it is true that we are, in some essential way, the sum of our own interests and affections, then the challenge, in terms of our creative practice, is simply *to notice what we notice*, acknowledging the people and places, the habits and attitudes and experiences, that are for us inspiring—and then to base our actions on that clarity.

"Hurry up and finish it," my good friends said. "Hurry up and finish that book on slowing down." The difference between a "quick fix" and a "slow one" is that a quick fix is all too often cheap and nasty and impermanent, whereas a slow fix, at its best, may last a lifetime. The suggestions I am making here are by no means major. Some cost a small amount of money; most are free. *Walking, talking, dreaming, drawing, spending time with children.* All that is necessary is that we see them as worth doing, and value them enough to follow through.

There is joy to be found in the most minuscule of choices, in the pockets of slowness concealed inside each ordinary day: ten minutes in the morning in which to write down our dreams, five minutes in the late afternoon in which to stand by a window and watch the changing colors of the sunset, another pause before bed for a brief moment of prayer. Such things do not demand an inordinate commitment. From outside, our lives may look much as they have always done. We alone will recognize the small, rejuvenating pleasures, the invisible sustenance: the difference between skimming a text and taking the time to read it slowly and in depth; between emailing our friend, and making time to sit with her and talk; between rushing through our days, and honoring "the space between," allowing space to muse and brood and wonder and exult, to bask in our accomplishments.

When I was a student, I owned a portable typewriter, a little blue-green Olivetti. Last month, I woke from a dream in which its hard metal shell had been transformed into some kind of rough sacking—a coarse brown hessian. The typewriter had become soft—squashy—*slow.* My fingers plunged and squelched among the keys. It was (only just!) possible to type. But in order to do so, I had to give the task my undivided attention. I had to engage on a very literal level—given the dream's own punning undertow—with the resistance (and the sustenance) of the material world.

Returning to ourselves as material beings reminds us to place less emphasis on the flickering tickertape of verbal commentary, and to focus instead on older, steadier, more grounded pleasures. It is helpful, perhaps, to think in terms of "coming to our senses," reinhabiting ourselves as living, breathing creatures, not just a three-pound brain tilted sideways above strained shoulders and neglected legs. In his recent book, *Becoming Animal,* David Abram reminds his readers that ultimately, "All our knowledge is carnal knowledge." Each of us can return to our body in the way that suits us best: via the scented steam of a long hot bath, or the hands of a wise masseuse, or more actively through dance or yoga lessons, a fierce hike in the winter along a frozen river. A stretch of solitude can be helpful too, especially when accompanied by a media fast. Once again, the simple mantra is *refuse & choose.*

A little ease, a little spaciousness. Such things aren't casual. Slowly we return to the immediate present, to the flowers on the table, to the cat's soft fur. Time spreads out around us, a slow and rippling pool. There is time to watch and listen, time to remember. *World enough & time.* Our animal selves, so long ignored, settle back into the breathing landscape of the earth itself.

The book is done, and we look up, *alive, alive.*

Tactics

‧ The English naturalist Roger Deakin used to walk around his area of Suffolk, describing what he saw to an imaginary medieval friend. If you had such a friend, what might you point out to him or her?

‧ If there were a box you could fill with whatever makes you happiest—a box you would open again in extreme old age—what would you put into it? For myself, I think, I would put light, all the varieties of light, and conversations with beloved friends.

‧ *Consider the following quotations:*

"Fast learns, slow remembers. Fast proposes, slow disposes. Fast is discontinuous, slow is continuous. . . . Fast gets all our attention, slow has all the power."

STEWART BRAND

"If you can't get rid of the skeletons in your closet, you'd better teach them to dance."

GEORGE BERNARD SHAW

BIBLIOGRAPHY SOURCES & SUGGESTIONS FOR FURTHER READING

Books that were used in reference to specific chapters, are cited under the chapter headings below. Those that especially inspired me, and to which I returned again and again, are listed in the General Bibliography. I would like to pay special tribute to Jay Griffiths, author of the incomparable *A Sideways Look at Time*. Her book is a classic, a one-woman encyclopedia, witty, original, dazzlingly comprehensive. I also found great sustenance in the work of David Abram, Robert Grudin, Marion Milner, and Adrienne Rich.

GENERAL BIBLIOGRAPHY

Abram, David. *The Spell of the Sensuous: Perception and Language in a More-than-Human World* (New York, Vintage Books, Random House, Inc. 1996).

Claxton, Guy. *Hare Brain, Tortoise Mind: Why Intelligence Increases When You Think Less* (London, Fourth Estate, 1997).

Field, Joanna. (pseudonym of Marion Milner). *A Life of One's Own* (Los Angeles, Jeremy P. Tarcher, 1981).

Griffiths, Jay. *A Sideways Look at Time* (New York, Jeremy P. Tarcher, Penguin Putnam Inc., 1999).

Grudin, Robert. *Time and the Art of Living* (New York, Ticknor & Fields, 1982).

Kern, Stephen. *The Culture of Time and Space, 1880-1918* (Cambridge, MA, Harvard University Press, 1983).

Partridge, Eric. *Origins: A Short Etymological Dictionary of Modern English* (New York, Crown Publishers, 1983).

Picard, Max. *The World of Silence*, translated by Stanley Goodman (Washington DC, Regnery Gateway, 1948, 1986).

Rheingold, Howard. *They Have a Word for It: A Lighthearted Lexicon of Untranslatable Words and Phrases* (Los Angeles, Jeremy P. Tarcher, Inc., 1988).

Rich, Adrienne. *What Is Found There: Notebooks on Poetry and Politics* (New York, W.W. Norton & Co., 1993).

Slouka, Mark. "Quitting the Paint Factory. On the Virtues of Idleness," *Harper's Magazine*, November 2004.

Yutang, Lin. *The Importance of Living* (New York, HarperCollins, 1937, 1998).

REFERENCES

INTRODUCTION

Abram, David. *The Spell of the Sensuous: Perception and Language in a More-Than-Human World* (New York, Vintage Books, A Division of Random House, Inc., 1996).

Brand, Stewart. *The Clock of the Long Now: Time & Responsibility* (New York, Basic Books, 1999).

Eno, Brian. Quoted by Stewart Brand, *op. cit.*

Merton, Thomas. Quoted by David Abram, *op. cit.*

Schor, Juliet B. *Plenitude: The New Economics of True Wealth* (New York, Penguin Press, 2010). See Schor for up-to-date information on U.S. "crazy-busy-ness."

Thoreau, Henry David. *The Heart of Thoreau's Journals,* edited by Odell Shepard (New York, Dover Publications, Inc., 1961).

Thornton, Mike. *Meditation in a New York Minute: Super Calm for the Super Busy (Sounds True* catalogue, Spring 2006).

CHAPTER 1: HURRY SICKNESS

Abram, David. *The Spell of the Sensuous: Perception and Language in a More-Than-Human World* (New York, Vintage Books, A Division of Random House, Inc., 1996).

Arendt, Hannah. Quoted by Oliver Sacks, *op.cit.*

Cave, Damien. "In Recession, Americans Doing More, Buying Less," *New York Times,* 3rd January 2010.

De Graaf, John, ed. *Take Back Your Time: Fighting Poverty and Overwork in America* (San Francisco, Berrett-Koehler Publishers, Inc., 2003).

Dossey, Larry. *Time, Space and Medicine* (Boulder & London, Shambhala, 1982).

Honoré, Carl. *In Praise of Slowness: How a Worldwide Movement is Challenging the Cult of Speed* (San Francisco, HarperSanFrancisco, 2004).

"Hurry sickness". This phrase originated with Larry Dossey, *op. cit.*

Jackson, Maggie. *Distracted: The Erosion of Attention in the Coming Dark Age* (Prometheus Books, Amherst, NY, 2008).

Merton, Thomas. Quoted by David Abram, *op. cit.*

Nabokov, Vladimir. Quoted by Mark Slouka, *op. cit.*

Reynolds, Nigel. "Hyphen falls victim to the email society," *The Daily Telegraph,* 21st September 2007.

Roethke, Theodore. *On Poetry and Craft* (Port Townsend, WA, Copper Canyon Press, 2001).

Role of work. Lindsay Potvin, "Americans rethinking role of work amid painful recession, says COB researcher," Florida State University College of Business, 18th October 2010.

Sacks, Oliver. "Speed" in *The Best American Spiritual Writing, 2005,* edited by Philip Zaleski (Boston, New York, Houghton Mifflin 2005).

Schindler, Katja. Conversation with Rowland Russell, Glenbrook, NH, October 2006.

Schor, Juliet. *The Overworked American: The Unexpected Decline of Leisure* (New York, Basic Books, 1992).

Schor, Juliet B. *Plenitude: The New Economics of True Wealth* (New York, Penguin Press, 2010).

Slouka, Mark. "Quitting the Paint Factory. On the Virtues of Idleness," *Harper's Magazine,* November 2004.

SlowLab describes itself as a laboratory for "slow design" thinking and creative activism, exploring slower rhythms of engagement with people, places, and things in order to realize new scenarios for community, sustainability and renewal. See www.slowlab.net.

Stafford, William. "The Way It Is" in *Early Morning: Remembering My Father, William Stafford,* by Kim Stafford (St. Paul, MN, Graywolf Press, 2002).

Paris demonstrators. Quoted in *The Week,* 6th January 2007.

Swift, Jonathan. *Gulliver's Travels.* Quoted by James Gleick in *Faster: The Acceleration of Just About Everything* (New York, Pantheon Books, 1999).

Take Back Your Time Day. October 24th. See http.//www.timeday.org.

Thoreau, Henry David. *The Heart of Thoreau's Journals*, edited by Odell Shepard (New York, Dover Publications, Inc. 1961).

Utne Reader. "How to Stop Time. Rip up your schedule and take back your life." (January-February 2003).

Work & leisure hours in the United States. See John de Graaf, also Judith Schor, *op.cit.*

Zen teaching story. This is widely quoted. I read it first in *Zen Flesh, Zen Bones,* compiled by Paul Reps (Harmondsworth, Penguin Books Ltd., 1971).

CHAPTER 2: THE INFINITELY HEALING CONVERSATION

Abram, David. *The Spell of the Sensuous: Perception and Language in a More-than-Human World* (New York, Vintage Books, Random House, Inc., 1996).

Buber, Martin. In Anthony Molino, *op. cit.*

Decline in friendship. See Susan Jacoby, *op. cit.*

Court reporters on talking faster. See John de Graaf, ed. *op. cit.*

Carr, Nicholas. *The Shallows: What the Internet Is Doing to Our Brains* (New York, W.W. Norton & Co, 2010).

Davis, Miles. See Stephan Rechtschaffen, quoting the trumpet player Miles Evans, *op. cit.*

De Graaf, John, ed. *Take Back Your Time: Fighting Poverty and Overwork in America* (San Francisco, Berrett-Koehler Publishers, Inc., 2003).

de Tocqueville, Alexis. See Robert Putnam, *op. cit.*

"Down the tube." A 2008 international survey of 27,500 adults between eighteen and fifty-five found that people were spending 43 percent of their leisure time on line. See Nicholas Carr, *op. cit.*

Eliot, T.S. *The Four Quartets* (New York, London, Harcourt Brace & Co., 1943, 1971).

Emerson, Ralph Waldo. "Table Talk," in *Uncollected Essays,* edited by Clarence Gohdes (New York, William Edwin Ridge, 1932).

Entrainment. An eerie synchronization of brain waves has been not-ed among people who talk well together. Scientists also report sim-ilarities in sentence structures, speaking rates, physical gestures, and posture. See *The Week,* 13th August 2010.

Epstein, Joseph. *Friendship: An Exposé* (Boston, New York, Houghton Mifflin, 2006).

Friendship seen as giving rise to "greater self-awareness" etc. In Anthony Molino, *op. cit.*

Ginsberg, Allen. In *Writers at Work: The Paris Review Interviews,* with an introduction by Alfred Kazin (New York, Viking Press, 1967).

Gleick, James. *Faster: the Acceleration of Just About Everything* (New York, Pantheon, 1999).

Graham, W. S. *Selected Poems* (London, Faber & Faber, 1996).

Griffiths, Jay. *A Sideways Look at Time* (New York, Jeremy P. Tarcher, Penguin Putnam, 1999).

Gulkarov, Arthur & Ishak. Quoted by Warren Lehrer and Judith Sloan, *op. cit.*

Hazlitt, William. "On Going a Journey" in Phillip Lopate, *op cit.*

Implanting device for perpetual Internet connection. See *The Week,* 4th June 2010.

Inuit woman's words. In Jerome Rothenberg, *op. cit.*

Jackson, Maggie. *Distracted: The Erosion of Attention in the Coming Dark Age* (Prometheus Books, Amherst, NY, 2008). A quarter of the U.S. population now says they have no close confidant, more than double the number in 1985. Americans now average twenty-three core ties and twenty-seven less significant ties, plus thou-sands or even millions of more casual connections.

Jacoby, Susan. *The Age of American Unreason* (New York, Pan-theon Books, 2008).

Keats, John. *Complete Poems and Selected Letters of John Keats* (New York, Modern Library, 2001).

Lehrer, Warren & Judith Sloan. *Crossing the Boulevard: Strangers, Neigh-bors, Aliens in a New America* (New York, W.W. Norton & Co., 2003).

Lochhead, Liz. "Men Talk" in *True Confessions and New Clichés* (Edinburgh, P.D. Meany, 1985).

Lopate, Phillip, ed. *The Art of the Personal Essay: An Anthology from the Classical Era to the Present* (New York, Anchor Books, Doubleday, 1994).

Lynton, Norbert. *Kenneth Armitage* (London, Methuen, 1962).

Mansfield, Howard. Personal interview, Hancock, NH, 13th March 2007.

Marinetti, Filippo. Quoted by Mark Slouka, *op.cit.*

Merton, Thomas. Quoted by David Abram, *op.cit.*

Miller, Stephen. *Conversation: A History of a Declining Art* (New Haven, CT, Yale University Press, 2006).

Molino, Anthony, ed. *The Couch and the Tree: Dialogues in Psychoanalysis and Buddhism* (New York, Farrar, Straus and Giroux, 1998).

NPR (National Public Radio). June 23rd, 2006. Debbie Elliott spoke with sociology professor Lynn Smith-Lovin of Duke University about a new survey documenting America's growing social isolation.

Oldenberg, Ray. *The Great Good Place: Cafés, Coffee Shops, Bookstores, Bars, Hair Salons, and Other Hangouts at the Heart of a Community* (New York, Marlowe, 1999).

Oswald, Alice. "The Universe in time of rain makes the world alive with noise" in *A Green Thought in a Green Shade: Poetry in the Garden*, edited by Sarah Maguire (London, The Poetry Society, 2000).

Parker-Pope, Anna. "What Are Friends For? A Longer Life," in *The New York Times*, 20th April 2009.

Partridge, Eric. *Origins: A Short Etymological Dictionary of Modern English* (New York, Crown Publishers, 1983).

Patchett, Ann. *Truth & Beauty: A Friendship* (New York, HarperCollins Publishers Inc., 2004).

Powdthavee, Nattavudh. "Putting a price on friends, relatives and neighbors. using surveys of life-satisfaction to value social relationship" in *The Journal of Socio-Economics*, Vol. 37, #4, August 2008.

Putnam, Robert D. *Bowling Alone: The Collapse and Revival of American Community* (New York, Simon & Schuster, 2000). Informal socializing fell by a third in the U.S. between the 1970s and 2000, with an especially large decline in the 1990s. With the recession, this is now beginning to change.

Stephan Rechtschaffen. *Time Shifting: Creating More Time to Enjoy Your Life* (New York, Main Street Books, Doubleday, 1996).

Research on response to women's talk in class. Quoted by Mary Ann Sieghart in "Women on top? You've got to be joking," in *The Independent*, 15th July 2010.

Rich, Adrienne. *The School Among the Ruins* (New York, W.W. Norton & Co., 2004). All quotations in "Fastforward Commercial" are from Rich's "USonian Journals 2000," unless otherwise noted.

Rich, Adrienne. *On Lies, Secrets and Silence: Selected Prose 1966-1978* (New York, W.W. Norton & Co., 1979).

Rich, Adrienne. *What Is Found There: Notebooks on Poetry and Politics* (New York, W.W. Norton & Co., 1993).

Rothenberg, Jerome, ed. *Shaking the Pumpkin: Traditional Poetry of the Indian North Americans* (Garden City, NY, Doubleday & Co. Inc., 1972).

Russell, Bertrand. Quoted by Joseph Epstein, *op. cit.*

Simmell, Georg. Quoted by Joseph Epstein, *op.cit.*

Slouka, Mark. "Quitting the Paint Factory. On the Virtues of Idleness," *Harper's Magazine,* November 2004.

Steele, Richard. In Phillip Lopate, *op.cit.*

Speed of talk. See James Gleick, *op.cit.*

Swift, Jonathan. "Hints Towards an Essay on Conversation" in *English Essays, From Sir Philip Sydney to Macaulay,* edited by Charles W. Eliot (London, P.F. Collier, 1937.

Yeats, William Butler. *The Autobiography of William Butler Yeats* (New York, Collier Books, Macmillan Publishers Inc., 1965).

3: CHILD TIME

Abolishment of recess. see Lowell Monke, *op.cit.* It is worth pointing out that when Thoreau himself taught school, along with his older brother John, the two of them took their students on long walks in the woods; recess was thirty minutes instead of ten. See Robert Sullivan, *op.cit.*

Abram, David. *The Spell of the Sensuous: Perception and Language in a More-than-Human World* (New York, Vintage, Random House, Inc., 1996).

Association for the Study of Literature and Environment, www.asle.org.

BB. *The Little Grey Men* (New York, HarperCollins, 1942).

BB, *Down the Bright Stream* (London, Eyre & Spottiswood,1948).

Berenson, Bernard. Quoted by Cobb, *op. cit.*

Berry, Thomas. Quoted in the newsletter of the E.F. Schumacher Society, Winter 2003-2004.

Carr, Nicholas. *The Shallows: What the Internet is Doing to Our Brains* (New York, W.W. Norton & Co., 2010).

Center for Ecoliteracy, 2522 San Pablo Avenue, Berkeley, CA 94702. Tel. (510) 845-4595. info@ecoliteracy.org.

Chawla, Louise, *In the First Country of Places: Nature, Poetry, and Childhood Memory* (Albany, NY, State University of New York Press, 1994).

Children and Nature Network. www.childrenandnature.org.

"Children's dictionary drops 'nature words.'" Posted by Koert van Mensvoort, 4th February 2009. http.//www.nextnature.net/.

Chudacoff, Howard. *Children at Play: An American History* (New York and London, New York University Press, 2007).

Cobb, Edith. *The Ecology of Imagination in Childhood* (New York, Columbia University Press, 1977).

Coles, Robert. *The Spiritual Life of Children* (Boston, Houghton Mifflin, 1990).

Connecting-With-Nature. www.connecting-with-nature.net.

Corporate logos. Richard Louv, *op.cit.*

Davies, Matthew A. "Nintendo Thumb" in *The Original Vermont Observer,* November 3rd, 2006.

Dickinson, Emily. *The Complete Poems of Emily Dickinson,* edited by Thomas H. Johnson (London, Faber & Faber, 1975).

Earth period. the phrase is taken from David Sobel's book, *Children's Special Places: Exploring the Role of Forts, Dens and Bush Houses in Middle Childhood* (Tucson, AZ, Zephyr Press, 1993).

Ecopsychology Institute. www.centerchange.org.

Eisner, Elliot. "The Three Curricula That All Schools Teach" in *The Educational Imagination* (New York, MacMillan, 1985).

Emerson, Ralph Waldo. *The Selected Writings of Ralph Waldo Emerson,* edited by Brooks Atkinson (New York, The Modern Library, 1964).

Fout, Janet. In Richard Louv, *op. cit.* Thoreau's mother was just such an "active listener," a fact that very likely influenced her son. "My mother was telling tonight," Thoreau wrote in his journal, on a spring day in 1857, "of the sounds she used to hear summer nights when she was young and lived on Virginia Road,—the lowing of cows or cackling of geese, or the beating of a drum as far off as Hildreth's, but above all Joe Merriam whistling to his team, for he was an admirable whistler. Says she used to get up at midnight and go and sit on the door-step when all in the house were asleep and she could hear nothing in the world but the ticking of the clock in the house behind her." Quoted by Robert Sullivan, *op.cit.*

George, Jean Craighead. *My Side of the Mountain* (New York, D.F. Dutton, 1959).

Ginzburg, Natalia. *A Place to Live,* translated by Lynne Sharon Schwartz (New York, Seven Stories Press, 2002).

Gopnik, Adam. "Bumping into Mr. Ravioli" in *Through the Children's Gate: A Home in New York* (New York, Alfred A. Knopf, 2006).

Hallowell, Edward M. *CrazyBusy: Overstretched, Overbooked, and About to Snap! Strategies for Coping in a World Gone ADD* (New York, Ballantine Books, 2006).

Heaney, Seamus. *Preoccupations: Selected Prose 1968-1978* (New York, The Noonday Press, Farrar, Straus and Giroux, 1980).

Henry, Julie. "Words associated with Christianity and British history taken out of children's dictionary," *The Telegraph*, 6th December 2008.

Home habitat. *The Independent*, 23rd September, 2004.

Jackson, Maggie. *Distracted: The Erosion of Attention in the Coming Dark Age* (Amherst, NY, Prometheus Books, 2008). Jackson claims that although children "are bathed in an average of nearly six hours a day of non-print media" they are often unable "to synthesize or assess information, express complex thoughts or analyze arguments."

James, William. quoted by Richard Louv, *op. cit.*

Evelyn Fox Keller. *A Feeling for the Organism: The Life and Work of Barbara McClintock* (New York, W. H. Freeman & Co., 1983).

Kroeber, Theodora. *Ishi: In Two Worlds* (Berkeley, University of California Press, 1963).

Lash, Joseph P. *Eleanor and Franklin: The story of their relationship based on Eleanor Roosevelt's private papers* (New York, W.W. Norton & Co., 1971).

Learning in the Real World. 725 Main Street, #232, Woodland, CA 95695-3406. Tel. (530) 661-9240. www.realworld.org.

Lee, Dorothy. *Freedom & Culture* (New Jersey, Spectrum Books, Prentice Hall, 1959).

Lopez, Barry. speaking at the Roger Tory Peterson Institute at a gathering of teachers and nature writers, Jamestown, NY, Fall 1994.

Lorde, Audre. quoted in an interview by Louise Chawla, *op. cit.*

Louv, Richard. *Last Child in the Woods: Saving Our Children from Nature Deficit Disorder* (Chapel Hill, NC, Algonquin Books, 2005).

McKibben, Bill. *The Age of Missing Information* (New York, Random House, 1992).

Mill, John Stuart. *The Autobiography* (Cambridge, Cambridge University Press, 2004).

Mitchell, Stephen. *Hope and Dread in Psychoanalysis* (New York, Basic Books, 1993).

Monke, Lowell. "Charlotte's Webpage," *Orion*, September-October 2005.

Morris, Edmund. *The Rise of Theodore Roosevelt* (New York, Putnam, 1979).

Muir, John. *Nature Writings: The Story of My Boyhood and Youth, My First Summer in the Sierra, the Mountains of California, Stickeen, Selected Essays by Muir* (The Library of America, Penguin Books, U. S.A., 1997).

Nabham, Gary Paul, and Stephen Trimble. *The Geography of Childhood: Why Children Need Wild Places* (Boston, Beacon Press, 1994).

Natural History Network is a national non-profit organization designed to support the teaching and practice of natural history. See www.naturalhistorynetwork.org.

Nature words removed. http.//www.nextnature.net/.

No Child Left Inside. My conversation with John Elder, Clare Walker Leslie and John Tallmadge took place in October 2006, when "No Child Left Inside" was hardly more than a pipedream. A year later, on September 19th, 2007, the House of Representatives passed the NCLI Act with strong bipartisan support. This helps schools teach the basics of environmental education, provides funds and training for teachers, and does its best to ensure that students are indeed environmentally literate. See www.eenclb.org and www.cbf.org.

Orr, David. "Loving Children. A Design Problem" (Oberlin, OH, *Designer Builder,* October 2000).

Peterson, Roger Tory, speaking at the Roger Tory Peterson Institute to a gathering of teachers and nature writers, Jamestown, NY, Fall 1994.

Piaget, Jean. Quoted by Edward M. Hallowell, *op. cit.*

Pyle, Robert Michael. *The Thunder Tree: Lessons from an Urban Wildland* (New York, Houghton Mifflin, 1993).

Pyle, Robert. "Eden in a Vacant Lot. Special Places, Species, and Kids in the Neighborhood of Life" in "Spots of Time. Multiple ways of being in nature in childhood" in *Children and Nature: psychological, sociological, and evolutionary investigations,* edited by Peter H. Kahn, Jr. and Stephen R. Kellert (Cambridge, MA, MIT Press, 2002).

Revery/reverie. André Breton characterized reverie as "a magical young girl, unpredictable, tender, enigmatic, provocative, from whom I never seek an explanation of her escapades." Quoted by Edward Hirsch, in *How to Read a Poem and Fall in Love with Poetry* (New York, Harcourt, Inc., 1999).

Rich, Adrienne. *Of Woman Born: Motherhood as Experience and Institution* (New York, W.W. Norton & Co, 1976).

River of Words, 2547 8ᵗʰ Street, Berkeley, CA 94710, U.S.A. Tel. (510) 548-POEM (7636). Website. www.riverofwords.org.

Roosevelt, Eleanor, in *The Soul's Code: In Search of Character and Calling,* by James Hillman (New York, Random House, 1996).

School hours. Quoted by Elliot Eisner, *op. cit.*

Smith, Robert Paul. Quoted by Gary Paul Nabham, *op.cit.*

Snyder, Gary. *Turtle Island* (New York, New Directions, 1974).

Snyder, Gary, *The Practice of the Wild* (New York, North Point Press, Farrar, Straus and Giroux, 1990).

Stafford, Kim. "A Separate Hearth" in *Having Everything Right: Essays of Place* (Lewiston, ID, Confluence Press, 1986).

Stratton Porter, Gene. *A Girl of the Limberlost* (New York, Dell Publishing Co., 1986).

Stratton Porter, Gene. *Coming Through the Swamp: The Nature Writings of Gene Stratton Porter,* edited and with an introduction by Sydney Landon Plum (Salt Lake City, University of Utah Press, 1996).

Sullivan, Robert. *The Thoreau You Don't Know: What the Prophet of Environmentalism Really Meant* (New York, HarperCollins, 2009).

Teenage texting. today's teenagers typically send or receive a message every few minutes during their waking hours. See Nicholas Carr, *op.cit.*

Thoreau, Henry David. *The Heart of Thoreau's Journals,* edited by Odell Shepard (New York, Dover Publications, Inc., 1961).

Ward, Colin. *The Child in the Country* (London, Bedford Square Press, 1988).

Wilson, E.O. quoted in Richard Louv, *op.cit.*

Wordsworth, William. *The Prelude* (London, Penguin, 1850, 1976).

Working children. See, www.stolenchildhoods.org.

Wright, Lawrence. *Clockwork Man: The Story of Time, Its Origins, Its Uses, Its Tyranny* (New York, Horizon Press, 1968). Wright points out that the first British Factory Act, in 1819, limited a nine-year-old to twelve hours work a day. "The Children's Charter" of 1833 forbade child employment under the age of nine. That year the Commissioners took the evidence of a youth who had begun work in a mine at the age of eight. Chained to a coal tub and bent double, he pulled it though the low galleries for anything up to fourteen hours. Some started such work at the age of six.

4: IN PRAISE OF WALKING

As a student of English and American literature (and a committed walker), I have long been familiar with most of the poems and essays mentioned here. Nonetheless, my sections on Wordsworth and Keats, on the nineteenth-century essayists, on Frank O'Hara and on Virginia Woolf, have inevitably been influenced by Rebecca Solnit's *Wanderlust: A History of Walking*. I am particularly grateful for her account of Wordsworth's work practices (as given by one of the Grasmere locals), and for the statistics on walking in midtown and Lower Manhattan. I was also moved by the humor with which she treats the "rambling men," and her clear-sightedness as to the difficulties faced by the female walker.

Abbey, Edward. *The Journey Home: Some Words in Defense of the American West* (New York, Dutton, 1977).

Bradbury, Ray. *The Stories of Ray Bradbury* (New York, Knopf, 1980).

Clark, Thomas A. *In Praise of Walking* (Pittenweem, Moschatel Press, 2004).

Clark, Thomas A. *One Hundred Scottish Places* (Eindhoven, The Netherlands, Parnassus Press, 1999).

Clark, Thomas A. *The High Path* (Pittenweem, Moschatel Press, 2003).

Clark, Thomas A. *The Hundred Thousand Places* (Manchester, U.K., Carcanet Press Ltd., 2009).

Clark, Thomas A. *Tormentil and Bleached Bones* (Edinburgh, Polygon, 1993).

Clark, Thomas A. Personal interview, Pittenweem, Fife, 9th April, 2005. In summer 2010, the Ingleby Galley in Edinburgh exhibited a large, site-specific wall painting entitled "The Hidden Place," created by Thomas A. Clark. This showed an alternative map of Scotland, with more than a hundred place names replaced by English phrases translated from Gaelic, Pictish, Norse, English, French, Latin, and Scots. "Each becomes a piece of condensed folk poetry, revealing the riches of the past with a quiet lyricism; *bay of the bent grass, place of pebbles, ridge of tears.*" info@inglebygallery.com.

Commuting. see Nick Paumgarten, *op.cit.*

Damasio, Antonio. See Stephen Johnson's article, "Antonio Damasio's theory of thinking faster and faster. Are the brain's emotional circuits hardwired for speed?" *Discover,* May 2004.

De Quincey, Thomas. *Recollections of the Lakes and the Lake Poets,* edited by David Wright (Harmondsworth, Penguin Books, 1972). De Quincey notes that "Wordsworth's person was always worst in a state of motion," for, as the country people said, " 'he walked like a cade'—a cade being some sort of insect which advances by oblique motion." Indeed, his walk had a "wry or twisted appearance," and had been known to edge his companions towards the side of the road. Coleridge too walked in an oddly crooked fashion, and even Dorothy Wordsworth, whom De Quincey praises for "the glancing quickness of her motions," had "a stooping attitude when walking."

Driving. the American photographer Edward Weston said he refused to drive faster than thirty-five mph, because otherwise he couldn't see. See Terry Tempest Williams. *Finding Beauty in a Broken World* (New York, Pantheon Books, 2008).

Emerson, Ralph Waldo. "Notes on Walking" in *Ralph Waldo Emerson: Essays and Lectures* (New York, Library of America, 1983).

Emerson. *The Selected Writings of Ralph Waldo Emerson*, edited by Brooks Atkinson (New York, The Modern Library, 1964).

Gallagher, Winifred. *Rapt: Attention and the Focused Life* (New York, Penguin Books, 2009).

Girdner, John H., *Newyorkitis* (New York, The Grafton Press, 1901). Swarthmore psychologist Barry Schwartz points out that New York recently placed at the very bottom of a list of America's happiest cities. See Gallagher, *op. cit.*

Hazlitt, William. "On Going a Journey". see Lopate, Phillip, *op. cit.*

Honoré, Carl. *In Praise of Slow* (London, England, Orion Books, 2005).

Iyer, Pico. *The Global Soul: Jet-lag, Shopping Malls and the Search for Home* (London, Bloomsbury, 2000). Among the many branches of the Slow Movement is a new trend called Slow Travel, which aims to reduce the ecological costs of such journeys, as well as to enhance the traveler's own enjoyment.

Joyce, James. Quoted by Nancy Willard in *Telling Time: Essays on Writing* (New York, Harcourt Brace & Co., 1993.)

Keats, John. *Selected Letters*, edited by Robert Gittings (Reading, Berkshire, Oxford University Press, 2002). Icolmkill and Staffa are small islands off the west coast of Scotland. Icolmkill is perhaps more familiar as Iona.

Kundera, Milan. *Slowness*, translated from the French by Linda Asher (New York, HarperCollins, 1995).

Levertov, Denise. "The Mutes" in *Being Alive: the sequel to Staying Alive*, edited by Neil Astley (Tarset, Northumberland, 2004).

Lopate, Phillip, ed. *The Art of the Personal Essay: An Anthology from the Classical Era to the Present* (New York, Anchor Books, Doubleday, 1994). Includes Richard Steele's "Twenty-four Hours in London," William Hazlitt's "On Going a Journey," Henry David Thoreau's "Walking," and Virginia Woolf's "Street Haunting."

Mansfield, Katherine. Quoted by Padma Hejmadi in *Room to Fly: A Transcultural Memoir* (Berkeley, University of California Press, 1999).

"Mr. Toad" from Kenneth Grahame's *The Wind in the Willows*. Quoted by Pico Iyer, *op. cit.*

O'Hara, Frank. *The Selected Poems* (New York, Vintage Books, 1974).

O'Hara, Frank. *Lunch Poems* (San Francisco, City Lights Books, 1964).

O'Hara, Frank. *Standing Still and Walking in New York: Frank O'Hara*, edited by Donald Allen (Bolinas, CA, Berkeley, Gray Fox Press, 1975).

Partridge, Eric. *Origins: A Short Etymological Dictionary of Modern English* (New York, Crown Publishers, 1983).

Paumgarten, Nick. "There and Back Again. The Soul of the Commuter," *New Yorker*, 16th April 2007.

PEN is the world's oldest international and human rights literary organization, founded in 1921. One hundred and one countries are members of International PEN, of which Scottish PEN is one.

Robinson, Tim. *Stones of Aran: Pilgrimage* (London, Penguin Books, in association with the Lilliput Press, 1990).

Saunter: There are disagreements even now about the derivation of this word. *The Oxford Dictionary of World Histories* claims that the original (Middle English) sense was "to muse or wonder," whereas Eric Partridge refers it back to the Middle French *s'aunter.* "to advance oneself, move forward." See *The Oxford Dictionary of World Histories: The life stories of over 12,000 words,* edited by Glynnis Chantrell (Oxford, Oxford University Press, 2002) and Partridge, *op.cit.*

Solnit, Rebecca. *Wanderlust: A History of Walking* (New York, Penguin Putnam, Inc., 2000).

Speed of walking. "The ever-quickening pace of modern life," *The Week*, 19th May 2007.

Stafford, William. *You Must Revise Your Life* (Ann Arbor, The University of Michigan Press, 1986).

Steele, Richard. "Twenty Four Hours in London," see Phillip Lopate, *op. cit.*

Stevenson, Robert Louis. "Walking Tours" in *Virginibus Puerisque and other papers* (New York, Charles Scribner & Sons, 1912).

Walking. there can be no question that walking is good for us, especially walking outside in the natural world. "Urban parks conferred postive effects, though green areas with water were even more beneficial." See *The Week*, 21st May 2010. "Just sitting," on the other hand, has a deleterious effect. A recent study reported that sitting for prolonged periods actually shortens your life span. Those who sat for more than six hours a day were nearly 20 percent more likely to die over the fourteen year study period than those who sat for less than three hours daily. See *The Week*, 24th December 2010-7th January 2011.

Thoreau, Henry David. "Walking" in *Excursions* (New York, Corinth Books, 1962).

Whitman, Walt. In *Walt Whitman: Prose Works, 1892*, 2 vols., edited by Floyd Stovall (New York, New York University Press, 1963-64).

Woolf, Virginia. "Street Haunting," see Phillip Lopate, *op. cit.*

Woolf, Virginia. *A Room of One's Own* (London, Hogarth Press, 1967).

Wordsworth, Dorothy. *Journals of Dorothy Wordsworth*, edited by Mary Moorman (London, Oxford University Press, 1976).

Wordsworth, William. *The Prelude: A Parallel Text*, edited by J.C. Maxwell (Harmondsworth, Penguin Books, 1976).

5: THE ART OF LOOKING

Agassiz, Louis. I first read this story in Ezra Pound's *ABC of Reading* (London, Faber & Faber, 1973) where the fish is described as a sunfish. It also appears in Guy Davenport, *op. cit,* and in "Coming to Our Senses," *Orion*, Autumn 1997. Agassiz used to commission Thoreau to supply him with snakes and fish and snapping turtles, so Shaler's sunfish may well have originated in Walden Pond. Again, see Davenport, *op. cit.*

Attention Restoration Theory (ART) argues that people can focus better after spending time outside in nature; even looking at natural scenes is said to help. Nature offers "soft fascinations" that allow us to bask in "effortless attention" while gazing up at the sky, or listening to the leaves rustling overhead. See Rachel and Stephen Kaplan, *The Experience of Nature: A Psychological Perspective* (Cambridge, Cambridge University Press, 1989).

Bash, Barbara. *True Nature: An Illustrated Journal of Four Seasons in Solitude* (Boston & London, Shambhala, 2004). See also "True Nature—a Visual Blog" by Barbara Bash. This can be found at barbarabash.blogspot.com.

Bash, Barbara. Personal interview, Rosendale, NY, 26th August 2006.

Berenson, Bernard. Quoted by Edith Cobb in *The Ecology of the Imagination* (New York, Columbia University Press, 1977).

Berger, John. *The Shape of a Pocket* (London, Bloomsbury, 2001).

Calvino, Italo. *Six Memos for the Next Millennium* (Cambridge, MA, Harvard University Press, 1988).

Carr, Emily. *Growing Pains: An Autobiography*, with a foreword by Ira Dilworth (Toronto, Canada, Irwin Publishing, 1971).

Chamberlain, Gethin. "Darfur Through the Eyes of Innocents," *The Scotsman*, 4th May 2005.

Children's drawing. In Peter Steinhart, *op.cit.*

Chuang-tzu. quoted by Calvino, *op.cit.*

Clark, Thomas A. Personal interview, Pittenweem, 9th April 2005.

Clottes, Jean & David Lewis-Williams. *The Shamans of Prehistory: Trance and Magic in the Painted Caves*, translated from the French by Sophie Hawkes (New York, Harry N. Abrams, 1998).

Clottes, Jean. *Chauvet Cave: The Art of Earliest Times*, translated from the French by Paul G. Bahn (Salt Lake City, The University of Utah Press, 2003).

Davenport, Guy. *The Geography of the Imagination: Forty Essays by Guy Davenport* (New York, Pantheon Books, 1992).

Edwards, Betty. *Drawing on the Artist Within* (New York, Simon & Schuster, 1986).

Field, Joanna (pseudonym of Marion Milner). *A Life of One's Own* (Los Angeles, Jeremy P. Tarcher, 1981).

Franck, Frederick. *The Zen of Seeing: Seeing and Drawing as Meditation* (New York, Vintage Books, 1973).

Franck, Frederick. *Zen Seeing, Zen Drawing: Meditation in Action* (New York, Bantam Books, 1993).

Glancey, Jonathan. "Gift of Nature," *Guardian Education,* 1ˢᵗ October 2002.

Graham, Jorie. *Erosion* (Princeton, NJ, Princeton University Press, 1983).

J.F. Hendry. *The Sacred Threshold: A Life of Rilke* (Manchester, England, Carcanet, 1983).

Hinchman, Hannah. *A Life In Hand: Creating the Illuminated Journal* (Salt Lake City, UT, Peregrine Smith Books, 1991).

Jackson, Maggie. *Distracted: The Erosion of Attention in the Coming Dark Age* (Amherst, NY, Prometheus Books, 2008).

Jamison, Kay Redfield. *Exuberance: The Passion for Life* (New York, Vintage Books, Random House, 2004).

Jung, C.G., in Malchiodi, *op.cit.*

Kabat-Zinn, Jon. *Coming to Our Senses: Healing Ourselves and the World Through Mindfulness* (New York, Hyperion, 2005).

Kunitz, Stanley with Genine Lentine. *The Wild Braid: A Poet Reflecting on a Century in the Garden,* (New York, W.W. Norton & Co, 2005).

Malchiodi, Cathy A. *The Soul's Palette: Drawing on Art's Transformative Powers for Health and Well-Being* (Boston & London, Shambhala, 2002).

Matisse, Henri. Quoted in "Cézanne to Picasso. Ambroise Vollard, Patron of the Avant-Garde," Metropolitan Museum of Art, New York, September 2006-Janaury 2007.

McEwen, Rory. See C. Oscar Moreton, *op.cit.*

Henry Moore. Quoted in "Moore at Kew," Kew Gardens, London, September 2007-March 2008.

Moreton, C. Oscar. *Old Carnations and Pinks,* with eight color plates by Rory McEwen (London, George Rainbird, in association with Collins, 1955).

Picasso, Pablo. Quoted by Judith Thurman, *op.cit.*

Rilke, Rainer Maria. *Letters on Cézanne,* translated by Joel Agee (New York, North Point Press, Farrar, Straus & Giroux, 1985, 2002).

Rilke, Rainer Maria. *Letters of Rainer Maria Rilke,* translated by Jane Bannard Greene and M.D. Herter Norton (London, W.W. Norton & Co., 1972).

Rilke, Rainer Maria. *The Selected Poetry of Rainer Maria Rilke,* edited and translated by Stephen Mitchell, with an introduction by Robert Hass (New York, Vintage International, 1989).

Ruskin, John. *Praeterita* (London, Rupert Hart-Davis, 1949).

Ruskin, John. see *Ruskin's Drawings:* Nicholas Penny (Oxford, Ashmolean Museum handbooks, 1997).

Siegel, Bernie, in Cathy A. Malchiodi, *op.cit.*

Steinhart, Peter. *The Undressed Art: Why We Draw* (New York, Vintage Books, 2004).

Smyth, Jim. Quoted by Peter Steinhart, *op.cit.*

Taubman, Mary. *Gwen John* (London, Scholar Press, 1985).

Thurman, Judith. "First Impressions. What does the world's oldest art say about us?" *The New Yorker,* 23rd June 2008.

Weschler, Lawrence. *Everything that Rises: A Book of Convergences* (San Francisco, McSweeney's Books, 2006).

Williams, Terry Tempest. "Ode to Slowness" in *Red: Passion and Patience in the Desert* (New York, Pantheon Books, 2001).

Yeats, William Butler. *The Autobiography of William Butler Yeats* (New York, Collier Books, Macmillan Publishing Co., 1965).

The Campaign for Drawing was founded in 2000, and has been an independent charity since March 2006. Sue Grayson Ford is the director, and can be reached at The Campaign for Drawing, 7 Gentleman's Row, Enfield, EN2 6PT, 0208 351 1719. You can get further information at info@drawingpower.org.uk. See too www.thebigdraw. org.uk. Discussions are held at www.drawing.org.uk.

See too, the Studio in a School programs in New York, where educators are partnered with professional artists, guiding students to develop their own creative vision. Studio in a School, 410 West 59th Street, New York, NY 10019, tel. (212) 765-5900. www.studioinaschool.org.

6: THE INTENSEST RENDEZVOUS

Augustine of Hippo, Saint. *The Confessions* (Oxford, New York, Oxford World Classics, 1998).

Arcana, Judith. *Grace Paley's Life Stories: A Literary Biography* (Urbana and Chicago, University of Illinois Press, 1993).

BB. *The Little Grey Men* (London, Puffin Books, 1962).

BB. *Down the Bright Stream* (London, Eyre & Spottiswoode, 1948).

Baca, Jimmy Santiago. Quoted by Adrienne Rich, *op. cit.*

Bach, Gerhard and Blaine Hall. *Conversations with Grace Paley* (Jackson, MI, University Press of Mississippi, 1997).

Berensohn, Paulus. Personal interview, Guilford, VT, 1st September 2006.

Bellow, Saul. *Humboldt's Gift* (New York, The Viking Press, 1975).

Books sold in U.S. *Harper's Magazine,* June 2007.

Carr, Nicholas. *The Shallows: What the Internet is Doing to Our Brains* (New York, W.W. Norton, 2010).

Chang Ch'ao. Quoted by Lin Yutang, *op.cit.*

Chudacoff, Howard P. *Children at Play: An American History* (New York & London, New York University Press, 2007).

Csikszentmihalyi, Mihalyi. *Creativity: Flow and the Psychology of Discovery and Invention* (New York, HarperCollins, 1996).

Eco, Umberto, interviewed by Adam Gopnik in *PEN America* 10. *Fear Itself* (April/May 2009).

Emerson, Ralph Waldo. *The Selected Writings of Ralph Waldo Emerson,* edited by Brooks Atkinson (New York, The Modern Library, 1964).

Grudin, Robert. *On Dialogue: an essay in free thought* (Boston, New York, Houghton Mifflin, 1996).

Hamill, Sam. *New York Poem* from *Dumb Luck.* Boa Editions, New York, 2002.

Ings, Simon. *The Eye: A Natural History* (London, Bloomsbury, 2007).

Jackson, Maggie. *Distraction: The Erosion of Attention in the Coming Dark Age* (Prometheus Books, Amherst, NY, 2008).

Jacoby, Susan. *The Age of American Unreason* (New York, Pantheon Books, 2008).

Keats, John. *Selected Letters,* edited by Robert Gittings (Oxford, New York, Oxford University Press, 2002).

Koch, Kenneth. "I'm a writer who likes to be influenced" in "The Ecstasy of Influence. A Plagiarism," by Jonathan Lethem, *Harper's Magazine,* February 2007.

Ku Ch'ienli (now anglicized as Guangqi) and Chin Shengt'an (now anglicized as Jin Shengtan), both quoted by Lin Yutang, *op. cit.*

Kunitz, Stanley with Genine Lentine. *The Wild Braid: A Poet Reflecting on a Century in the Garden,* (New York, W.W. Norton & Co., 2005).

Le Guin, Ursula K. "Staying Awake. Notes on the alleged decline of reading," *Harper's,* February 2008. It has been pointed out that if the average human lifetime is reckoned as about sixty-two years, it is only in the last six lifetimes that most of us have encountered the written word.

Levertov, Denise. *Light Up the Cave* (New York, New Directions, 1981).

Lusseyran, Jacques. *And There Was Light* (New York, Parabola Books, 1987).

Lusseyran, Jacques. *What One Sees Without Eyes: Selected Writings of Jacques Lusseyran* (New York, Parabola Books, 1999).

Machiavelli, Niccolo, in Robert Grudin, *op.cit.*

Oliver, Mary. *Blue Pastures* (New York, Harcourt Brace & Co., 1995).

Opie, Iona and Peter. *The Oxford Nursery Rhyme Book* (Oxford, The Clarendon Press, 1955).

Pinksy, Robert in conversation with Charles Simic, J.F.K. Library, Boston, 28th January, 2008.

Prose, Francine. *Reading Like a Writer* (New York, HarperCollins, 2006).

Reading statistics, as given in Jackson, *op.cit.* These figures are continually changing. Nicholas Carr claims that by 2008, the time the average American (over the age of fourteen) devoted to reading had fallen to 143 minutes a week, a drop of 11 percent since 2004. See Carr, *op.cit.*

"Reading the Sutras by Moonlight" is inscribed by Yuxi Simon (d. 1337), a Chinese priest of the Yuan dynasty, though the painter himself is unknown. Wang Fenchen was a poet of the Song dynasty (960-1279).

Rich, Adrienne. *What Is Found There: Notebooks on Poetry and Politics* (New York, W.W. Norton & Co. 1993).

Rukeyser, Muriel. Quoted by Denise Levertov in *The Poet in the World* (New York, New Directions, 1973).

Simic, Charles. *Orphan Factory: Essays and Memoirs* (Ann Arbor, The University of Michigan Press, 1998).

Slow reading. In 1887, Friedrich Nietzsche described himself as a "teacher of slow reading." More recently, the Oxford historian Keith Thomas wrote about his own slow reading in the *London Review of Books.* "I don't think using a search engine to find certain key words in a text is a substitute for reading properly. You don't get a proper sense of the work, or understand its context. And there's no serendipity—half the things I've found in my research have come when I've luckily stumbled across something I wasn't expecting." Quoted by Patrick Kingsley in "Why the Rush? The art of reading slowly" in *The Guardian,* 15th July 2010.

SS. the Schutzstaffel or Protection Squadron, a major paramilitary organization under Hitler and the Nazi Party.

Stafford, William. *Even in Quiet Places,* afterword by Kim Stafford (Lewiston, ID, Confluence Press, 1996).

Stevens, Wallace. *Selected Poems* (London, Faber & Faber Ltd., 1953, 1972).

Strand, Mark. "Slow Down for Poetry," *The New York Times Book Review,* 15th September 1991.

Strand, Mark. Quoted by Mihalyi Csikszentmihalyi, *op.cit.*

Sullivan, Robert. *The Thoreau You Don't Know: What the Prophet of Environmentalism Really Meant* (New York, HarperCollins, 2009).

Tate, James, ed. *The Best American Poetry, 1997* (New York, Scribners, 1996).

Wang Fenchen. Quoted in "Awakenings. Zen Figure Paintings in Medieval Japan," The Japan Society, Spring 2007.

Williams, William Carlos. *Selected Poems,* edited by Robert Pinksy (New York, Library of America, 2004).

Woolf, Virginia. *A Writer's Diary,* edited and with an introduction by Leonard Woolf (New York & London, Harcourt, Brace, Jovanovich, 1954, 1981).

Woolf, Virginia. Quoted by Alain de Botton in *How Proust Can Change Your Life* (New York, Vintage International, Random House, 1997).

Yeats, William Butler. *The Celtic Twilight: Faerie and Folklore* (London, A. H. Bullen, 1902).

Yutang, Lin. *The Importance of Living* (New York, HarperCollins, 1937, 1998).

7: A FEAST OF WORDS

Baldwin, James, interviewed by Studs Terkel in *Voices of Our Time: Five Decades of Studs Terkel Interviews* (The Chicago Historical Society, 1993). Baldwin was in Switzerland, working on his book *Another Country,* and surrounded by "white snow, white mountains, white faces." He listened to Bessie Smith every day, he said, and "corrected things according to what I was able to hear . . . the voice, the beat, the intonations." He needed the beat, he said, "and Bessie had the beat."

Blythe, Ronald, ed. *The Pleasures of Diaries: Four Centuries of Private Writing* (New York, Pantheon Books, 1989). It is worth pointing out that Chinese and Japanese literature provides a *two-thousand year* record of diaries, journals, pillow books, and other "confessional" writings. See *Nine Gates: Entering the Mind of Poetry, Essays,* by Jane Hirshfield (New York, HarperPerennial, 1998).

Carr, Nicholas. *The Shallows: What the Internet is Doing to Our Brains* (New York, W.W. Norton, 2010).

Cather, Willa. Quoted in *The Mountain Stands Alone: Stories of Place in the Monadnock Region*, edited by Howard Mansfield (Hanover, NH, University Press of New England and the Monadnock Institute of Nature, Place and Culture, 2006).

Clouds. "Each cloud the weight of a hundred elephants." See Rob Brezsny's "Beauty and Truth Lab" at Truthrooster@gmail.com.

Coleridge, Samuel Taylor. *The Notebooks of Samuel Taylor Coleridge, vol.1, 1794-1804*, edited by Kathleen Coburn (Princeton, NJ, Princeton University Press, Bollingen Foundation, 1957).

de Balzac, Honoré. quoted by Stefan Klein, *op.cit.*

de Botton, Alain. *How Proust Can Change Your Life* (New York, Vintage, 1998).

Deakin, Roger. *Notes from Walnut Tree Farm* (London, Hamish Hamilton, an imprint of Penguin Books, 2008).

Fadiman, Anne. *At Large and At Small: Familiar Essays* (New York, Farrar, Straus & Giroux, 2007).

Fountain, Gary, and Brazeau, Peter, ed., *Remembering Elizabeth Bishop: An Oral Biography* (Amherst, MA, University of Massachusetts Press, 1994).

Fountain Pen Hospital. This magical store has been in existence for more than fifty years, and describes itself as "the ultimate source for fine writing pens." It is to be found at 10 Warren Street, New York, NY 10007. Tel. (212) 964-0580 or (800) 253-7367. info@fountainpenhospital.com.

Friedman, Donald, with essays by William H. Gass and John Updike, *The Writer's Brush: Paintings, Drawings, and Sculpture by Writers* (Minneapolis, Mid-List Press, 2007). Apart from Gerard Manley Hopkins, and the others listed above, there are many other writer-artists, among them Emily and Charlotte Bronte, Robert Louis Stevenson, W.B. Yeats, Elizabeth Bishop, William Carlos Williams, and Allen Ginsberg.

Hampl, Patricia. *Blue Arabesque: A Search for the Sublime* (New York, Harcourt, 2006).

Heaney, Seamus. *The Spirit Level* (New York, Farrar, Straus & Giroux, 1996).

Hopkins, Gerard Manley. *The Notebooks and Papers of Gerard Manley Hopkins,* edited by Humphrey House (London and New York, Oxford University Press, 1937).

Irish monks. *Antaeus: Journals, Notebooks and Diaries,* #61, edited by Daniel Halpern, (Tangier, London, New York, Autumn, 1996). See also *A Celtic Miscellany, translations from the Celtic Literatures* by Kenneth Hurlstone Jackson (Harmondsworth, Penguin Books, 1971).

Jackson, Maggie. *Distracted: The Erosion of Attention in the Coming Dark Age* (Prometheus Books, Amherst, NY, 2008).

Jean, Georges. *Writing: The Story of Alphabets and Scripts,* translated from the French by Jenny Oates (New York, Harry N. Abrams, Inc., 1992).

Keats, John. *Complete Poems and Selected Letters of John Keats,* with an introduction by Edward Hirsch (New York, Modern Library, 2001).

Kern, Stephen. *The Culture of Time & Space, 1880-1918* (Cambridge, MA, Harvard University Press, 1983).

Klein, Stefan. *Time: A User's Guide,* translated by Shelley Frisch (London, Penguin Books, 2008).

Letters. Nicholas Carr points out that the volume of mail sent through the U.S. postal service dropped at its fastest pace ever during 2009. Nicholas Carr, *op. cit.*

Mansfield, Katherine. See Patricia Hampl, *op.cit.*

McEwen, Christian. *In the Wake of Home* (Dublin, NH, Meadowlark Press, 2004).

Milosz, Czeslaw. *To Begin Where I Am: Selected Essays,* edited by Bogdana Carpenter and Madeline G. Levine (New York, Farrar, Straus & Giroux, 2001).

Mann, Thomas, "Tristan" in *Death in Venice and Seven Other Stories* (New York, Vintage, 1963).

Oliver, Mary. *Blue Pastures* (New York, Harcourt Brace & Co., 1995). The poet William Blake would have approved of Mary Oliver's precision. "To generalize," he wrote, "is to be an Idiot. To Particularize is the alone distinction of merit." Quoted by Jane Hirshfield in *Nine Gates: Entering the Mind of Poetry* (New York, HarperPerennial, 1998).

Rich, Adrienne. *What Is Found There: Notebooks on Poetry and Politics* (New York, W.W. Norton & Co., 1993).

Potter, Beatrix, in *Beatrix Potter: A Life in Nature* by Linda Lear (London, Allen Lane, 2006).

Stafford, Kim. *Early Morning: Remembering My Father* (St. Paul, MN, Greywolf Press, 2002).

Stafford, Kim. *The Muses Among Us: Eloquent Listening and Other Pleasures of the Writer's Craft* (Athens and London, University of Georgia Press, 2003).

Stafford, William. *Writing the Australian Crawl: Views on the Writer's Vocation* (Ann Arbor, University of Michigan Press, 1978).

Stafford, William. *Even in Quiet Places*, afterword by Kim Stafford (Lewiston, ID, Confluence Press, 1996).

Steinman, Michael, ed. *The Element of Lavishness: Letters of Sylvia Townsend Warner & William Maxwell, 1938-1978* (Washington, DC, Counterpoint, 2001).

Sullivan, Robert. *The Thoreau You Don't Know: What the Prophet of Environmentalism Really Meant* (New York, HarperCollins, 2009).

Thoreau, Henry David. *The Heart of Thoreau's Journals,* edited by Odell Shepard (New York, Dover Publications, Inc., 1961). See too, Robert Sullivan, *op. cit.* Thoreau was always well supplied with pencils, but there were times when he had difficulties in acquiring the perfect notebook. "I cannot easily buy a blank-book to write thoughts in," he wrote. "[T]hey are commonly ruled for dollars and cents." Quoted by Howard Mansfield in *In the Memory House* (Golden, CO, Fulcrum Publishing, 1993).

Valéry, Paul. "Poetry and Abstract Thought," translated by Denise Folliet, in *Toward the Open Field: Poets on the Art of Poetry 1800-*

1950, edited by Melissa Kwasny (Middletown, CT, Wesleyan University Press, 2004).

Van Doren, Mark. *The Dialogues of Archibald MacLeish and Mark Van Doren* (New York, E.P. Dutton & Co., Inc. 1964).

Walker, Alice. "Finding Celie's Voice," *Ms.*, December, 1985.

White, Gilbert, in Ronald Blythe, *op. cit.*

Woolf, Virginia. *The Waves* (London, The Hogarth Press, 1931, 1972).

Woolf, Virginia. *A Writer's Diary*, edited and with an introduction by Leonard Woolf (New York and London, Harcourt, Brace, Jovanovich, 1954, 1981).

Woolf, Virginia. *The Diary of Virginia Woolf*, Vol.Two, 1920-1924, edited by Anne Olivier Bell, assisted by Andrew McNeillie (New York and London, Harcourt Brace Jovanovich, 1978).

Woolf, Virginia. *Congenial Spirits: The Selected Letters of Virginia Woolf*, edited by Joanne Trautman Banks (New York and London, Harcourt Brace Jovanovich, 1989).

Yutang, Lin. *The Importance of Living* (New York, HarperCollins, 1937, 1998).

8: THE SPACE BETWEEN

Bell, Alexander Graham. Quoted in Howard Mansfield, *op.cit.*

Best ideas. Jane Hirshfield quotes from a letter of Mozart's, in which he describes his own creative process. "When I am, as it were, completely myself, entirely alone, and of good cheer—say, traveling in a carriage, or walking after a good meal, or during the night when I cannot sleep; it is on such occasions that my ideas flow best and most abundantly." See *Nine Gates: Entering the Mind of Poetry, Essays*, by Jane Hirshfield (New York, HarperPerennial, 1998).

Berensohn, Paulus. *Finding One's Way With Clay: Pinched Pottery and the Color of Clay* (New York, Simon & Schuster, 1972).

Berensohn, Paulus. personal interview, Guilford, VT, 1st September 2006.

Campaign to Protect Rural England. For information about the map published by CPRE see *The Weekly Telegraph*, 25th-31st October 2006.

Campbell, Joseph. *The Power of Myth*, with Bill Moyers (New York, Anchor Books, A Division of Random House, Inc., 1991).

Carlson, Richard and Joseph Bailey. *Slowing Down to the Speed of Life: How to Create a More Peaceful, Simpler Life from the Inside Out* (Harper San Francisco, 1997).

Carr, Nicholas. *The Shallows: What the Internet is Doing to Our Brains* (New York, W.W. Norton, 2010).

Claxton, Guy. *Hare Brain, Tortoise Mind: Why Intelligence Increases When You Think Less* (London, Fourth Estate, 1997).

Colapinto, John. "The Interpreter" in *The New Yorker*, 16th April, 2007.

De Quincey, Thomas. *Suspiria De Profundis* (Boston, Ticknor, Reed & Fields, 1850).

Fisher, M.F.K. *Last House: Reflections, Dreams & Observations, 1943-1991* (New York, Pantheon Books, 1995).

Flat-rock approach. The story of Edgar Anderson, head of the Missouri Botanical Gardens in St. Louis, is quoted by William Mac-Leish, *op.cit.*

Gendlin, Eugene T. *Focusing* (New York, Bantam Books, 1981).

Graham, Jorie. In Molly McQuade, *op. cit.*

Green talk. M.F.K. Fisher seems not to have known this (at least not consciously), but the writer Elif Batuman reports that "Among the alchemists and kabbalists, the perfect language that would unlock ultimate knowledge was known as either "the green language" or "the language of birds." See Elif Batuman, *The Possessed* (New York, Farrar, Straus and Giroux, 2010).

Gregory, Peter N. & Susannne Mrozik, eds. *Women Practicing Buddhism: American Experiences* (Boston, Wisdom Publications, 2008).

Groning, Philip. *Into Great Silence*, Bavaria-Filmkunst Verleih, 2005.

Hejmadi, Padma. *Room to Fly: A Transcultural Memoir* (Berkeley, University of California Press, 1999).

Hirshfield, Jane. In Peter N. Gregory and Susanne Mrozik, eds. *op. cit.*

Jackson, Maggie. *Distracted: The Erosion of Attention in the Coming Dark Age* (Amherst, MA, Prometheus Books, 2008).

James, William. Quoted by William Powers, *op.cit.*, and also by Nicholas Carr, *op.cit.*

Japanese school of Sumi painting. Quoted by Padma Hejmadi, *op. cit.*

Joseph's poem is quoted by Christian McEwen in *The Alphabet of the Trees: A Guide to Nature Writing*, edited by Christian McEwen and Mark Statman (New York, Teachers & Writers Collaborative, 2000).

Kafka, Franz. *The Collected Aphorisms,* translated by Malcolm Pasley (London, Penguin Books, 1994).

Kostelanetz, Richard. *John Cage: Documentary Monographs in Modern Art* (New York, Praeger Publishers, 1970).

Kufu. Quoted by Guy Claxton, *op.cit.*

Lao-tzu. *Tao Te Ching*, A new English version, with foreword and notes, by Stephen Mitchell (New York, Harper & Row, 1988).

Lohr, Steve. "Slow Down, Brave Multitasker, And Don't Read This in Traffic," in *The New York Times*, 25th March 2007.

Ma. First described for me by Howard Mansfield, personal interview, Hancock, NH, 13th March 2007. See too, Howard Mansfield, *op.cit.*

MacDowell. The situation has changed since my last visit. Guests at the MacDowell Colony can now respond to email in the library, freeing Colony Hall for convivial conversation.

MacLeish, William. *The Day Before America: Changing the Nature of a Continent* (Boston, Houghton Mifflin, 1994).

Mansfield, Howard. *The Same Ax, Twice: Restoration and Renewal in a Throwaway Age* (Hanover and London, University Press of New England, 2000).

McQuade, Molly, ed. *By Herself: Women Reclaim Poetry* (St. Paul, MN, Graywolf Press, 2000).

Merton, Thomas. *The Way of Chuang Tzu* (New York, New Directions, 1969).

Molino, Anthony, ed. *The Couch and the Tree: Dialogues in Psychoanalysis and Buddhism* (New York, North Point Press, Farrar, Straus & Giroux, 1998).

Monk, Meredith. Personal interview, Peterborough, NH, 24th February 2007.

Monk, Meredith. See also "Buddhism and Creativity," a conversation between Jane Hirshfield and Meredith Monk, moderated by Pat Enkyo O'Hara, 2005, in Peter N. Gregory and Susanne Mrozik, *op.cit.*

Monk, Meredith. *impermanence*. ECM Records, Munich, 2008.

Multitasking. It is worth pointing out just how dangerous this can be. More than five thousand Americans were killed in 2009 as a result of trying to text or use their cell phones while behind the wheel. See *The Week,* 8th October 2010. Texting while driving is even more dangerous than driving drunk. A recent study by *Car and Driver* found that it took a driver an extra seventy feet to come to a complete halt when texting, as opposed to only an extra four feet when driving drunk. *The Week,* 15th October 2010.

Oliver, Mary. *Winter Hours: Prose, Prose Poems, and Poems* (Boston, New York, Houghton Mifflin, 1999).

Picard, Max. *The World of Silence,* translated by Stanley Goodman (Washington, DC, Regnery Gateway, 1948, 1986).

Powers, William. *Hamlet's BlackBerry: A Practical Philosophy for Building a Good Life in the Digital Age* (New York, HarperCollins, 2010).

Revill, David. *The Roaring Silence: John Cage: A Life* (New York, Arcade Publishing, 1992).

Stein, Gertrude. "Reflection on the Atomic Bomb," 1946. *Yale Poetry Review,* 1947.

Supertasking. See *The Week,* 23rd April 2010.

Taliesin, chief bard of Britain and a Celtic shaman, was a historical figure who lived in Wales during the latter half of the sixth century. See *Taliesin: The Last Celtic Shaman* by John Matthews, with additional material by Caitlin Matthews (Rochester, VT, Inner Traditions, 2002).

Von Durckheim, Karlfried Graf. *The Japanese Cult of Tranquility* (York Beach, ME, Samuel Weiser, 1974).

Wakin, Daniel J. "An Organ Composition for the Very, Very Patient" in *The New York Times*, 5th May, 2006.

Winnicott, D.W.. *The Maturational Process and the Facilitating Environment* (London, Tavistock Press, 1960).

Yutang, Lin. *The Importance of Living* (New York, William Morrow, 1937, 1998).

9: LEARNING TO PAUSE

Blake, William. *The Complete Poetry and Prose of William Blake*, edited by David V. Erdman (New York, Anchor Books, Doubleday, 1998).

Carmichael, Alexander. *Carmina Gadelica: Hymns & Incantations* (Hudson, New York, Lindisfarne Press, 1992, 1994).

Chadwick, David. *Crooked Cucumber: The Life and Zen Teaching of Shunryu Suzuki* (New York, Broadway, 1999).

Chatwin, Bruce. *The Songlines* (New York, Viking Penguin, Inc., 1987).

Chesterton, G. K. "On Lying in Bed" in *Tremendous Trifles* (London, Methuen, 1909).

Chronobiology. my information is drawn from *Time: A User's Guide* by Stefan Klein, translated by Shelley Frisch (London, Penguin Books, 2008).

Dossey, Larry. *Healing Words: the Power of Prayer and the Practice of Medicine* (San Francisco, HarperSanFrancisco, 1993).

Eckhart, Meister. *Meister Eckhart from Whom God Hid Nothing: Sermons, Writings & Sayings*, edited by David O'Neil, foreword by David Steindl-Rast (Boston, London, Shambhala, 1996).

Eddie, Bill. Personal communication, Edinburgh, Spring 2005.

Gallagher, Winifred. *Rapt: Attention and the Focused Life* (New York, Penguin Books, 2009).

Greenland ice story. *The Best American Spiritual Writing, 2004,* edited and introduced by Jack Miles (New York, Houghton Mifflin, 2004).

Hass, Robert. *Praise* (New York, Ecco Press, 1979).

Heschel, Abraham Joshua. *The Sabbath* (Boston, MA, Shambhala Publications, 1951, 2003).

James, William. *The Varieties of Religious Experience: A Study in Human Nature* (Glasgow, William Collins Sons & Co, 1977).

Kundera, Milan. *Slowness,* translated by Linda Asher (New York, HarperCollins, 1995).

"Let me fall . . . " lyrics by Josh Groban, in Cirque du Soleil.

Merton, Thomas. *Thoughts in Solitude* (Boston & London, Shambhala, 1993).

Metta meditation. I have seen many accounts of *metta* meditation. My favorite can be found in *Teachings on Love* by Thich Nhat Hanh (Berkeley, CA, Parallax Press, 1998).

Mono-time. The word is drawn from *A Sideways Look at Time* by Jay Griffiths (New York, Jeremy P. Tarcher, Penguin Putnam Inc., 1999).

Muir, Edwin. *Scottish Journey* (Edinburgh, Scotland, Mainstream Publishing, 1996).

Muller, Wayne. *Sabbath: Finding Rest, Renewal, and Delight in Our Busy Lives* (New York, Bantam Books, 1999, 2000).

Partridge, Eric. *Origins: A Short Etymological Dictionary of Modern English* (New York, Crown Publishers, 1983).

Negative rumination. "When you aren't doing anything in particular, but are just 'at rest,' your brain's so-called default mode kicks in. This baseline mental state often leads to inward-looking, negative ruminations that tend to be, as [neuroscientist Richard] Davidson puts it, 'all about my, me, and mine.' " See Gallagher, *op. cit.* See also Tolle, *op.cit.*

Plum Village. Personal journal, September 2004.

Rebar. see Silverman, Justin Rocket. "Park it right here, on 8th Ave. bench" *amNew York,* 22nd September 2006.

Reid, Alastair. *An Alastair Reid Reader: Selected Prose and Poetry* (Hanover, NH, Middlebury College Press, 1994).

Rumi, Jelaluddin. *The Essential Rumi,* translated by Coleman Barks (Edison, New Jersey, Castle Books, 1997).

"Slow Down, Finding your natural rhythm in a speed-crazed world," *Utne Reader,* March-April 1997.

St. John the Evangelist. *Introduction a la Vie Devoté de Charles Forot,* my translation (Paris, Librarie Garner Freres, ND.)

Stafford, William. *Even in Quiet Places* (Lewiston, ID, Confluence Press, 1996).

Steindl-Rast, Brother David. *Gratefulness, the Heart of Prayer: An Approach to Life in Fullness* (New York, Paulist Press, 1984).

Strimling, Arthur. Personal interview, New York, 3rd October 2006.

Thich Nhat Hanh. *The Long Road Turns to Joy: A Guide to Walking Meditation,* (Berkeley, CA. 1996, Parallax Press).

Thoreau, Henry David. Quoted by John Daniel in *Rogue River Journal: A Winter Alone* (Berkeley, CA, Counterpoint, 2005).

Tolle, Eckhart. *The Power of Now: A Guide to Spiritual Enlightenment* (Novato, CA, New World Library, 1999).

Unhappiest hour in America. Quoted by Gallagher, *op. cit.*

U.S. National Recreation and Parks Association 1992 survey. Quoted by David Loy and Linda Goodhew in "Consuming Time," in *Hooked! Buddhist Writings on Greed, Desire, and the Urge to Consume,* edited by Stephanie Kaza (Boston & London, Shambhala, 2005). It is perhaps worth pointing out here that Americans take only fourteen vacation days a year, whereas some Europeans take as many as thirty-nine. See Gallagher, *op.cit.*

Waskow, Arthur. "Can America Learn from Shabbat?" in *Take Back Your Time: Fighting Overwork and Time Poverty in America,* edited by John de Graaf (San Francisco, Berrett-Koehler Publishers Inc., 2003).

Wilde, Oscar. *Prose Writing and Poems* (London, Dent, 1955).

Yeats. William Butler. *The Autobiography of William Butler Yeats* (New York, Collier Books, Macmillan Publishing Co. Inc., 1965).

10: ACROSS THE BRIDGE OF DREAMS

Agassiz, Louis, in Walter de la Mare, *op. cit.*

Alvarez. A. *Night: Night Life, Night Language, Sleep, and Dreams* (New York, London, W.W. Norton & Co., 1995).

Angier, Natalie. "Cheating on Sleep. Modern Life Turns America into the Land of the Drowsy," *New York Times,* 15th May, 1990.

Armour, Stephanie, "Lack of sleep catches up with today's workforce" in *USA Today,* 3rd March 2008. Lack of sleep has a deleterious effect on other creatures too. To give just one example, sleep-deprived honeybees waggle-dance less accurately. See *Harper's Magazine,* February 2011.

Aristides. Quoted by David Coxhead and Susan Hiller, *op. cit.*

Barasch, Marc Ian. *Healing Dreams: Exploring the Dreams That Can Transform Your Life* (New York, Riverhead Books, Penguin Putnam, 2000).

Blum, David. *Appointment with the Wise Old Dog: Dream Images in a Time of Crisis* (video, 29 minutes). This must be ordered directly from David Blum's widow, Sarah Blum, at P.O. Box 104, Medina, WA 98039-0104.

Borges, Jorge Luis. *The Preface to Dr. Brodie's Report* (New York, E.P. Dutton, 1972).

Bronte, Emily. *Wuthering Heights* (New York, New American Library, 1959).

Carpenter Co. Labs. www.sleepbetter.org.

Chesterton, G. K. "On Lying in Bed," in *Tremendous Trifles* (London, Methuen, 1909).

Coleridge, Samuel Taylor. *The Notebooks of Samuel Taylor Coleridge, vol. 1, 1794-1804,* edited by Kathleen Coburn (Princeton, NJ, Princeton University Press, Bollingen Foundation, 1957).

Coxhead, David and Susan Hiller. *Dreams: Visions of the Night* (London, Thames & Hudson, 1989).

De la Mare, Walter. *Behold This Dreamer!* (London, Faber & Faber, 1939, 1984).

Emerson, Ralph Waldo. In "Demonology," *The Complete Works of Ralph Waldo Emerson,* Vol. 10, (Boston, Houghton Mifflin & Co., 1903-4).

Epel, Naomi. *Writers Dreaming* (New York, Carol Southern Books, 1993).

Flaubert, Gustave, in Walter de la Mare, *op. cit.*

Godwin, Malcolm. *The Lucid Dreamer: A Waking Guide to the Traveler Between Worlds* (New York, Simon & Schuster, 1994).

Hillman, James. *Blue Fire: Selected Writings by James Hillman,* edited by Thomas Moore (New York, Harper & Row, 1989).

Jung, Carl Gustav. The *Essential Jung,* selected by Anthony Storr (Princeton, Princeton University Press, 1983).

Kahlo, Frida. *The Diary of Frida Kahlo: An Intimate Self Portrait,* with an introduction by Carlos Fuentes (New York, Harry N. Abrams, Inc. 1995).

Krippner, Stanley, ed. *Dreamtime & Dreamwork: Decoding the Language of the Night* (Los Angeles, Jeremy P. Tarcher, Inc., 1990).

Matthews, Caitlin. *The Way of the Celtic Tradition* (Hammersmith, London, Element, HarperCollins, 1989, 2003).

Matthews, John, editor. *The Bardic Source Book: Inspirational Legacy and Teachings of the Ancient Celts* (London, Blandford Press, 1998).

Matthews, John. *Taliesin: The Last Celtic Shaman* (Rochester, VT, Inner Traditions, 1991, 2002).

Monaghan, Patricia. *The Red-Haired Girl From the Bog: The Landscape of Celtic Myth & Spirit* (Novato, CA, New World Library, 2003).

National Sleep Foundation. a nonprofit organization supporting public education, sleep-related research, and advocacy related to sleep deprivation and sleep disorders. See www.sleepfoundation.org.

Partridge, Eric. *Origins: A Short Etymological Dictionary of Modern English* (New York, Crown Publishers, 1983).

Rheingold, Howard. *They Have a Word for It: A Lighthearted Lexicon of Untranslatable Words and Phrases* (Los Angeles, Jeremy P. Tarcher, Inc., 1988).

Rothenberg, Jerome, ed. *Shaking the Pumpkin: Traditional Poetry of* the *Indian North Americas* (Garden City, New York, Doubleday & Co., 1972).

Rumi, Jelaluddin. *Open Secret,* versions by John Moyne and Coleman Barks (Putney, VT, Threshold Books, 1984.)

Russell, George. Quoted by Malcolm Godwin, *op.cit.* Russell was a poet and mystic, and a leader of the Irish literary renaissance. In 1888, he took the name "AE," an abbreviation of "Aeon," meaning an eternal being that is an intermediary between the world and the supreme being of whom it is a part.

Schor, Judith. *The Overworked American: The Unexpected Decline of Leisure* (New York, Basic Books, 1992).

Sleep deprivation. See Natalie Angier, *op. cit.*

Steindl-Rast, David. *Gratefulness: the Heart of Prayer: An Approach to Life in Fullness* (New York, Paulist Press, 1984).

Stevenson, Robert Louis. "A Chapter on Dreams" in *The Lantern-Bearers and Other Essays,* selected with an introduction by Jeremy Treglown (New York, Farrar, Straus and Giroux, 1988).

Sullwold, Edith. In *Sacred Stories: A Celebration of the Power of Stories to Transform and Heal,* edited by Charles and Anne Simpkinson (HarperSan Francisco, 1993).

Tubman, Harriet, Elias Howe *et. al.* See Stanley Krippner, *op.cit.*

Van der Post, Laurens. *Jung and the Story of Our Time* (New York, Pantheon, 1975).

Vaughan, Henry. "The World," in *The New Oxford Book of English Verse,* edited by Helen Gardner (Oxford, Clarendon Press, 1972).

Walker, Alice. "Finding Celie's Voice," *Ms.,* December 1985.

Wallace, Anthony F.C. "Dreams and the Wishes of the Soul. A Type of Psychoanalytic Theory Among the Seventeenth Century Iroquois" in *Magic, Witchcraft and Curing,* edited by John Middleton (New York, The Natural History Press, 1967).

Williamson, Robin. *The Wise and Foolish Tongue: Celtic Stories and Poems* (San Francisco, Chronicle Books, 1991).

Yutang, Lin. *The Importance of Living* (New York, William Morrow, 1937, 1998).

11: A UNIVERSE OF STORIES

Abram, David. *The Spell of the Sensuous* (New York, Random House, 1997).

Abram, David. "Earth Stories" in *Resurgence*, #222, January-February 2004.

Beebe, William, ed. *The Book of Naturalists: An Anthology of the Best Natural History* (Princeton, Princeton University Press, 1988). It should be noted that Beebe's facts are somewhat out of date. The Andromeda Galaxy is in fact 2,500,000 *light years* from Earth.

Berensohn, Paulus. In *M.C. Richards: The Fire Within,* produced by Richard Kane and Melody Lewis-Kane (Kane Lewis Productions). KaneLewis@aol.com.

Benjamin, Walter. *Illuminations,* edited and with an introduction by Hannah Arendt (New York, Schocken Books, 1969). There is a lovely story about Thoreau that might almost have been invented to illustrate Benjamin's point about the "seeds." Apparently, Thoreau loved ruins, and when he heard that a certain pre-Revolutionary house was being demolished, he set off to examine it, posthaste. By the time he got there, only the foundation remained. But there, in the basement, he came across some seeds—seeds of a plant that no longer grew locally. Thoreau took the seeds, and planted them. They thrived. And the plant was returned to Concord. See Robert Sullivan, *op.cit.*

Blythe, Ronald. *Akenfield: Portrait of an English Village* (New York, Dell Publishing Co., 1969).

Buber, Martin. Quoted by Marc Kaminsky in *What's Inside You It Shines Out of You* (New York, Horizon Press, 1974).

Chatwin, Bruce. *The Songlines* (New York, Penguin Books, 1988).

Cree stories in David Abram, *op. cit.,* and Katherine McNamara, *op. cit.*

Ensler, Eve. *Insecure at Last: A Political Memoir* (New York, Villard, 2006).

Isay, David. *Listening Is an Act of Love: A Celebration of American Life from the StoryCorps Project* (New York, The Penguin Press, 2007).

Jackson, Maggie. *Distracted: The Erosion of Attention in the Coming Dark Age* (Amherst, NY, Prometheus Books, 2008).

Keen, Sam, in *Sacred Stories: A Celebration of the Power of Stories to Transform and Heal*, edited by Charles and Anne Simpkinson (New York, HarperCollins, 1993).

Evelyn Fox Keller. *A Feeling for the Organism: The Life and Work of Barbara McClintock* (New York, W. H. Freeman & Co., 1983).

Kundera, Milan. *Slowness*, translated from the French by Linda Asher (New York, HarperCollins, 1996).

Lehrer, Warren and Sloan, Judith. *Crossing the Boulevard: Strangers, Neighbors, Aliens in a New America* (New York, W.W. Norton, 2003).

Mansfield, Howard. Personal interview, Hancock, NH. 13th March 2007.

Mansfield, Howard. *In the Memory House* (Golden, CO, Fulcrum Publishing, 1993).

Mansfield, Howard. *Turn & Jump: The Divorce of Time and Place* (Camden, ME, Down East Books, 2010).

McNamara, Katherine. *Narrow Road to the Deep North: A Journey to the Interior of Alaska* (San Francisco, Mercury House, 2001).

Merleau-Ponty, Maurice. Quoted by David Abram, *op.cit.*

Merwin, W.S., in *Being Alive, the sequel to Staying Alive*, edited by Neil Astley (Northumberland, Bloodaxe Books, Ltd., 2004).

Meyerhoff, Barbara. *Number Our Days* (New York, Simon & Schuster, 1978).

Meyerhoff, Barbara. Story told to me by Arthur Strimling, New York, early 1990s.

McClintock, Barbara. Quoted by Linda Hogan in *Listening to the Land: Conversations about Nature, Culture and Eros*, edited by Derrick Jensen (San Francisco, Sierra Club Books, 1995).

Ostranyenie. See *The Alphabet of the Trees: A Guide to Nature Writing*, edited by Christian McEwen and Mark Statman (New York, Teachers & Writers Collaborative, 2000). Harvard psychologist

Ellen Langer suggests using such "defamiliarization" with those closest to us. "Imagine that you've had the same spouse for many years. If you look for a way in which he's different today, you'll find something. That makes him more interesting and, probably, more likable." Quoted by Winifred Gallagher in *Rapt: Attention and the Focused Life* (New York, Penguin Books, 2009).

Paley, Grace. *Begin Again: Collected Poems* (New York, Farrar, Straus & Giroux, 2001).

Paley, Grace. *Conversations with Grace Paley,* edited by Gerhard Bach & Blaine H. Hall (Jackson, MS, University Press of Mississippi, 1997).

Paley, Grace. Interviews with Christian McEwen, New York, April 1992; Thetford, VT, May 2001.

Porche, Verandah. *The Body's Symmetry* (New York, Harper & Row, 1974).

Porche, Verandah. Personal interview, Guilford, VT, 16th April 2007.

Putnam, Robert D., *Bowling Alone: The Collapse and Revival of American Community,* (New York, Simon & Schuster, 2000).

Robinson, Tim. *Setting Foot on the Shores of Connemara & Other Writings* (Dublin, The Lilliput Press, 1996).

Sorrowless Fields. Personal communication, John McEwen, 29th June 2007.

Sullivan, Robert. *The Thoreau You Don't Know: What the Prophet of Environmentalism Really Meant* (New York, HarperCollins, 2009).

Watching television. Details quoted by Maggie Jackson, *op.cit.* See also Putnam, *op.cit.*

12: A DAY SO HAPPY

Abrams, Linsey. Memorial gathering in honor of Grace Paley and Jane Cooper. Teachers & Writers Collaborative, New York, 17th April 2008.

Adams, Guy, "Meet the Natives" in *The Independent Magazine,* 8th September 2007.

Auden, W. H. *The Collected Poems of W.H. Auden,* edited by Edward Mendelson (New York, Modern Library, 2007).

Basho. Quoted by Phil Cousineau, *op. cit.*

Bellow, Saul, in *The Paris Review Interviews,* introduced by Alfred Kazin (New York, Viking Press, 1967).

Blake, William. "I want! I want!" line-engraving, printed in black ink, in *For the Sexes, The Gates of Paradise* (Fitzwilliam Museum, Cambridge).

Chadwick, David. *The Life and Zen Times of Shunryu Suzuki* (New York, Broadway, 1999).

Consumerism. By the winter of 2010, 93 percent of American consumers claimed to have changed their spending habits. Retailers at Christmas were looking forward to "frugal splurging." *The Week,* 24th December 2010-7th January 2011.

Cousineau, Phil. *The Art of Pilgrimage: The Seeker's Guide to Making Travel Sacred* (Berkeley, CA, Conari Press, 1998).

Csikszentmihalyi, Mihalyi. *Flow: The Psychology of Optimal Experience* (New York, Harper & Row, 1990). See also Gallagher, *op.cit.*

The Dalai Lama and Paul Eckman. *Emotional Awareness: Overcoming the Obstacles to Psychological Balance and Compassion* (New York, Times Books, Henry Holt & Co., 2008).

Descartes, René. Quoted in *The Best Spiritual Writing 2000,* edited by Philip Zaleski (New York, HarperCollins, 2000).

Dunmore, Helen. "Glad of these times" in *Being Alive: the sequel to Staying Alive,* edited by Neil Astley (Tarset, Northumberland, Bloodaxe Books, Ltd., 2004).

Eckhart, Meister. *Meister Eckhart from Whom God Hid Nothing,* Foreword by David Steindl-Rast (Boston and London, Shambhala, 1996).

Enantiodromia. The word originated with Heraclitus, and was later taken up by Carl Jung. See *Jung and the Story of Our Time* by Laurens van der Post (New York, Pantheon, 1975).

Gallagher, Winifred. *Rapt: Attention and the Focused Life* (New

York, Penguin Books, 2009). Gallagher praises the "wide-angle perspective on life" that, in Csikszentmihalyi's terms, allows people to be "surprised by something every day." She also points out that the kind of concentrated joyful focus I've been describing is not especially common. "About 20% of people flow once or more each day; about 15%, never; the great majority, only occasionally."

Gandhi. Quoted by Eknath Easwaran in *Gandhi the Man* (Tomales, CA, Nilgiri Press, 1997).

Green, Penelope. "This is Your Brain on Happiness" in *O*, March 2008.

Griffin, Susan. See "To Love the Marigold" in Loeb, *op. cit.*

Happiness. In a recent study, the Princeton psychologist Daniel Kahneman asked 909 working women to keep a written record of everything they had done and felt the previous day. He discovered that job security and marital status had relatively little effect on their sense of satisfaction. What really made a difference was *the degree of choice they had about how they spent their time.* It is also worth noting that despite their generally lower socioeconomic status, *women savor more than men.* [My emphasis.] See Gallagher, *op.cit.*

Harrington, Anne and Zajonc, Arthur. *The Dalai Lama at MIT* (Cambridge, MA, Harvard University Press, 2006).

Houston, Fiona. Personal interview, Traquair, Peebleshire, Scotland, 25th April 2005.

Houston, Fiona J. *The Garden & Cottage Diaries: My Year in the Eighteenth Century* (Glasgow, Scotland, Saraband, 2009).

Jackson, Maggie. *Distracted: The Erosion of Attention in the Coming Dark Age* (Amherst, NY, Prometheus Books, 2008).

James, William. Quoted by Rebecca Solnit. *op.cit.*

Krech, Greg. *Naikan: Gratitude, Grace, and the Japanese Art of Self-Reflection* (Berkeley, CA, Stone Bridge Press, 2002).

Lanchester, John. "Pursuing Happiness," *New Yorker*, 27th February 2006.

Loeb, Paul Rogat, ed. *The Impossible Will Take a Little Longer: A Citizen's Guide to Hope in a Time of Fear* (New York, Basic Books, 2004).

Maia. Numerous conversations, ongoing.

Meditation. More narrowly focused practices, such as following the breath, have been found to help meditators concentrate better in their daily lives, as well as improving short-term memory. Broader, more receptive practices help smooth transitions from one task to the next; they also reduces stress. See Gallagher, *op. cit.*

Milosz, Czeslaw. *New and Collected Poems, 1931-2001* (New York, Ecco Press, 2001).

Neruda, Pablo. "Childhood and Poetry," quoted in *Neruda & Vallejo: Selected Poems,* edited, with a new preface, by Robert Bly (Boston, Beacon Press, 1993).

Nye, Naomi Shihab. "Rebellion against the North Side" in *Words Under the Words: Selected Poems* (Portland, OR, Eighth Mountain Press, 1995).

O'Keeffe, Georgia. Quoted by Maggie Jackson, *op.cit.*

Paley, Grace. *Fidelity* (New York, Farrar, Straus and Giroux, 2008).

Partridge, Eric. *Origins: A Short Etymological Dictionary of Modern English* (New York, Crown Publishers, 1983).

Revel, Jean-François and Ricard, Matthieu. *The Monk and the Philosopher: A Father and Son Discuss the Meaning of Life,* translated from the French by John Canti (New York, Schocken Books, 1998).

Ricard, Matthieu. *Happiness: A Guide to Developing Life's Most Important Skill,* translated by Jesse Browner (New York, Little, Brown & Co., 2006).

Rinpoche. Tibetan for "precious jewel."

Rilke, Rainer Maria. *The Poet's Guide to Life: The Wisdom of Rilke,* edited and translated by Ulrich Baer (New York, The Modern Library, 2005).

Seligman, Martin. *Authentic Happiness* (New York, Free Press, 2002).

Schueler, Jon. *The Sound of Sleat: A Painter's Life,* edited by Magda

Salvesen and Diane Cousineau (New York, Picador, 1999).

Socrates. Quoted by Alain de Botton in *Status Anxiety* (New York, Pantheon Books, 2004).

Solnit, Rebecca. "The Uses of Disaster. Notes on bad weather and good government" in *Harper's Magazine,* October 2005.

Tharp, Twyla. *The Creative Habit: Learn It and Use It for Life* (New York, Simon & Schuster, 2003). It is worth emphasizing that such generosity is strongly correlated with personal well-being. Psychologist Chris Peterson points out that good-hearted, altruistic people are "happier and healthier and live longer than people who pursue all the latest toys but never have enough." Quoted by Gallagher, *op. cit.*

Thoreau, Henry David. *Walden and Civil Disobedience* (New York, The New American Library of World Literature, 1960).

Tsesse. Quoted by Lin Yutang, *op. cit.*

Tsongkhapa. In Anne Harrington, *op. cit.*

Unhappy Americans. Quoted by Bret Stephens in *The Wall Street Journal,* reporting a recent study by the World Health Organization. *The Week,* 24ᵗʰ March 2007.

Vanuatu. See Guy Adams, *op. cit.*

White, E. B. Quoted by Twyla Tharp, *op. cit.*

Wu-Men. In *Art & Nature: An Illustrated Anthology of Nature Poetry,* selected by Kate Farrell (New York, Little, Brown & Company, 1992).

Yutang, Lin. *The Importance of Living* (New York, William Murrow, 1937, 1998).

Zagajewski, Adam. "Try to Praise the Mutilated World" in *Without End: New & Selected Poems* (New York, Farrar, Straus & Giroux, 2002).

Zinn, Howard. *You Can't Be Neutral on a Moving Train* (Boston, Beacon Press, 1995).

AFTERWORD

Abram, David. *Becoming Animal: An Earthly Cosmology* (New York, Pantheon Books, 2011).

Emerson, Ralph Waldo. *The Selected Writings of Ralph Waldo Emerson,* edited by Brooks Atkinson (New York, The Modern Library, 1964).

Influences arcing across time, described by Robert Hass as "poetry in action." Quoted by Robert Sullivan, *op.cit.*

Jackson, Maggie. *Distracted: The Erosion of Attention in the Coming Dark Age* (Amherst, NY, Prometheus Books, 2008).

James, William. Quoted by William Powers, *op.cit.*

Matthews, William, in *Antaeus: Journals, Notebooks and Diaries,* #61, edited by Daniel Halpern (Tangier, London, New York, Autumn, 1996).

Powers, William. *Hamlet's BlackBerry: A Practical Philosophy for Building a Good Life in the Digital Age* (New York, HarperCollins, 2010).

Sullivan, Robert. *The Thoreau You Don't Know: What the Prophet of Environmentalism Really Meant* (New York, HarperCollins, 2009).

PERMISSIONS

"For the Children" By Gary Snyder, from *Turtle Island*, copyright ©1974 by Gary Snyder. Reprinted by permission of New Directions Publishing Corp., New York, NY.

"Gatha" from *The Long Road Turns to Joy: A Guide to Walking Meditation*, ©1996 by Thich Nhat Hanh. Reprinted by permission of Parallax Press, Berkeley, California.

"Song of an Initiate," translated from Spanish and Huichol by Jerome Rothenberg, reprinted from *Shaking the Pumpkin: Traditional Poetry of the Indian North Americans*, Doubleday (New York, NY), ©1972. Reprinted by permission of Jerome Rothenberg.

"New York Poem" by Sam Hamill from *Dumb Luck* ©2002 by Sam Hamill. Reprinted by permission of Boa Editions, Rochester, NY

"Haiku of Basho's" on p. 13 {A Crow/....} from *The Essential Haiku: Versions of Basho, Buson & Issa*, Edited and with an Introduction by Robert Hass. Introduction and selection ©1994 by Robert Hass. Unless otherwise noted, all translatios ©1994 by Robert Hass. Reprinted by permission of HarperCollins Publishers, New York, NY.

"Gift" (9 1.) From *New and Collected Poems: 1931-2001* by Czeslaw Milosz. ©1988, 1991, 1995, 2001 by Czeslaw Milosz Royalties, Inc. Reprinted by permission of HarperCollins Publishers, New York, NY.

"Poem" by Wu-Men (p. 47) from *The Enlightened Heart: An Anthology of Sacred Poetry*, Edited by Stephen Mitchell. © 1989 Stephen Mitchell. Reprinted by permission of HarperCollins Publishers, New York, NY.

"Number 91" (The Breeze at Dawn . . .) and "Number 116" (Take someone who doesn't keep score . . .) by Jalāl al-Dīn Rūmī (Maulana), from *Open Secret: Versions of Rumi*, translated by John Moyne, Coleman Barks. ©1984 John Moyne and Coleman Barks, Threshold Books. Reprinted by permission of Coleman Barks.

ACKNOWLEDGMENTS

This book could not have been written without an immense amount of kindness, generosity, and hands-on practical support. I would especially like to thank Maia for her fine-tuned ear in matters of the spirit, Simon for his love and constancy, and Alesia for her good soups and brilliantly timed presents. Don and Maria lent me their house in Vermont, and allowed me to stay there for the best part of seven years. Verandah Porche, Stephanie Wolfe-Murray, Alastair Reid and Leslie Clark, Linda Winston, Kate Stevens and John Hoffman put me up for extended stretches of time, shared innumerable meals, and were always ready for another cup of tea. Barbara Mor believed in me long before I could manage that for myself. Huge thanks, too, to my original agent, Rob McQuilkin. Without his faith and kindness (not to say his bright watch-maker's eye), this book would never have come into existence.

I would also like to thank my tribe of friends for all of the years of rich wide-ranging conversation, in particular, Eleanor Adams, Pat Anderson, Barbara Bash, Hosie Baskin, Susan Bonthron, Sarah Buttenwieser, Edite Cunha, Tess Darwin, Susan Davis, Anna Dembska, Charlene Ellis, Adam Ganz, Janice Gould, Pru Grand, Don Guttenplan, Andrea Hawks, John Hoffman, Parker Huber, Terry Iacuzzo, Randy Kehler, Mariel Kinsey, Simon Korner, Maia, Alesia Maltz, Maria Margaronis, Annabel McCall, Katherine McNamara, Barbara Mor, Jo Morissey, Aurora Levins Morales, Pat Musick, Kathy O'Rourke, Roz Parr, Susie Patlove, Verandah Porche, Amy Pulley, Sarah Rabkin, Tessa Ransford, Jane Rasch, Joy Seidler, Ann Stokes, Arthur Strimling, Fred Taylor, David Te Selle, Paki Weiland, Linda Winston, and Stephanie Wolfe-Murray.

And to my family too, in particular, my mother Brigid McEwen, my sisters Helena and Isabella, my brother John, my uncle Johnny, and my aunt, the late Clare Wagg.

I would also like to thank the following people for allowing me to interview them, and in many cases, to quote them in this book. Special thanks to Barbara Bash, Paulus Berensohn, Thomas A. Clark,

Guy Claxton, Fiona Houston, Parker Huber, Maia, Howard Mansfield, John McEwen, Meredith Monk, Grace Paley, Verandah Porche, Amy Pulley, Alastair Reid, Rowland Russell, Sarah Schulman, and Arthur Strimling.

My cats, Sophie and Noushka, dozed and idled as I worked, and kept me cheerful company throughout. The staff at the Forbes Library in Northampton, Massachusetts, were unfailingly kind and efficient. Kirsty Bain, Sarah Bauhan, Jane Eklund and Henry James at Bauhan Publishing, and the magnificent publicist Scott Manning, could not have been more helpful. Thank you, one and all.

In 2007, its centennial year, I spent two peerless months at the MacDowell Colony. I have never had so clear and joyful a focus in my work. May we all enjoy such generous support.

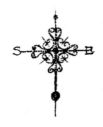

BAUHAN PUBLISHING LLC
70 Main Street,
Peterborough, NH 03458 USA

Typeset in Minion Pro by Kirsty Anderson
Cover Design by Henry James